Three Cheers for Loose Balls

"[With] irrepressible personality and charm, [Williams's]
coming-of-age story, on court and off, proves more compelling
than the usual-suspects parade of the game's outsized egos."
—*The New Yorker*

"This brash collection of anecdotes and rants shows that
[Williams] can be as cruel as he is kind."
—*Publishers Weekly*

"Jayson Williams is refreshingly candid about race, sex, money,
and alcohol in the NBA . . . a nice insider's view of
professional basketball."
—*New York Times Book Review*

"Comedy, drama, reality, and so much more . . . A must-read for
those who want to know . . . about . . . life in the NBA."
—Marcus Camby

"Enormous humor, refreshing candor, and surprising
reflection . . . Williams holds nothing back . . . It's difficult to
remember another professional athlete being so honest about
his own struggle to become a worthy human being . . .
NBA Commissioner David Stern should hand this book to
every rookie whose name is called out on draft night."
—*Des Moines Register*

"The most frank, funny, and controversial sports book since
Ball Four . . . a richly human coming-of-age tale embedded in
a hilariously candid exposé about the larger-than-life world
of professional basketball . . . Even reading the index evokes
laughter . . . Earnest, outrageous, and profound . . . *Loose
Balls* is the fastest, freshest, and funniest book ever about
life inside the Big Show."

—*Fort Meyers News-Press* (Florida)

LOOSE BALLS

Easy Money, Hard Fouls, Cheap Laughs,

and True Love in the NBA

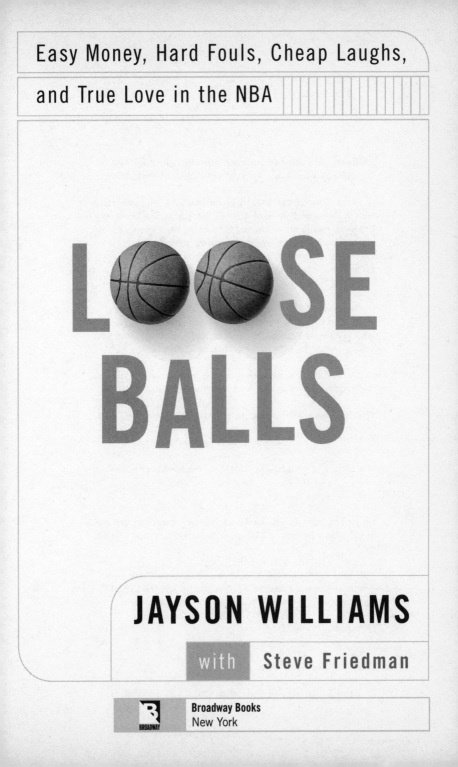

LO⬤⬤SE
BALLS

JAYSON WILLIAMS

with Steve Friedman

Broadway Books
New York

A hardcover edition of this book was originally published in
2000 by Doubleday, a division of Random House, Inc.

Broadway Books titles may be purchased for business or
promotional use or for special sales. For information, please
write to: Special Markets Department, Random House, Inc., 1540
Broadway, New York, NY 10036.

BROADWAY BOOKS and its logo, a letter B bisected on the diagonal,
are trademarks of Broadway Books, a division of Random House, Inc.

First Broadway Books trade paperback edition published 2001.

Designed by Patrice Sheridan

The Library of Congress has cataloged the hardcover edition as
follows:

Williams, Jayson.
Loose balls: easy money, hard fouls, cheap laughs, and true love
in the NBA / by Jayson Williams with Steve Friedman.—1st ed.
p.   cm.
Includes index.
1. National Basketball Association.   2. National Basketball
Association—Corrupt practices.   3. Violence in sports—United States.
4. Discrimination in sports—United States.   I. Friedman, Steve.   II. Title.
GV885.515.N37W54   2000
796.332'64'0973—dc21
99-41569
CIP

ISBN 0-7679-0569-5

01   02   03   04   05   10   9   8   7   6   5   4   3   2   1

For Linda and Laura

Contents

Acknowledgments

A book like this owes much to many people. Though there are too many to thank by name, I want to mention a few.

First, my parents, who blessed me with love and discipline and great expectations. My childhood friends, guys like Boogie and Marcus and George, and my brother, Victor, who all stuck with me in good times and bad. My coaches, especially Paul "Doc" Nicelli, Bob Oliva, Lou Carnesecca, Ron Rutledge, Butch Beard, Paul Silas, and Clifford Ray, teachers who helped turn a troubled kid into a man. The scores of men and women in the media who taught me about the power of the press and the rewards of straight talk—particularly Don Imus and Rocky Allen, men I count as friends. My longtime friend and lawyer Oscar Holt, a steady guide through the fast money and fleeting fame of professional basketball.

Finally, in a book about the NBA, the people I want to thank most are the guys in the league—the coaches, refs, and, especially, the players. These are the men I bang, foul, grab, and try to beat eighty-two nights a year, while they bang, foul, grab, and try to beat me. Without these guys—my opponents, teammates, friends, and occasional enemies—this book could never have been written. So, to the guys who provided me with my best and funniest material, thanks.

And, *especially* to you power forwards, muscly centers, and other sensitive big men, no offense intended. Really.

INTRODUCTION

This is how it works when you're an NBA veteran who can think:

I'm guarding Patrick Ewing. I'm pushing him, he's pushing me, and we're both watching Charlie Ward—one of the Knicks' point guards—bring the ball up the court.

I say, "Yo, Patrick, you guys need a point guard who can get the ball up the court faster."

Patrick doesn't say anything, just keeps muscling and pushing and shoving.

Then I say, "Man, your point guards, Charlie and Chris Childs, by the time they get you the ball, you ain't got much time to make your shot."

Maybe he still won't say anything, but now he's not pushing me so hard.

Then I say, "Gee, they're freezing you out, Patrick, they done made you into a rebounder. How do you like that? You're a role player now. You're making a hundred million, and you're a damn role player. Man, I don't know many role players who get those

1

nice sneaker contracts, who do those nice Pepsi commercials. I don't think you'll be doing no Pepsi commercials if your point guard keeps going like this."

Then Patrick's muttering. Then he's saying, "Damn, man. Jay, you know, you're right. Damn."

Next time-out I look over at the Knicks' bench, and Patrick is yelling at his point guards to get him the ball.

When the game starts again, I start again. And now I'm all sympathetic. And I'll tell you something about a lot of guys in the NBA. You give 'em a sympathetic ear, they lose their minds they're so happy. A lot of guys, by the end of the game, they're unloading *all* their problems on me. Sometimes it's about a teammate, how "he's spoiled, he's selfish, he don't pass me the ball." Sometimes it's about how mean their coach is.

Before you know it, with a lot of centers (and I'm not talking about Patrick here), you know what his girlfriend's favorite color is or what his wife's going to be wearing that night. And then he's telling you about his money problems. When a guy you're guarding starts talking about what he did that pissed his girlfriend off, or how he just lost a big chunk of change on something stupid, then you know that your sympathetic conversation has worked just perfect.

This is how it works when you're a young man with a lot of money and not a lot of sense:

Springtime of 1991, and the Philadelphia 76ers are in the play-offs. I might be a dumb, bench-warming rookie, but I'm smart enough to see that we're not going to make it very far. So I ask Charles Barkley, my drinking buddy and teammate, how much extra money we'll be earning if we lose in the first round. Because I'm thinking about summer vacation.

"Fifty-five," he says.

"Whoa!" I say.

The day we lose I go down to the neighborhood and I get seventeen kids I grew up with and I tell everybody to go and pack for a week—we're getting out of here. I hire limousines to pick everybody up in front of their buildings. I got the whole first-class section of the airplane. Put it all on my American Express. We fly down to Puerto Rico, get seven suites. After a week it's time to come back and we're all sitting in the first-class cabin again. I notice that everybody has alcohol. Everybody's drinking from those little bottles of liquor they serve on the plane, but I don't see any stewardess and these guys are holding bottles by the hundreds. Bags of bottles. I'm thinking, "What's going on here?" I ask some of the guys, "Hey, man, how'd you get all that alcohol already? I didn't see no stewardess come by."

And one of my pals says, "Hey, Jay, check this out. Would you believe it? Every time we would clean out the refrigerator and leave the hotel and go down to the beach, I mean *every* time, we'd come back and they'd filled it back up. We were doing this like three or four times a day."

"Nooooo!" I say. "No, please, say you didn't." But sure enough, they did. They had been cleaning out the fridge three times a day, in seven rooms, including the $300 bottles of champagne. I felt sick. I must have drunk twenty of those bottles on the way back to New York. Just trying to ease the pain.

At the time, my father was paying all my bills. I gave him my money, he paid my bills. So a few days after I get back, my father comes knocking on the door upstairs in my house. He's yelling.

"Jayson, wake up, wake up!"

"What's the matter, Daddy?" I say. "What's the matter?"

"Somebody stole your American Express card," he says. "The idiot just took seventeen people to Puerto Rico. But don't worry. I'm gonna call the police and the credit card company. We'll nail that boy who stole from you. You're not gonna have to pay for that low-down dog's crime."

He keeps going, keeps yelling, and I say, "No, no, Dad. Dad, that was me."

He stops.

"You make five hundred thousand dollars a year," he says, "and you go to Puerto Rico, take seventeen people, spend forty-one thousand dollars on your friends in seven days?"

We're all in the kitchen now. My mom's up now, too, making coffee. I don't know what to say. He looks over at my mother, says, "Barbara, your boy must be on drugs."

I try to ease my dad's concern a little. I tell him, "Don't worry about it. I'm getting fifty-five thousand for the play-offs."

He says, "Jay, I don't care. You can't be spending that kind of money in one week. That's almost one-tenth of your regular pay-check, son."

He's pissed off. He's disappointed in me. Working hard and saving money have always been important to my dad. He doesn't speak to me for three weeks. We eat breakfast every morning, he doesn't even look at me he's so pissed off. Finally the check comes for the play-offs. And here comes my dad knocking on the door. This time it's six o'clock in the morning and at first he's all soft and cheerful. He says, "Your check is here, Mr. World Traveler." Then he starts yelling, real loud. *And it ain't fifty-five thousand, it's fifty-five hundred, you dumb s.o.b.*

The next day I go see Charles Barkley.

"Charles," I say, "I thought you told me the play-off check was fifty-five thousand."

He says, "That's a damn lie. I told you it was fifty-five. I thought even *you* would know it was fifty-five hundred. As much as you played, you should have got fifty-five dollars."

And this is how it works when you're on the road, trying to relax:

The New Jersey Nets are playing the SuperSonics in Seattle, probably the whitest city in America. Two of my friends on the Nets, Armen Gilliam and P. J. Brown, and I are going to see *Pulp Fiction*. The Ham—that's what we call Armen, which is short for Hammer, as in Arm & Hammer—is real proud, pretending he's a Harvard kind of guy even though he went to UNLV. Armen would *never* listen to rap music. And don't even *think* about using the n-word around him. There are about a hundred people in the movie and three blacks—me, Armen, and P. J. And as soon as that part comes on where the one guy blows the other guy's brains out in the car—it was an accident, you know—Armen stands up, yelling, "Senseless violence! This is just senseless. It makes no sense . . . That guy didn't have to die . . . These are the movies that are ruining America!"

And all the white people just turn around and look at Ham and they must have been thinking, Oh, my goodness!

Armen walks out. Then he calms down, he comes back in, and this is the part when the black guy is getting bucked by another guy in the movie. Ham walks back in about two minutes before that part. And when that comes on, he stands up again.

"Oh, my Lord," he says. "This is disgusting! This is despicable!"

He gets to the aisle, and he's walking out again, and this old white lady is walking behind him—and the whole movie theater is pissed off at the Ham by now. Ham sees the lady coming behind him and tries to open the door for her.

"You're leaving, too?" he says, all polite.

And the lady says, "I'm not leaving, square-ass! I'm going to the bathroom!"

I love basketball. I love the competition and the teamwork and, yes, the chance to perform at the highest level and to get paid well for it. But I love other things about the game, too. The mind games. The nutty rivalries—sometimes even between teammates. Some pregame routines that would make your eyes pop. The crazy characters. People and things I might not have believed if I hadn't seen them, and lived them, since I entered this league ten years ago.

If you're reading this book, you probably love basketball, too, but even if you watch forty games a week on TV—maybe *especially* if you watch forty games a week on TV—there's a lot about the NBA you have never noticed.

When you see a team shooting layups, loosening up for a game in midseason, you probably don't notice some of the players looking into the stands, picking out the best-looking women, deciding which ones they'll send the ball boy over to with an invitation to meet outside the locker room after the game.

When you see a European player make a spin move to the basket, and his defender kind of stumble away from him, you don't notice that guy kind of gagging because the European guy stinks so bad. (At least until he's been here a while and learns about the American custom of using deodorant.)

When you see teammates ignoring each other on the court, you *definitely* don't notice that one player threatened to kick the other's butt the day before, until that other player pulled out the machete he's carried since he was a kid and ended the discussion.

When you see 580-degree spin moves and reverse dunks and a bunch of tall millionaries hugging and high-fiving, you're probably not noticing the groupies and the feuds and backbiting in the league. And when you see those "I Love This Game" television spots and the smooth sneaker commercials, you don't notice how tough, immature, mean, worried, funny, pissed off, scared, and downright insane some of the players in this league really are.

I notice because I'm one of them. I've been one of them for ten years. Ten years, and a lot of beers and barroom brawls, and some scrapes with the law and too many fights, and some yelling matches with coaches, and a bunch of headlines. Ten years, and three teams and too many coaches, and a bunch of interviews and one All-Star Game (as I write this) and a seven-year, $100-million contract.

These days a lot of people think I'm a funny, quotable, hardworking, community-minded team leader—all true, and all reasons I got that nice contract. Before that, a lot of people thought I was a loudmouth, bench-warming, hard-drinking attitude problem—also all true, and all of which probably helps explain the three teams.

But what a lot of people don't know is that my mom's white and my dad's black; that when I was twelve years old, my oldest sister, Linda, was attacked by a guy with a knife and got AIDS from the blood transfusion afterward; that she gave the virus to my other sister, Laura, and that both died; that each had a little child, and I adopted both; and when they had kids, I became a grandfather when I was twenty-seven years old; that I went to high school with a bunch of tough Italian guys who helped me cheat on the SATs, and that the FBI tried (and failed) to get me to rat out my friends; that I quit the St. John's basketball team twelve times; that I've been fighting since I was about six years old; that I first broke my thumb in a barroom brawl that Charles Barkley got me mixed up in (he got me mixed up in a lot of stuff); and that I worry so much about my family that I call my mom and my dad both at least a few times a day, and if they don't answer, I get anxiety attacks and can't breathe.

I'm going to tell you all about all of that, too, in addition to the little head games and sneaky tricks NBA players use, and which players hate each other, and who the best coaches are, and why some guys won't pass to other guys, and who the toughest guys in the league are, and the cheapest and dumbest and craziest. And smelliest. I'm no better than any of them. But while I might not be as famous as Larry Bird or Magic Johnson or Black Jesus in Sneakers himself, Michael Jordan, and while I'm not as crazy as Dennis Rodman or as well dressed as Pat Riley or as smart as Phil Jackson or as rich as Patrick Ewing, one thing I am, and anyone who knows me will tell you this, is honest. And I don't think anyone else has ever been completely honest about life in the NBA.

Chapter 1

Dumb & Dumber Don't Even
Begin to Describe It—
My Years with the
Philadelphia 76ers
(Following a Brief Detour
in the Desert)

 The only thing I knew about Phoenix
when I came out of college was it was
hot and it had a lot of pickup trucks.
So when the Suns drafted me out of St.
John's in 1990, and when the guy at the
podium said, "Going to the Suns is Jayson Williams," I said, "Oh,
no, I'm not. No, I'm not." Actually I didn't just say it. I yelled it.

Unfortunately, the TV cameras happened to be focusing on me
at that moment, scowling and waving my arms, yelling, "Oh, no,
I'm not." I don't think that helped me with the Phoenix fans.

I waited two months before going out there. The night before
the trip, I went to a party at Tunnel, a New York City nightclub. I
had my last drink at 5:30 A.M. The plane left a little after 6:00 A.M.
Then I was drinking on the plane, and when I got to Phoenix, I had
some drinks from the minibar in the hotel room. Then I passed out.
And you know how sometimes when you wake up in a hotel room,
you don't know where you're at? That was what it was like, but
worse. I look outside and there's nothing but desert. And as far as
I knew I was still in New York. I had forgotten all about the plane

ride. So I look outside and there was nothing but desert, and the heat just smacked me. It was 122 degrees that day. And the heat just knocked me down. I get up and there's the desert again. I think I'm still in New York and all I see is desert.

"Holy smokes," I say, "they dropped the bomb."

Now I'm all bug-eyed, trying to call the front desk, ask what the emergency evacuation plans are, who bombed the city, are the phone lines down, can I get in touch with my parents? And I hear a loud knock on the door. I answer it in my underwear. It's Jerry Colangelo, owner of the Phoenix Suns. I'm sweating—stinking, I'm sure, like a distillery. I can feel the alcohol coming out of my pores.

Jerry looks at me.

"Jayson?" he says.

But I'm still in New York. At least I think I'm in New York.

"What happened?" I yell. "They dropped the bomb on us. Where am I? I need to get in touch with my parents to make sure they didn't get hit by the bomb. Can you get me a phone line?"

Jerry's still looking at me.

"Oh, my," he says. "We've got a problem."

When Big Daddy Lost His Voice

A few weeks later they call me to the office, Jerry Colangelo and his boys. I'm overweight, out of shape, and I hadn't played basketball in a while, because I had a broken foot my senior year of college. Also, I'm continuing to hate Phoenix. Jerry tells me I have an attitude problem. Then he insults St. John's, my alma mater. I think Jerry's *trying* to piss me off.

"Screw you!" I say. Then I knock everything off Jerry's desk. Tell him I'm going home.

He says he'll meet me at the hotel, we can work things out, we *have* to work things out. But I don't even go to the hotel. I just go straight to the airport, then fly home, to my father.

I figure he'll be happy to see me, so when I knock on his door and he opens it, I'm all smiles.

"Dad," I say, "I'm home!"

"What the hell are you doing here?" he says. "You're supposed to be in Phoenix."

"Dad, they were treating me real bad out there. They're calling me 'boy.'"

Now I'm crying.

"They're talking down to me, yelling at me, criticizing me, saying I'm the worst player in camp."

My dad puts his hand on my shoulder.

"Jay," he says, "let me tell you something. You're my son, and I don't care what, you ain't never got to do something you don't want to do. You don't want to go out to Phoenix, you ain't got to go."

As soon as he says that, *briiing! briiing!*

I pick up the phone and it's Jerry Colangelo.

My dad's asking who it is, and I'm telling him don't worry, I'll handle it. And Jerry's yelling at me. He's saying, "Son, you don't come to Phoenix, we're going to give you the minimum, a hundred and fifty thousand. And you're never going to make more than that in this league."

My father sees my face and he says, "Let me speak to him. Let me have him."

"Dad," I say, "don't worry about it, man. I got him."

But my dad says, "Boy, I told you. You ain't gotta do nothing you don't want to do. Now, let me talk to him."

So I give my father the phone.

"Yeah, this is Big Daddy," he says, all belligerent. That's my father's nickname, Big Daddy. "What do you want?"

Then there's quiet.

"Oh, yeah?" he says again, but not so belligerent.

More quiet.

"Oh, yeah?" Real quiet now. "Ohh. Oh, man. Okay. Okay, thank you."

My dad hangs up the phone. Then he says, "Son, you've got to get your butt on the next plane back to Phoenix."

Car Trouble

When I'm back in Phoenix, because I'm the team's first-round draft pick, the team gives me a Pontiac Grand Prix. The second-round pick gets a Cadillac. I'm pissed off about that. So I take that Grand Prix and I drive into the parking lot and crash into every pole I can see, then I gave the car back to them.

So the owners tell me—they're being real cute—"You know, that car we gave you might have been too little. So we're gonna give you a big ol' Grand Marquis."

But I crash that one up, too. So finally they give me an LTD. Real Barnaby Jones model.

The day I get the car I have to go to the airport to pick up my brother Victor. I get there early, so I have a few drinks. For some reason I get drunker drinking at airports and Yankee games than anywhere else in the world. So when Vic finally arrives, I'm a little drunk, but we get in the LTD anyway, and I drive him back to the hotel.

One thing Arizona has, in addition to a lot of desert and pickup trucks, is these wide roads. Not just highways, but regular roads. I mean, eight lanes wide! My advice to anyone visiting Arizona is, if you're going to make a left and the light says yellow, don't do it.

I go to make a left turn on a yellow light and I'm halfway across the road and here comes a pickup truck from the other direction going eighty. I can see he's going to hit us, right on the passenger side. I hold on tight, tell Vic, "You gotta take this one for the team, bro."

Knocks us right into a telephone pole and knocks Victor right out. And before the ambulance gets there, I hear this *creeeeeeeeak* noise, and then Victor wakes up. And he's up about two seconds and then *Booooom!* The telephone pole drops right down on top of the LTD, right on Victor's side, hits him right on the head. Victor's gotta get sixty stitches; they gotta shave half his head.

So the owners see Victor, they see the LTD they gave me, they see me, and they say that's enough, we're shipping you out to Philadelphia.

A Game of Inches

Before signing me up, the Sixers' top guys meet with me in a Midtown hotel in New York City. They had heard I was fat, out of shape. They were worried about the broken foot, too. It was Harold Katz, then the owner, and Gene Shue, then the general manager. They wanted me to run up and down in the hotel ballroom. They thought I might be damaged goods. I told 'em I understood their concerns, but I had a better idea. Instead of running up and down in a damn ballroom, why didn't I run up and down on a basketball court for them? I said, "We can go to a park by my house." They thought that was a great idea and we agreed to go on down there.

Harold and Gene didn't know it, but the park we were going to was down on the Lower East Side, right next to the school I went to, P.S. 137. And before we drove down there, I called the principal, and I told him what's happening.

So when we get to the park, he's let the whole school out early, and there's nine hundred kids in the park, surrounding the court, hanging on the chain-link fence, screaming and yelling and cheering, "Williams! Williams! Williams! Williams!"

And I'm running and dunking and jumping, up and down and up and down. I'm flying! It's like one of those bad made-for-TV movies. I mean, I'm two feet above the rim, scraping my elbows on metal. And the kids are screaming and Harold and Gene are happy about the whole thing. They're talking to each other.

"Holy smokes!" they're saying. "We got a steal with this guy!"

Harold and Gene spent the next two years watching me miss layups, stumble around, saying, "What the heck happened at that park? Was that an optical illusion or what?"

They told Charles Barkley they were confused, because they'd seen me playing about two feet above the rim.

Charlie says, "You seen who? Doing what? When?"

What Harold and Gene and Charlie didn't know is that the basket at that park is only nine feet high.

The View from the Bench

My years with Philadelphia, I wasn't a factor at all. Off the court, I was hanging with Charlie, who was taking years off my life in bars and on the court—well, I was on the bench, not the court. And what I learned on the Sixers was that it's not the first seven guys on the team it's important to motivate, to get to buy into the team. They're going to be motivated anyway, playing all those minutes, being in the rotation. The critical players to motivate on any pro team are the last five. If the last five guys on the team buy into what the coach is trying to do, they're going to push the first seven guys. If the seventh guy's not playing well, and the twelfth guy is always trying hard, the seventh guy will play harder, because he doesn't want that twelfth guy to come in—he doesn't want to be like Wally Pipp was for Lou Gehrig.

I learned this with the Sixers, because that's *not* the way it was there. The last three or four guys on the team knew we weren't going to play, so we didn't care that much. And when we went to the play-offs that year, in '91, the first thing that was on a lot of the guys' minds—the guys who never played—was, "Let's get the hell out of here. You know we're not going to the championship, so let's get the hell out of here. Let's lose in the first round and get the hell out and start summer vacation."

How Mr. Magoo Cheated Death

Dogs hate cats. Gorillas hate tigers. I guess some parakeets even want to kick some canaries' asses. You know how it is. Well, Charles Barkley had it out for Armen Gilliam. I mean, it was like a cobra and a mongoose or something. When we all played for the Sixers, Charlie would stay out all night drinking and carrying on, and he'd be talking about Armen, what he was going to do to him in practice the next day. He'd be out with Rick Mahorn, who didn't drink but who also had a thing for Armen. And I was there, too. They'd be talking stuff about Armen. "I'm gonna take that freak's head off, I'm gonna kill that guy," stuff like that. And I'd say, "Yeah, Charlie, yeah," or "Uh-huh, Horn, you bet," while Charlie and I ordered some more cranberry juice and Absolut.

Then at practice the next day, they'd be chasing Armen around, trying to set a blind-side pick on him, get him with an elbow, and you know what? Charlie and Rick were so tired they couldn't even catch him—Armen never drank—and the Ham was bouncing around the court like Mr. Frigging Magoo, just *boing, boing, boing.* I don't think Armen ever knew Charlie and Rick were trying to kill him. To this day I don't think he knows.

Breakfast of Champions

Charles Barkley might have been one of the twenty greatest players of all time, and he might get quoted the most, but the man had some strange habits. A lot of days, when Charlie was too hungover to practice, or injured, or just tired, everyone would be running up and down the court, going hard in a scrimmage, except Charlie. While we all sprinted and sweated, Charlie would be sitting on his stationary bike—always the same one—pedaling at about one mile an hour, watching us and eating. Eating! And always the same thing. Every morning on the way to practice Charlie would stop at McDonald's and buy two big orders of pancakes and two big orders of sausage. After a while, he had the Sixers build a special tray on his favorite stationary bike to hold his pancakes and sausages, which he ate while he watched the rest of the team practice.

One day we're running the floor extra hard, because we'd lost the night before, and there's Charlie, sitting on his bike stuffing pancakes in his big mouth. Didn't even use a fork—just folded a sausage in between a couple pancakes with his hands and crammed it in. He's yelling. He's yelling mostly at Armen Gilliam.

"C'mon, Ham," he's yelling, "start running the floor." And pancake bits are flying out of Charlie's mouth while he's yelling, and juice is dribbling down his chin.

And Armen Gilliam, who never cursed at anybody, hears Charlie, and he turns to me while we're running. "Can you believe this sonofabitch?" Armen says. "He's telling me to run the floor and he's got pancakes flying out of his mouth!"

Killers

On the 76ers everybody used to call me Al Capone. I was a tough kid, and the other players thought I was a little street, a little slick. I'd gone to Christ the King High School in Middle Village, Queens, and that's where some tough kids, from tough families, went, and I became friends with them. I mean *tough*. When you read in the papers about the "prominent New York crime families," that's these guys' dads. And these guys were all named Sal and Vinnie and Frankie. And the guys on the 76ers knew that. I used to give these tough guys and some of my other high school buddies tickets to the games. One night they were sitting next to Charles Barkley's wife, Maureen, in the stands. Charlie saw that, and he told Harold Katz, the Sixers' owner, that I had killers sitting near his wife.

And that pissed me off because all these guys—my friends— were doing was minding their own business. They probably didn't say eight words the whole time. Didn't bother her one bit. I even asked Maureen about it. She said nobody bothered her. But Charlie went and told Harold Katz about these "killers."

So when we played the New York Knicks a few days later, in New York, I had Charles Barkley come down to the Manhattan bar I owned, Big Daddy's. I brought him over, showed him around, introduced him to everybody. And then I said, "Charlie, I want you to meet some of my high school friends. Charlie, these are the guys who were sitting near your wife last week who you called killers. This is so-and-so and this is so-and-so."

Man, Charlie turned into a stuttering freak. He sounded like Daffy Duck. "Uh-buh, uh-buh, uh-buh, no, I never said that. I never said that." One time in my life I remember Charlie shutting up, that was it.

T-t-t-t-talking the Talk

A lot of the Sixers didn't like each other those years. Charles Barkley and Rick Mahorn had their thing for Armen, and Charlie also had a problem with Charles Shackleford, and nobody liked the owner, Harold Katz. Katz had something in common with Shack, which is they both stuttered. And when they got mad, they *really* stuttered. And when those two were arguing about something, you couldn't believe it. If you were watching, you didn't hear nothing, because they couldn't finish a word. All you saw was saliva going all over the room.

Shack was a funny guy, and he came from South Carolina, so of course he had issues. I was born in South Carolina, and I never met a person from that state who didn't have issues. He was sensitive, and he had the stuttering thing, and he didn't ever want to fight anyone, but watch out if he got really mad. One time in practice he threw the ball into Armen Gilliam in the post, and like always, Armen didn't throw it back to him. Hammer was only one nickname we had for Armen. The other was Black Hole, because once a ball got into him, it disappeared, just like things do in real black holes in outer space.

This time, though, Shack said something. Then Armen said something, and Shack cursed at him.

Then Armen said, "Don't talk to me like that."

One thing you never do to Armen Gilliam is you never curse him. He did not like to be cursed at. He got really personal with that.

So Shack said, "Uh, uh, uh, uh, fu-fu-fu-fu . . ."

And Armen said, "Didn't I tell you don't curse me? You cursed me for the last time."

Later in the locker room Shack had his head down and he was tying his shoes. But Armen was ready to go. He wanted to fight. He walked over and said, "Let's go, fella. We're going to go back in the boiler room, and I'm going to lock the door. And there's only one man coming out of there."

Armen didn't curse or drink, but he would punch you four times before you knew what hit you. He was tough. But, like I said, Charles Shackleford was from South Carolina, and you know what that means. Issues.

So even though Shackleford didn't want to fight, he had no choice. So he said, "Okay, no problem."

Armen went in the boiler room, and then a couple minutes later Shack followed him, and he was carrying a big old black duffel bag.

The door closed and we were all standing outside, because now we all knew there was going to be a fight. The boiler room was right across from our locker room. Everybody was waiting and watching the door.

And after about a minute Armen Gilliam just about rips that door off its hinges and he comes running out, hollering, "He's crazy, he's crazy!" I've never seen Hammer run so fast.

Charles Shackleford had a big machete knife with him in that duffel bag. A big machete knife with holes in it, the kind they use to cut sugarcane in South Carolina, the kind he used when he cut cane with his father. That knife must have been two feet long, with holes in it. Those holes cut down the wind resistance in the sugar-cane fields.

Shack walks out of that door with his machete, and he sees us all looking at him. He says, "Da-da-da-da-dat boy has to be m-m-m-more careful who he's messing with."

Now, Shack would never, *ever* actually use that thing on any-body. I know that. He knows that. He's told me that. But Armen didn't know it. And Armen never messed with him again.

What Did You Call Me?

Teammates get into it with each other sometimes. Sometimes they even yell at each other on the court. But the Philadelphia 76ers is the only team I've ever seen where two players started physically fighting with each other during a game. I was one of them.

We were playing the Houston Rockets in a preseason game. I was guarding Otis Thorpe, and Manute Bol was guarding Hakeem

Olajuwon. And Otis and I were arguing about something or another, and it was getting pretty heated.

So while Otis and I were having words, Otis set a pick on Hakeem's man, Manute, and Hakeem ran down the lane for an alley-oop pass. I was supposed to switch with Manute on that play and push Hakeem away from the basket. But I was too busy arguing with Otis. In fact, we were wrestling with each other then, and I had my hands around his neck.

So Hakeem runs to the basket and Manute tries to recover, and Hakeem dunks on him. And Manute looks bad and gives me a look. He says, "Don't let that happen again."

And the next play they do the same thing, because Otis and I are still wrestling around. And Manute looks at me again, and he says, "You are the world's most toofus American." He was trying to say "most stupid," but he had trouble with the language.

I say, "Don't call me a stupid American no more, Manute."

But he does. "You are a toofus American," he says.

So I jump up on his neck, because he was so tall, seven feet six inches, and I wrestle him down like a big anaconda. We're on the floor, and I'm choking him. And Dick Bavetta, the ref, is blowing the whistle, but he doesn't know what to do, because we're on the same team.

Someone on our team calls time out, and I go out of the game. I don't play any more that night. Manute stays in, though. But he never called me a toofus American after that.

When the Sixers traded me at the beginning of the 1992 season, I thought I'd never play with a crazier bunch of guys again in my life.

Then I arrived in New Jersey.

Chapter 2

The Meanest, Funniest, Smelliest, and Softest Players in the League and How Larry Bird's Better Than Most People Think, Hakeem Is Nastier, and Michael Jordan Is Much, Much, *Much* Meaner

 You don't need me to tell you who the greatest scorer is in the NBA, or the best free-throw shooter, or the player with the most assists or steals or double doubles or triple doubles. All you need for that is a newspaper or a computer or a TV.

What I can tell you about are the players other players fear most in the final minutes of a game, the strongest players, the funniest players, the rudest players, the most irritating cheaters, and the biggest hypocrites.

Cheapest

Armen Gilliam was frugal. Nah, frugal isn't the word. This boy was damn cheap. He had short arms and deep pockets. He was a special kind of guy. When I played for the Sixers, he lived next door to me, in a $400,000 condo. But his lights were never on. So I never believed Armen *had* lights. And he used to store food in

21

the snow. Especially his cranberry juice. It was always in the snow; I guess he was saving on the cost of a refrigerator. I can still see that big five-gallon bottle of cranberry juice in the snow. And then one day he had company, because I heard people over there, and I go outside to look, and I see he *does* have lights. And then I trip over something, and I see Armen's whole apartment going dark. I had tripped over an extension cord that he had run under my patio and was stealing my lights. That boy was *more* than frugal.

Most Imaginative Approach to Fan Relations

The Nets are playing the Lakers a couple years ago in the Meadowlands. And before the game, Nick Van Exel comes over to me, and he gives me one of his jerseys and says, "Here, man, give this to your kid."

"Whoa, thanks, man," I say. "I have a grandson and I'll give it to him." I thought that was real nice of Nick. You know, he's got the bad rep—little wild man from that tough Cincinnati program, bumping refs, bad temper, all that—and here he is giving me one of his jerseys for little Alex.

So the game starts, and this one fan, this fat white guy, he keeps hollering at me. The whole damn quarter he won't shut up. I can't hear what he's saying, just that he's hollering. And he's yelling at Nick, too, just won't let up. So after the first quarter I yell up to him.

"What?" I yell.

He yells back. "That's my goddamned jersey."

I yell, "What jersey?"

He yells, "*My* jersey."

So I walk up a few steps to him to try to straighten things out.

"What the hell you yelling about?" I say.

The fat guy points at the Nick Van Exel jersey sitting on my chair, where I put it.

"Nick Van Exel took that jersey from me," he says. "I asked him to sign it, and he snatched it out of my hand."

So I say, "Well, why are you yelling at me and cursing me?"

He says, "That's *my* jersey."

I say, "Oh, yeah? If it was—now it's mine."

I'm thinking, This guy's crazy. Nick might be a little off, but there's no way he'd steal some fan's jersey before a game.

So midway through the fourth quarter, right before a free throw, I say to Nick, "Nick, who did you get that jersey from?"

He says, "The guy right there," and he points to the fat guy. "Dude kept yelling at me to hurry up and sign it, and I got ticked off. That's when I gave it to you."

Nick's got something to learn about fan relations. But I'll tell you what: My little grandson loves his Nick Van Exel jersey.

Most Chutzpah

Sam Cassell is a point guard who looks to shoot first and pass second. But his teammates don't mind, because he's a great shooter and a great scorer. He always wants the ball when the game's on the line. Sam says, "As long as they're talking about me, I'm still around. You know, good or bad."

I remember when Cassell signed with the Nets. We're practicing and I've got an open fifteen-footer and I'm about to shoot, and here's Sam, yelling, "Shoot, man, you'll make it. Don't worry, shoot that ball. Shoot that ball."

And I remember saying, "Sam, you're darned right I'm going to shoot that ball. You know, you just got here one day, and you're already telling me to shoot that ball? I'll shoot the ball when I have a shot. Don't worry. I've been here seven years, you know?"

Least Patience

A lot of people think Hakeem Olajuwon is real easygoing because they don't see him yelling much and because of that nice-sounding Nigerian accent. But Hakeem has a temper. At practice one day, when the Rockets were supposed to be working on free throws, Hakeem takes the ball and starts shooting jumpers. So one of his teammates, a rookie then, he takes the ball from the net after Hakeem hits a jumper and he walks to the free-throw line to work on his free throws, like he's supposed to.

"Give the Dream his change," Hakeem says, which means give him the ball, 'cause he made the shot.

"But, dude," the rookie says, "we're supposed to be working on free throws."

Hakeem walks over to him and slaps him across the face. *Whop!* He said, "You don't do that! You must always give the Dream back his change!"

So yeah, the Dream does have a temper.

Worst Command of the English Language (Tie)

Let me explain about Yinka Dare. Yinka is from Nigeria, and there are some things Yinka just doesn't understand. The Nets were playing Minnesota in 1996, when they had Christian Laettner. I came out of the game, and Yinka, who was on the bench, asked me, "Jayson"—he always called me Jay-son, like it was two words—"what does the 'C' on Christian Laettner's jersey stand for?"

I'm thinking, Damn, Yinka Dare should know what the "C" on Christian Laettner's jersey stands for—it's for "Captain," anybody knows that. But I didn't say anything. I just looked over at him and thought, Let me figure this brother out.

So I say, "Yinka, what do you think the 'C' on Christian Laettner's jersey stands for?"

He looks over at Laettner, who's a white guy, and he looks back at me, and Yinka goes, "'Caucasian'?"

We're losing, so I can't be laughing on the bench. I put my head down, got a towel over my face. And then Benoit Benjamin, another NBA genius on the Nets' bench, looks over at me and he says, "Woooo, child. That Yinka Dare sure is silly, isn't he? Everybody knows 'caucasian' starts with a 'k'."

Hungriest

When Adrian Caldwell played with the Nets, management always gave him a hard time because he was so heavy. They were going to cut him because he ate too many donuts. His weight clause said he had to be 270 or less, or he'd get cut. And he'd been up around 285 at the time. John Calipari, the coach then, told Adrian if he caught him eating any more donuts, he'd get cut. So one day—it was over Thanksgiving—a bunch of Nets are serving food to the homeless in downtown Newark. While we were serving food there, Adrian was coming out with six plates for the homeless, but only serving five people. I believe that joker was eating the other plate of food. He put on eight pounds while we were feeding the homeless. And he got cut, which was a shame, because donuts or no donuts, he was a good player and the Nets could have used him that year.

Greatest Patron of the Arts

One night after a game in Portland, Chris Morris and I walk into a bar and a guy's playing the piano. Bar music, you know, nothing fancy.

Chris says to the guy, "Hey, can't you play some Picasso?"

You know, there aren't a lot of rocket scientists in the NBA.

Second Hungriest

Rick Mahorn did things his own way. When we were both playing for the 76ers, I saw him eating a hot dog on the bench, then right when he finished, he shoveled another one down. "Damn, man," I said, "what are you doing?"

He looks at me, takes a bite, says, "I got an upset stomach, man. This helps settle it."

I think, I don't want to know what he ate the night before.

He ended up getting fined $2,500 for eating on the bench, but he said it was worth it, that it cured him.

Smelliest

Most fans think the one thing most European players have in common is they're good jump shooters, but don't have much of a street game. I'll tell you what European players *really* have in common, and it's something all the guys in the league realize.

You can tell when you have a foreign player on your team when you get into a real closed space with him. That's when you know who's foreign and who's not. It's not that they smell bad naturally. But these guys, when they first get to the U.S., it takes them a while to adopt American customs, like deodorant. Anyway, a few years ago, when Chuck Daly was my coach with the Nets, during a time we weren't getting along, there were about five minutes left in a game and Chuck put me in to guard this European center who was seven foot something. I was pissed off at Chuck, and the game was out of reach, so I figured I'm going to let the big fella score a couple, you know? Let him get some confidence.

I let him score one, but I get caught up under one of his armpits. It smells like possum nuts! (Which, like I said, wasn't really his fault. Any NBA player who didn't use deodorant would smell bad. At least to the guys who *did* use it.) Well, I had high hair back then, an Afro, and I swear it made my hair stick out sideways. I get caught in his armpit, with this thick funk, and I'm looking like Alfalfa!

I say, "Damn!" and I gag and run back upcourt. The next time we're on defense, they throw the ball into the big fella in the post and he drop-steps and dunks. And Chuck is screaming at me, saying, "Can't you stop him?"

And I'm yelling back, "Hell no! I ain't gonna stop him. Let this sonofabitch get in the shower, then maybe I'll stop him. But for now, he's gonna score thirty in the next two minutes, 'cause I ain't going under them armpits again."

He ended up with about 14 points, and he scored them real fast.

Most Closeted

Armen Gilliam's father was a preacher. I remember going to watch his father give a sermon one time, and his father was saying how he didn't like anything that was on TV. And he said the stuff that was on TV was just bad, and he took the TV away from his family; he didn't want anybody in his family watching TV no more. And he threw it in the closet. I was sitting next to Armen's mom, the preacher's wife. And when he said that about throwing the TV in the closet, she said, "Oh, and it gets mighty crowded in that closet." Turns out she would take the family in there to watch TV.

Air Apparent

People want to know who the next Michael Jordan is. There was a player a few years ago, Harold Miner, people nicknamed him Baby Jordan. Now other people are saying Kobe Bryant is the next Jordan. What people still don't understand is there will never be another Michael Jordan. It's like if Jesus just made a mistake and made two great ballplayers into one. Like Michael's supposed to have a twin, but Jesus took all his energies and talents and stuff and put it into him, Michael.

Best Bad Dresser

Michael Jordan was the number one dresser. Scottie Pippen learned from Michael, so he was a good dresser. Kevin Willis always looks pretty sharp. I'll tell you who are the worst dressers—the white guys. They invented the grunge look about fifteen years ago. Guys like Jon Koncak. He'd be making $3 million a year back then and he'd step off the team plane like he just got off the surfboard.

The sharpest dresser and the worst dresser are the same person—Charles Oakley. He's got nice suits, but they're always purple and yellow and stuff. He got the best suits but the worst colors. But he's 6'10", 265, so nobody tells him about it.

Biggest Animal Lover

When Armen Gilliam and I lived next door to each other in '92, I bought my son—really my late sister's son, who I adopted—a little dalmatian. And on the second day the dalmatian disappeared. My son cried for about a whole day and a half. He was twelve years old then. We went to sleep and he comes into my room—he called me Uncle Jay—yelling, "Uncle Jay, Uncle Jay, I hear the dog, I hear the dog." So we go down to the basement, I hear the dog, "Woof! Woof!" But it's coming from next door. It's coming from Armen's house. So I knock on Armen's door, and my dog comes running out.

I say, "Armen, what the hell are you doing with my son's dog? You kidnapped my son's dog."

And he says, "I opened the door and the dog ran in."

I say, "Gee, Armen, you could've opened the door and let the dog run back out. My son's been crying for two days."

Jim McMahon used to live next door to us, too, on the other side. And I told Jim McMahon about Armen kidnapping my dog. And after that, every time Armen came home from practice, Jim McMahon's two little boys would be playing in the yard and McMahon would come out—I'd never noticed before that McMahon was cross-eyed without those sunglasses on—and get his sons. He'd just run out without his glasses on. You know, you'd never see Jim without his glasses on; that's how nervous he was. He thought Armen was going to kidnap his kids, so he used to make his kids come in the house when Armen came home. He didn't want his kids playing in the yard. He didn't want them to be locked down in Armen's basement.

An Officer and a Gentleman, but Not Much on Small Talk

When I was on the way to the rookie combine, where all the rookies show their stuff, I got to sit next to David Robinson. I thought it was the biggest thrill. Here was a guy who was a naval officer, straight-A student, gymnast, musician, and a great player. I grew up on the Lower East Side of New York City—not exactly the suburbs—so I figured we could learn things from each other.

I was thinking, This is going to be a great conversation. He said, "Are you going to the rookie combine?" I said, "I sure am, man." I said, "David, I just want to tell you, I'm a big fan of yours." And he said, "Thank you very much." And I just looked away for a second, and I was getting set to ask him another question. And I turned around and he had on headphones and he had a piano keyboard in front of him. He played that damn keyboard for four hours. Didn't say another word to me, except at the end of the flight. Then it was, "Good luck."

Great player, great guy, doesn't talk a hell of a lot.

Most Innovative Ideas About Grooming

I had a teammate with the 76ers named Mike Gminski. Mike helped me a lot in my game. He would sit down and say, "Hey, bro, you know, you've got to calm down a little bit." Got me to focus.

One year, though, Mike grew a beard. And someone said, "Why did you grow a beard?" He said, "Black players think white players are better if they have beards." And I told him, "Hey, Mike, in that case, you should grow an Afro, too. And while you're at it, you should grow about another twenty inches on your vertical jump."

Worst Memory

Hakeem Olajuwon will embarrass you. I remember playing against him a few years ago, and after, I heard him tell some radio guys, "That number 55 plays so physical and he's going to be a very good player." And people heard, and they told me, "Hakeem—he don't even know your name."

So the next time we're in Houston, I grab a rebound in front of him, and I say, "You remember my name now?"

And he says, "I remember your name. You're Jayson Wilson."

Hakeem *likes* to embarrass people. He'll do it with stuff like forgetting your name. But he also has the best feet in the league, from all that soccer, so when you lean on him one way, he'll kick back and you fall down. He loves that. Hakeem has a very big ego that people don't know about. Partly, that's because what happens with foreigners when they come to this country is that they all think they know more than Americans. My father used to own a gas station in Harlem, and the West Indian guys used to come in there. And all they did was pump gas, but they knew more than my father, who owned the gas station for twenty years. Used to piss my father off.

"Ain't that something?" he'd say. "He just got to this country, I've been here sixty-two years, and he's telling me how to run my business after the second day of work."

Best Actors

When I guard a guy, I don't fall down. It's me against him, man-to-man. But there are definitely floppers in the league. And I'm going to tell you the truth. The biggest floppers are mostly the white guys. It's mostly the white guys who beat up their bodies. Except for Dennis Rodman, by far the biggest flopper around. Now, you just look at Dennis Rodman with 100,000 tattoos on him, an earring coming out of every hole in his body, right? And he's supposed to be so strong. And as soon as you make a move, he flops. It's like, "Why did you mess with poor old clean innocent Dennis?"

Most players hate that flopping. We're like, "Stand up like a man and play this damn game." You know? It pisses me off and a lot of other players. But Dennis used that technique better than anyone. And it worked. He wanted to get you hot, because he knew you can't do anything angry.

Most Legendary, and Hardest to Love

Every day I wake up and give thanks to Magic Johnson, Larry Bird, Julius Erving, and, of course, Black Jesus in Sneakers himself,

Michael Jordan. Those guys made it possible for me to make the kind of money I'm making. Which isn't to say I necessarily loved them all that much on the court.

I remember the first time I played against Larry Bird. It was one of his last years, and Charles Barkley was already a star, but Larry was just killing Charlie. Then Armen took him, and he was killing Armen. I looked up from the Sixers' bench and I said, "How the hell is he doing this, that skinny-assed white boy?" I said to Jim Lynam, "Put me in the game, Coach."

He said, "You think you can handle him?"

I said, "Yeah, I can handle him."

He put me in the game and the first thing Larry does is get the ball, look at me, and say, "Hey, rookie," while he shoots a three-pointer in my face.

"Damn," I say, "he ain't gonna shoot the next one."

The next time he gets the ball, he fakes and I jump about three feet off the ground and he dribbles around me and hits a layup. Then the next time I play it straight up, and he raises up and hits another jumper. He scores like 14 points in six minutes. He messed my mind up so much, I didn't want to play basketball anymore. I just wanted to beat him up. I'd never been killed in a spurt that quickly.

So I'm back on the bench again and Charles Barkley is getting *his* ass ate up again. Jim Lynam looks down the bench at me and I just start staring up into the crowd. I have no eye contact with Jim. I do not want to go back in there and play Larry Bird again.

Magic was another player I didn't get off to such a great start with.

The first time I met him, I was a high school sophomore in New York City. The Lakers came to have a pregame shootaround at our gym, and Pat Riley, the Lakers' coach then, wouldn't let us in to watch. This is winter, and we're out there freezing our butts off, watching through the glass. When the shootaround was over, we all ran up to the Lakers. I asked Magic for his autograph. "Not now, kid, not now," he said.

I went home and I said, "Screw Magic. I'm a Julius Erving fan now." I threw away my Magic jersey and put on my Dr. J one.

Then a few years later, when I was playing against Magic for the first time, every time I got next to him under the boards, I knocked him down. And when there was about thirty seconds left in the game, he comes up to me, and he says, "Damn, Jay, why you beating me up like this?"

I said, "Do you remember you came over to practice at a high school in New York City one time?"

"No, I don't remember," he said.

And I said, "I asked you for your autograph and you didn't give it to me."

And he said, "What's your mother's name?"

I said, "First you ignore me when I'm just a kid and now you wanna start insulting my mom? Screw y—"

"Nah," Magic says, "I want to try to make it up for you. I want to give you an autographed jersey for your mom. And if there's anyone else you want one for, I'll do that, too."

So Magic gave me autographed jerseys for my mom and my son, and I went back to being a Magic fan again. (I still liked the Doc, of course. I never played against him, but he told me when I came into the league I should work on my fifteen-foot jump shot and learn to swim underwater, that it would help my conditioning.)

As for Black Jesus in Sneakers himself, all I can say is that for everything that's been written and said about him, the fact is Michael Jordan was underrated. Not for his skills and athletic ability and what a great player he was, but for his coaching ability and his toughness. I mean, he was always telling the other Bulls what to do and making sure they did it. And as for toughness, Michael Jordan was by far the toughest player I ever saw in the NBA. You know, he does those commercials and he'll be smiling for the TV cameras, knowing he's going to make another $60 million off the court, but all the time he's smiling, he's mumbling something like, "If you foul me like that one more time I'm gonna rip your throat out." I've heard him say that a lot of times. Michael understands the world. Michael understands that he can't just go out there and rip somebody's face off on the court, but he'll catch you after the game and he'll put you right on your back. Michael's hard. He's a hard guy.

And everyone knew it. I mean everyone. I heard Michael curse out a referee one time after a call he didn't like. Michael cursed him out, then said, "Now, don't do that again. You did that before." And the referee said something, and Michael said, "Shut up, man, I don't want to hear that no more. Now, don't make that call again." And the referee just walked away. And he didn't make that call again.

And his teammates knew it, too. Scotty Burrell told me when he was with the Bulls, he'd practice hard every single day, I mean *hard*. I asked him why he was killing himself like that. He said Michael said he'd beat anyone up who didn't practice hard. He said, "If I don't go hard, Michael Jordan would have busted my ass."

I said, "Scotty, ain't you a grown man?"

He said, "Yeah, but it was Michael Jordan, and I believed him."

When you were playing against Michael Jordan, you didn't want to look him in the eye. Because if you looked at him in the eye, he took it as a challenge, somewhat like a Doberman pinscher would. So during the game, soon as he looked at me, I looked straight to the ground. He was looking for a reason, he was looking for any incentive to beat you. So what I'd do with Michael, especially in the play-offs, was come in and act like, "Uh, ho, ho-hum," like this game doesn't mean nothing to you, then you try to sneak up in the end and beat him. His eyes just look right through you, as if he could read your brain or what play you're doing. He's like Medusa that way.

You know, Michael Jordan said Charles Barkley would never win a championship because he doesn't have the commitment to win. He's a great player and a great guy, but I think you have to go out to every game and treat it like Jordan did, like every game's going to be your last. I think Charlie's one of the greatest players who ever played. But he doesn't treat every game the last four, five years like it's his last. And Charlie's not the easiest guy in the world to get along with. He rubbed Clyde Drexler the wrong way, he rubbed another couple guys the wrong way. Me and Charlie get along so well because I learned from all of Charlie's mistakes. I learned from all the good things he taught me, too. I'm just twice as smart as Charlie. I watched the good things he did and I put those into play, and I watched the bad things he did and I didn't put those into play.

Forever Young

When Manute Bol and I played on the 76ers together, I think he was about fifty-seven. Seriously. I asked him one time how old he was. He said he wasn't sure.

"Manute," I said, "don't you all have birthday parties in Africa?" He told me naw, what they do is put a little chop in the village tree each time one of the village kids gets a year older. So I said, "How many chops the last time you looked?

"I can't remember," he says. "They chopped the tree down, and that was a long time ago."

Strangest Anatomy

They say Arvydas Sabonis, the big center for the Trail Blazers, was the greatest player ever in his prime, back when he was in Europe. He's still the best passing big man in the game, by far. But back then, they say he was like Magic, but seven foot three inches. I'll tell you what Sabonis has that no one else does. That's a huge head. The human head is supposed to weigh about eight pounds. Well, Sabonis' head weighs about eighty-six pounds. That's the truth. That's a fact. When he leans his head on you, there's nothing you can do.

He's not a real strong guy, it's just that his head is so big. He's Fred Flintstone squared, you know—to the third power.

Dirtiest

You hear a lot of players bitching about John Stockton's hard picks and how he's dirty. But John Stockton never seemed dirty to me. The only problem with John Stockton is he wears them little shorts. Someone should tell the man the ABA days are over.

There are other players, though, I didn't respect and I never will. I never respected Bill Laimbeer. I give him credit for getting the most out of his ability, but he was dirty. No other player respects that. I'll tell you another player who's a dirty player, or who was a dirty player before we got him on our team, the Nets, in the 1997–98 season. Rony Seikaly is a holding guy. He isn't dirty to hurt you. He's dirty in that he knew all the little tricks. You go up for a rebound, he'd grab your hand, hold you. Things that would frustrate you.

You can't tell who's going to be dirty till you play them. I remember A. C. Green came over when I was with the Sixers and we were playing the Lakers and he asked me to sign an autograph for his niece, who he said loved me. So I signed it. Three plays into the game he elbowed me in the mouth, and me and him started fighting.

He's real religious, right? Well, I'll tell you, he might be religious, and he's a good player, but he ain't the cleanest player in the league, that's for sure.

Most Pious

Just because you say your prayers don't make you religious. You got to try to live the best you can. One player I knew was supposed to be a real Christian. He was supposed to be a really religious person, right? He'd been renting a house and the owners charged him $25,000 in damages when he was getting ready to leave. So he knocks on my door one night, asks me do I know Mafia people, can I go and have them burn that house down.

I told him to get out of my hotel room and don't ever come back.

I was raised going to church. I'm a believer. But as long as I'm talking about religion, here's a question: Why do more and more athletic teams have their little prayer sessions before and after games at half-court? Why pray in public? Why does everybody have to see you pray? I go visit sick kids ten o'clock at night but I don't tell anybody. I go visit sick kids six o'clock in the morning and no one comes along. I pray every morning and every evening, but I don't do it on Park Avenue. Why do you have to pray in front of everybody? Why don't you do it in your locker room? Why pray in the most famous arena in the world, Madison Square Garden? What is that all about? I think it would be more real if you did it in private, for yourself.

If you're going to pray before or after a game, at least include everyone, like the Charlotte Hornets do at home. Before every game there, they have a prayer, and everybody puts their heads down and prays. So do that in Madison Square Garden and I'll feel that it's more authentic. I'm not down on any of the Knicks, because all the Knicks that I know are good people. But it just seems like the praying they do is done for show more than it's done for praising the Lord. If you're going to praise the Lord, let everybody praise the Lord.

Undeserved Reputations

I think Rod Strickland's one of the nicest guys in the league. Yeah, I know he's got that bad-boy rep. Don't we all, from New York? It comes with the territory. Like cheesecake. And Shawn Kemp, another bad boy, in addition to being an unbelievable athlete, is one of the nicest guys I ever met. Great sportsman. But all those on-court moves make fans think he's got a big ego. He's always moving or grooving. He dunks, he moves his hands, he makes a good shot, he does the shimmy thing. He's got so much body language in everything he does, he's really a pleasure to watch. But a lot of fans don't think so.

I know he's got a bad rep, but I have never heard Shawn Kemp say one bad thing about anybody. And Shawn Kemp came into this league when he was only eighteen, and he persevered. He persevered through a lot of stuff. He was raw, and people didn't think he was going to make it. And he came in this league as a star, and he's going to go out as a star.

Tired, Not Lazy

Another player who's a little misunderstood is Derrick Coleman. Derrick and I got along from the day we met. That was in a classroom at a Dapper Dan tournament for the top high school players in the country. That night, I remember Derrick and I sneaking some beer, splitting a forty-ouncer, and Derrick passing out outside of my motel room, and me passing out right next to him.

We got along from that moment on. Now, Derrick played a lot of minutes his entire career. And I would say he's not a lazy guy, but more a tired guy. Neither one of us, me or Derrick, got a lot of sleep when we were young. We liked to run and have fun and party. And Derrick's line always was, "You want it now in practice, or you want it in the game? Which one do you want?" So Derrick comes into practice, he gets the shooting in, and then when contact drills start, he just does the first two or three plays. If scrimmage went to seven, he would just do the first 2 points, then let the younger guys, or the guys who don't play as much, get in. Coaches didn't like that too much. I can tell you Chuck Daly didn't like it a bit when we were both with the Nets. But I would never say that Derrick Coleman was lazy, because he played a lot of minutes all the way through high school, he played every minute in his college, every minute in the NBA. I think Derrick was just tired, and reasonably so.

Most Underrated

Just like a lot of people think some of the NBA's nicest guys are badasses, and some of the real bad dudes are upstanding citizens, they also have the wrong idea about talent. Partly this is because players get reps early, or because they don't talk much, or they say the wrong things, or whatever. But there are some great players in this league who fans don't appreciate.

I think P. J. Brown, who I played with in New Jersey and is now with the Miami Heat, is one of the most underrated players in the league. And he likes it that way. No one's out gunning for him. I'd say Horace Grant is underrated, but he made $10 million a year for the last five years, so if he's underrated, he sure ain't underpaid. Tyrone Hill—fierce rebounder, always goes hard—he's underrated. Nick Anderson with Sacramento is underrated. He's an incredibly talented player. No one talks a lot about the Davis boys—Dale and Anthony—but if you play against those two guys, you know you're in for a war. Those two guys, they play harder than anything, and they play all year long.

Now that Charles Oakley is out of New York, I'd say he's underrated, because he's a great player with a great heart. But you can't be a Knick and underrated. You play with New York, and you have a big rep automatically. Sometimes maybe bigger than you deserve, though I'm not going to name any names here, as I have to play against these guys for another six years or so.

Hold the Milk, Pass the Beer

The most underrated player I have ever seen—and this might surprise a lot of people—is Shawn Bradley. Shawn must be one of the most astonishing athletes I've ever seen besides Michael Jordan. To be seven foot six and be so coordinated, so quick, a good athlete, so mobile—you know, he's about a 95 or 90 on the golf course, good tennis player, was a great baseball player when he was young. I believe before Shawn leaves this game, he will be a Hall of Famer—he'll put up some Hall of Fame numbers. I really believe that.

But he's going to have to change his approach to the game. First, he's going to have to be less selfish. Now, I played with Shawn on the Nets, and I like him a lot, but I remember one game, a couple years ago, he looked at his box score—he had 18 points, eleven rebounds—and he was pretty happy. But the thing is, in that game every guy just came down the lane and dunked on him and did what they wanted to do. And he came out just being happy about his box score. Now, at the time it was early in the season, and people had been down on him for his bad stats, so it's understandable. But what Shawn has to learn is that when people are coming down the lane and dunking on him, especially when you're a so-called franchise player, then a box score with 18 and eleven doesn't mean anything.

The other thing about Shawn is if he wasn't so religious on the court, he'd be a better player. He should get to see some more of the outside elements to make him a little meaner.

It's not like he's Mr. Devout or anything anyway. I used to joke with him when we played golf. I'd say, "I don't care how religious you are. I don't care if you're Jesus himself. When you go out on that golf course everybody cheats." I'd ask him, "What'd you get, Shawn?"

"A six," he'd say.

I knew damn well Shawn got about an 8 on that hole, but, hey, he's seven foot six and got a six-foot-six driver. Who was I to argue with him?

A couple of beers wouldn't hurt him, either. You know, he'll put a couple of beers down and he'll get big like everybody else. Gain some weight. Drinking a lot of milk ain't helping him. And when you drink beer, a whole different character comes out in you. And sometimes you need to take that character and build from that. You take that character and say, "Wow, man, God, if I'm mean like this, why can't I be mean on the court like this?"

So if Shawn gets less selfish and maybe a little less devout on the court, and more mean, and has a few beers, he's going to be one of the all-time greats.

Of Fairy Tales and Fallaways

Now I'll tell you the most *overrated* basketball players in the world. They're the playground legends, the guys who built their reputations in the parks. Let me explain something about parks. Parks are like old ladies, and park stories are like old-lady stories. You sit down with some old ladies and play bridge, you know? At the first bridge table, one kid might have fallen down and got a splinter in his butt. By the time the story gets to that last table, that kid's going in tomorrow for hemorrhoid surgery. And that's how it is in the parks. I've played in parks—everybody blows everything out of proportion in parks.

Everyone in the NBA was a great park player. But when you get some kid who can dunk backward in the parks looking at an NBA game on TV, where it's so spread out, it looks easy to him. It's like a pretty good golfer watching the Masters, saying, "I can hit it further and straighter than that guy." He can't.

You have to understand, these park legends are playing with a thirty-five-year-old man on their team, and one of the guys on the other team is fifty years old.

That's how these legends are built. How many park legends have made it in the NBA? You can't count Connie Hawkins. He ain't no park legend if he played college ball, and he did. The park legend is somebody who didn't go to college, played in the park his whole life, and made it to the NBA. It's like Bigfoot. Fun to read about and watch silly TV shows about. But it doesn't exist.

Biggest Music Lover

Armen, who doesn't like to pay for things when he can get them free, asked my brother Victor if he could help him move a couple pieces of furniture one day. Ham figures since I'm his teammate and Victor's my brother, Victor will help for nothing. And he's right.

When Victor shows up, he's wondering why Armen has a twenty-four-foot-long U-Haul truck for just a "couple pieces of furniture." But Victor's a good guy. He spends all day helping Armen pack his stuff. Now, Armen plays a whole lot of instruments, and every time he picked one up to move it, he'd play a little something for my brother. If he picked up the bass, he played the bass. If he picked up the drums, he'd play the drums. The saxophone, same thing. My brother, he's a real nice guy, he's shy, he didn't want to say, "Look, man, I want to get out of here. Enough with all the music hoo-ha."

Victor keeps quiet until they both walk over to lift the piano. He's thinking, Man, how in the *world* are two people going to move this thing? And while he's thinking, Armen sits down at that piano, looks over at my brother, then hits a couple notes and starts singing from "Love on the Rocks." "'Pour me a drink,'" he sings, "'and I'll tell you some lies.'"

And my brother looks at Armen and says, "Aw, hell, that's it.

Man, I'm out of here. I'm not moving nothing else." So Armen pretty much gets the picture that he was taking advantage of the situation.

My brother thinks he's out and clear then. All he has to do is help Armen take the stuff to the new house—with no piano. They jump into this big U-Haul truck and they start driving, and Victor can see Armen is really enjoying driving this truck and really getting into shifting these gears. So they get on the highway, and all the while my brother is thinking, Man, I'm glad the music is over and I didn't have to lift that damn piano." And then Armen reaches into his shirt pocket and takes out this harmonica and starts playing something from Alabama.

Armen Gilliam, the truck-drivin', piano-playin', harmonica-blowin' preacher's son. Ain't nobody in the league like him. Thank goodness.

Greatest Trash Talkers

Talking trash is part of the NBA, but not nearly as much as a lot of fans think. About half the players don't say anything when they're playing. A bunch of others—if they're your friends—ask you what you're doing that night, and then there are some guys who just make the funny comments. Antoine Carr always had a good sense of humor on the court. Once, after I dunked hard on Greg Ostertag, Antoine acted all scared and said, "Goddamn, big fellow, you like to kill him." He's always funny on the court with his little comments. I don't know how much Ostertag was laughing, but everyone else thought it was pretty funny. And Patrick Ewing, who everyone thinks is this serious guy, he's got a great sense of humor. Whenever I play him, he says, "Aw, man, you playing me again?" He says, "They going to put your wild butt on me? Please don't hurt me." You know, he thinks I play way too aggressive. But he's a funny guy.

As for the trash talkers, there are a few in the league. Michael Jordan was always saying stuff. "You can't stop me. I can do whatever I want against you." And he was always right, too. Gary Payton is probably one of the big talkers now, and Vernon Maxwell, and of course Reggie Miller. Tim Hardaway is ruthless. He'll be talking the whole game. I remember one game a couple years ago, fourth quarter, he says, "You all ain't going to win this game. We're about to tear it up right now." And they did.

Alonzo Mourning talks some stuff. Nick Van Exel yaps a lot. And then you got some players, and I'm thinking of Shaquille O'Neal especially, who talk with their body language, playing the crowd. I think when people start playing the crowd, that bothers me more than anything else, because now they're trying to embarrass you. They're not talking to you, they're embarrassing you. Shaq's done that to me before, and we got into it. Took some swings at each other.

The Night Larry Made Doc Choke

As for really tormenting people, Larry Bird was about as good as anyone I ever encountered. And other players felt the same way. Remember when he first came into the league and he and Julius Erving were the big stars, and they were guarding each other one game and the refs threw Julius out because he was choking Larry? That picture must have been on every sports page in the country, and maybe some in China, too. Supposedly what happened was Larry had about 30 points going into the third quarter, and Doc had 8. And Larry, who had been talking smack all game, saying, "I'm gonna shoot now," and "I'm gonna light you up with a hook now," and then doing it, he starts with the really cruel stuff.

Whenever he gets close to Doc, he kinda whispers, "Thirty to eight, Doc, thirty to eight, Doc." And Doc was proud, and he lost it. And I think Larry probably laughed the rest of the game.

Code of Conduct

No player talks about another player's girlfriend or wife or mother, or anything like that.

There are some things we don't cross the line with. You have to understand that in this league you've got a lot of kids who make a lot of money and can easily spend it. And these kids come from neighborhoods where other people—for *not* a lot of money—could easily do very great bodily harm to somebody. Some of these kids in the league now have friends who would hurt someone just to impress you, or just to get in your good graces. Imagine what a kid like that would do for $10,000. And an NBA player can take $10,000 and throw that in twenty minutes in a crap game.

You see this in the record business more than anything. Hey, you see it in *all* entertainment businesses. NBA players know it. They know that peace is very fragile, so we watch what we say and do.

Chapter 3

Pleasures of the Flesh, Temptations of the Spirit, and How Charles Barkley Took Me Under His Wing and Proceeded to Shave Four Years off My Life

Suppose you're young, black, and good-looking, and you're making more money than you can count, and women are calling your hotel room at one o'clock in the morning—not just women, but *Sports Illustrated* swimsuit models. That's what it's like to be in the NBA.

Drinking and drugs exist in sports, too, just like they exist in all of society, but before I get to those, I want to talk about sex, because at least that doesn't end up with your butt in jail or in trouble with the police. At least most of the time.

Next time you watch a pro basketball game, watch us talking during the layup drills. See us sometimes looking in the stands? What's happening is the players are seeing if they spot a woman they might want to meet. If they do, most of the time they send a ball boy over. The ball boy goes over, says, "Here's a pass. Meet so-and-so at the gate after the game." And yeah, almost every time they show up. We're NBA players, so it's a status thing for these women.

45

There could be trouble if two guys are sending ball boys to the same woman, or to a woman who's sitting next to a guy, but most of the players are pretty respectful about that. Sometimes in the same markets, two guys on one team have their eye on the same woman, and that's dangerous. But most of the time players avoid that. The waters are plentiful, so why make waves?

Room Service

How plentiful? I was at my hotel in Phoenix after a game a couple years ago, and about one o'clock in the morning the phone rings. Lady says she's a swimsuit model for *Sports Illustrated*. She comes up to my room at 1:30, and it ends up she's telling the truth.

I spend a few nice hours with her. She's very materialistic; everything that came out of her mouth was money. She was talking about how she had a model friend who was married to a ballplayer who gives her $12,000 a month and mentioning another basketball player who gives her other model friend $10,000 a month to take care of his baby and to have another baby from her.

I spent about four hours with her and sent her on her way. Times like that, the NBA is FANtastic, brother.

Beds Are for Sleeping, Too

Just because sex is readily available doesn't mean we don't have standards. I took a young lady to training camp with me a few years ago, and we flew down together, to Florida. I'm six foot ten, and I laid myself across a few seats and took my shoes off. But this young lady lay down, and she still had her shoes on, big old boots. They were just all over the place. I thought it was very unladylike and I let her know. She smoked all the time, too, which I didn't appreciate.

And the worst thing, after you have relations, or sex, or whatever you want to call it, making love, whatever, I can't stand it when after you finish, they're always cuddled up on you. I have claustrophobia in the worst way. So when it's time for me to go to sleep,

I don't want nobody hugging me, I don't want nobody near me. I want an imaginary line right down the middle of the bed. But all night she'd cuddle up against me. She knows I have claustrophobia, and I can't sleep that close to anybody because I have bad dreams. But this young lady, she wouldn't stay on her side. That, and the combination of the cigarettes and her putting her feet up like a sailor, well, I put her on a flight after a few days. Sent her home early.

Standards, that's what I'm talking about.

Think of Us as IBM Salesmen

Every year, the beginning of the season, the league tells us about sex, about all the trouble we could get in. But you know what? We're the highest-profile athletes in the world. We're like rock stars. So, yeah, there's groupies everywhere. And yeah, there are guys who bring the girls. I've heard some people call them fixers. That's not accurate. You know what they really are. They're pimps. These guys, they say, "Hey, man, you remember me from four years ago?" and four years ago, you might have had too many beers, so you say, "Yeah, yeah," and then he says, "I'm gonna fix you up with this girl or that girl," and before you know it, you're upstairs and you're in trouble.

The thing is you can't tell a young rookie on the road not to go out. Maybe 10 percent of the rookies are going to stay in their hotel room and read a novel. The other 90 percent are going to be shaking their ass or watching someone else's ass shake.

And you can't blame the rookies, because it's no different than the guy who goes on the road for IBM. He ain't going to sit up in that hotel room, he's going to go out. It's not like he's going to commit adultery—well, he might try—but he's definitely going to go out. Guys in this league are no more sex addicts than the guy who's working for IBM who has to travel. It's just a lot easier for us. And when you're a rookie in the NBA, when you're just starting to be famous, you want to find out how famous you are. You want to get the best table in the house, the prettiest girl in the room.

Oprah

Or sometimes you want the most famous or powerful woman in the room. I've always had a thing for Oprah. Oprah fascinates me. Here's a woman from the South, self-made, built a business out of nothing, incredibly successful. And I admit it, I used to have a crush on Oprah. NBA players have time on their hands, and sometimes I'd catch her show and think, Yeah, I can see me and Oprah. And I figured I'd have no problem if I put the word out, even though I've read she's got that boyfriend and all. I figure I'm young, good-looking, articulate, and intelligent, plus I'm a professional athlete making some serious money.

Then a few years ago I read how much money Oprah was making. *Really* serious money. Millions and millions. And a few more millions. And after reading that, I took a look at myself in the mirror. And suddenly I wasn't so good-looking. In fact, I realized that to Oprah I wouldn't look like nothing more than chopped liver. That's what I'd be to Oprah—six foot ten inches of ugly old chopped liver. That woman is making some *serious* money.

Stormy Weather

I don't mean to imply that it's just the young guys looking for action. Some of the craziest guys in the league are the old men. When Clifford Ray was my assistant coach with the Nets, trying to teach me about hook shots, he was also always bragging about how big he was. Clifford played center in the NBA, so naturally he was tall, but that's not the kind of big he was bragging about.

He told me one time he was doing this woman and he had her in the bathroom of his hotel room. He said, "I was doing her from behind. I had one foot in the toilet bowl and I had the other foot in the bathtub and I was flicking on and off the lights and flushing the toilet."

When he's telling me this, I'm thinking, What the hell?

He said, "That was my action of thunder, lightning, and rain."

And I'm thinking, Oh, man. Here's a grown man, fifty-five years old, one foot in the toilet bowl and the other one in the shower, flushing the toilet and flicking the lights? And the league's worried about rookies?

The Virus

You might think from reading about these groupies and swimsuit models and Clifford's crazy-ass, stormy-weather routine that NBA players are irresponsible. Do guys act crazy? Of course they do. They're guys. But you know, after Magic Johnson announced he had the virus, I bet you that for that next five or six months, all the players' wives got a *whole* lot more attention. I think that really opened everybody's eyes. I already knew about it, with my two sisters having died of AIDS. But a lot of guys didn't know.

The thing is you've got to take care of yourself. And for a while, people did. The players were a lot more careful; you *know* condom stock went way up. But now you hear people saying, "Well, you can live twenty years with it, or thirty years." And it's hard sometimes when you're in a situation and you got a supermodel on your arm. When that happens, a lot of the guys say, "Well, she's a supermodel—she can't have AIDS."

I wouldn't care what she is. If I'm with a woman, I'm going through $100 worth of rubbers. I put so many rubbers on I look like John Holmes.

If I'm out, the first thing I do if a girl comes to my room is I knock on my teammates' doors. "You got rubbers?" I ask. "You got rubbers?" Maybe one of the guys will give me one, but then he'll say, "I need these other two," so I have to knock on another door. Because I wear two or three at once, I have to knock on a few doors. One time I was desperate, so I ended up knocking on Don Casey's door—he was about sixty years old at the time, then our assistant coach.

"You got rubbers?" I say. He's mumbling and rubbing his eyes. "What time's the bus go?" he mumbles. "What time's the bus go?" I'm asking for rubbers and he wants to know about the bus.

Sharks, Speed Traps, and the Joys of Fatherhood

I was reading in *Sports Illustrated* a few years ago about all the NBA players who had fathered illegitimate children. First off, I don't know that it's the media's—or anyone's—business how many kids you have, as long as you take care of them. But even so, one of the things that shocked me was how guys could be so brave to have all that unprotected sex. But I guess it's like a surfer. When he first goes in the water, he's worrying about a shark. A few weeks later he's patting that shark on the ass, he's chasing that shark. Same thing with some of these guys. I mean, they're more aware, but they still do stupid things. Sometimes it's just selfish, stupid guys. But I have no doubt that some of these girls trapped the guys into it—they wanted to have an NBA player's baby. But you know what? If you made a child, you have to support it. Even if a girl traps you into it, you still got caught and you've got a child. I mean, if you're riding down the highway and you're going eighty-five and you're caught in a speed trap, you've got to still pay the ticket. They trapped you, but you were speeding. If you weren't speeding, you wouldn't get that ticket.

Cheating, NBA Wives, and a Matter of Trust

Most guys I talk to in the NBA tell me, "Why would you, a young man, earning a lot of money, stuff thrown at you every day, why would you even think about getting married? And give away half your money?"

It's not just basketball players. Ninety-five percent of the athletes I've ever discussed it with say the same thing. Larry Holmes, one of my good friends who I visit at his house, he's always telling me, "Now, don't get married." Larry Holmes preaches it to me all the time in front of his wife, which she doesn't seem to appreciate too much, but I figure she and Larry work that out after I go home.

I was supposed to get married right before I signed my last contract, which turned out to be so big. I wanted to wait till the contract was signed, and I wanted to be absolutely sure about the marriage. I didn't want to sign my contract, get married, then three months later I'm divorced, and she gets 50 percent of $100 million. I mean, I love that "to serve and protect" stuff, but I don't love it *that* much.

As it turns out, I signed the contract, then we broke up.

Diamonds Are a Man's Worst Enemy

I don't want anyone to think I don't respect women or that I don't respect marriage. It's just the opposite. I think before it's all said and done we'll have a woman in the NBA. I'm not talking about refs. I'm talking about power forwards and point guards. You know why? Because the farmers keep feeding their animals all those hormones and steroids and stuff and the women keep eating the hamburgers, and that makes women a lot stronger than they used to be. I swear, sometimes when they kick me out of bed, you wouldn't believe how strong they are already. So they'll be in the NBA before too long, you mark my words.

As for marriage, I'm all for it. It's a great institution, but in the NBA it's tough.

What happens in the league is when your wife is home and you're out working and she's not working, she's sitting there and she's waiting on you to come home, and she's got all these wild fantasies of what you're doing. Especially if she doesn't have her own career, and she has a girlfriend who's telling her, "Well, you know, he made this much money, he's on the road, and I heard this about him and I heard that." Rumors can break up more marriages. Especially if your wife doesn't have anything to do. That's why it's better for an NBA wife to have her own career. Something to keep her mind occupied.

Because if her mind isn't occupied, there's trouble. And sometimes the trouble comes from the other wives. You got some wives who go into the players' wives' room after a game, and they're flashing a ten-carat diamond, and their husband's the star of the team, so they're acting like they're the star of the wives. They're not treating the other wives nice. That's why the only woman I know who goes into that room now after a game is my mother.

People always say it's the wives worrying. They ain't the only ones worrying. If you're not home, a lot of times you're worrying, too. It's a two-way street. The key is, if you don't want to cheat on your wife, you don't have to. You don't even have to cheat on your girlfriend if you don't want to. And they don't have to cheat on you. It's about trust.

Old Horses, New Tricks

You want a quick way to figure out who's married in this league? Look at the old-timers. Those old horses who have been playing twenty years aren't all playing because they love the game or they need the money. Some of them are playing because they don't know how to be home with the wife and kids. They've never *been* home. So how can they retire? They don't know how to bring a kid to school in the morning, they don't know how to cook breakfast, they don't know how to be a househusband.

I've seen some of these guys retire, and they stay home for the first time, and they watch their little boy, or their little girl, and they say, "Oh, man, that's Damien! That's a devil child. That ain't my kid."

Or they look at their wife in the kitchen, and they go, "Man, my wife got some fat calves!" Old horses like that, they have some learning ahead of them.

Yoo-Hoo!

We all get our ideas about sex growing up, so I guess I can't really talk about sex without mentioning the time my mother found out my father had been cheating on her. I was twelve years old then.

After my mom found out about my dad, she waited till he got home, when he was in the shower. My mom grew up in Brooklyn, was a little crazy. So when he was in the shower, she took his gun and shot three times into the bathroom. She was pissed off about that other girl.

My father ran out and pushed her down and ran into the bedroom. And my mom grabbed a butcher knife then and came running after him. I was just lying in bed, and my dad came into my room, yelling at me, "What we going to do?"

I said, "You mean, what *you* going to do? She mad at you, Pop, not me, right?"

My dad climbed out my window. This was in the late seventies when all the brothers were wearing cowboy boots, and one of his heels got caught on the windowsill and I had to try to loosen it. When I finally did, he fell and hit his head on our birdbath.

My mother heard him and came running out and he jumped into the Yoo-Hoo truck he had then. He had a Yoo-Hoo distributorship. My mother was chasing him with her butcher knife, trying to stab him through the window. And by then, I was hanging on the other side of the truck, because I figured if she was so tripped out and he got away, Mom might come after the guy who helped Dad escape out the window. Me.

I rode on the outside of that Yoo-Hoo truck for about thirty minutes, and it felt like it was going about sixty. I think my dad thought my mother must have still been behind us. Finally he stopped and pulled me in.

"Damn, Dad," I said.

That was the only time I ever saw my parents argue. That one time was plenty.

The Wings of Devils

Charles Barkley taught me more about basketball than anyone else. When I came to Philadelphia, he taught me how to run the floor, how to deal with the media. He taught me about charisma and about what happens if you're impatient, like Charlie was with people sometimes. You know, Charlie grew up in Alabama, where people move pretty slow, so maybe that's why he's impatient sometimes. I'm from New York, and you *better* be patient there, or you're going to kill every cabdriver you meet, or you're going to break your foot kicking someone's butt every day.

One thing I wish Charlie hadn't done was take me under his wing socially. He probably cost me about four years off my life. Because of Charles Barkley, my liver is about the size of two footballs. Charlie could drink. Man, could he drink. And the thing about Charlie, he would stay out all night. I mean *all* night. Once someone said to him, "Charlie, when you gonna sleep?" I'll never forget. He was all hungover, practicing three-pointers, hitting about eight in a row, with his eyes barely open, stinking of alcohol, could barely walk, and he says, "I'll sleep when I'm dead, man, I'll sleep when I'm dead."

A couple years ago Charlie said he was quitting drinking because it had been hurting his game. I love Charlie, I owe a lot to Charlie, but I think he was using drinking as an excuse to explain why his game wasn't as good as it used to be. Charlie was just getting older, and his skills were fading. And I think he knew it. But which would you rather be: a drunk or a basketball player who's not as good as he used to be? Charlie decided to go with being a drunk. Excuse me, a recovering drunk. Myself, I'd have to go with the bad basketball player.

I'm not saying that I think quitting drinking is a bad thing. I don't.

Chris Mullin quit drinking a few years ago. I asked him about it, and he told me, "I'll play ten years straight, won't ever drink, I'll make thirty million. Then I go back to the neighborhood. The same guys will be right where I left them, but I'll have thirty million to play with. But if I went there now and I started drinking—ten years go by and I'd be broke, I'd be miserable. So I'll stop for ten years, twelve years. When I retire, I'll go back and I'll have thirty million in the bank, and a big reason I'll have that is I quit drinking."

And that made a lot of sense to me.

You're Getting Sleepy. Verrrry Sleepy

No question I used to drink too much. I know that now. Maybe some of my old coaches knew it then. But the way a lot of them tried to get me to quit was ridiculous.

The Nets had me going to see one psychiatrist a few years ago. He did all the talking. He told me that his son was an airline pilot. I had to see this guy once a week, and after about a season all I knew was how to fly a plane. That's all he talked about. The coaches then were making ten out of twelve guys on the team go see him. Which was about right—we were a crazy team back then. We had what you call issues. Chris Morris was on that team. He used to write "Trade Me" on his sneakers. We had Derrick Coleman, Armen Gilliam, P. J. Brown, Sam Bowie, guys like that. We had an "all short bus" crew on that team. We were the short-bus crew of the league. You know, the normal kids go to school on the big bus. We were the short-bus crew.

Each one of us had a scheduled time to see the shrink in the morning, because practice started at noon. One guy would be there at 7:30 to 8:00, maybe another guy from 8:00 to 8:30 and so on.

The last appointment was 11:00 and I always tried to get that one. The shrink would be sitting there, and he'd be asking me how I felt and was I happy and such. So I used to let him go through his whole thing, the how-do-I-feel, the my-son-the-pilot, the whole deal. Then about 11:30, especially on those days I was hungover and really didn't feel like running up and down that damn floor, I'd say, "Oh, you know, I'm really having a problem with Jack Daniel's also."

Then he'd be going for five minutes or so on the deadly effects of Jack Daniel's, and then he's all concerned, like, "How's everything else in your life, buddy? How's everything going?" It would be 12:30 before he let me loose. And I'd walk into practice half an hour late, after a lot of the running drills were over, and everyone would be looking at me. The coaches were pissed. And I'd hold my hands out. I'd say, "Hey, this is what you all told me to do. You all told me to see the psychiatrist."

Old-Time Religion

I was raised Catholic, mostly by my mom, who's one of the most religious people I know. But when I was living down in Ritter, South Carolina, as a little boy, my Grandma Elvira, my dad's mother, tried to make me into a Methodist. Every Sunday she'd take me and my first cousin, whose name was Herman Lee but who everybody called Stinker, to the Methodist Church, and I'll tell you what: When those hymns started, your lips better be moving. Even if you didn't know the words, you'd better be saying something, or Grandma Elvira would whack you on the head.

Stinker was the son of my dad's sister, Loretta, who was the most beautiful woman I ever saw and who I had a big crush on. She was married to Herman Lee, Sr., and they used to fight all the time. Yelling, hitting, you name it. One time she was coming home in her car, a big Delta 88, and he was driving somewhere in his car, another big car, and as Aunt Loretta tells it, they saw each other and they couldn't help it, they just aimed straight at each other. *Boom!* To this day Aunt Loretta limps because of that one particular accident. Eventually they got divorced, which is a good thing. And she's been happily married to a really great guy for years, so that's a good thing, too.

Anyway, there's Grandma Elvira and me and Stinker sitting there in the eighth row and they're singing and I'm moving my lips so I don't get conked on the head, and then the preacher stops and he starts the laying on of hands. He'll walk down into the crowd and he'll smack his palm on someone's forehead and yell out, "Praise Jesus," and then that person will faint onto the floor and sometimes they'll start babbling. Talking in tongues they call it down there. So he whacks Grandma Elvira and she wobbles a little, but she don't go down. He whacks her again and she sways a little, but she don't go down. A third time—*whack!*—I mean, he hits her *hard*, and she falls to one knee and starts babbling a little, but Grandma Elvira won't go down. As religious as she was, she would never fall to the floor, and in fact she was proud of that. And so, naturally, were me and Stinker, both nine years old that summer. Every time the preacher would hit her and she'd wobble, we'd look at each other and whisper, "Gramma ain't going down."

So after he tries Grandma Elvira one more time then lays his hands on some other people and knocks a bunch of old people on the floor, the preacher yells out, "What man in this community needs savin'? Who amongst us is in dire trouble and needs the Lord's help?"

And a voice in the front row says, "I need help. I need saving."

Stinker and me know this is a familiar voice, and when the boy talking stands up, we see it's Fuzzy, which is what everybody calls this boy. Fuzzy and his family live in Possum Corner, not far from Ritter. Fuzzy's about nineteen years old at the time.

"What ails you?" the preacher booms out.

"Alcohol!" Fuzzy yells.

"Are you ready to give your life to Jesus?"

"Yes, I am!"

The preacher puts his hand on Fuzzy's forehead, softer than he was whacking the old folks, and he yells out, "Alcohol, leave this man. Satan, begone! Lucifer, get away from Fuzzy and don't ever come back!"

And then, I swear to God, Fuzzy vomits an eighty-foot orange stream. It's like a giant flame. Me and Stinker are all the way back in the eighth row, and we have to duck, but some of it still hits us. And the preacher is saying, "And if you ever take another drink, Fuzzy, if you ever let Satan into your body under the disguise of alcohol, you will go blind."

And on that day Fuzzy quit drinking. When my family left Ritter later that year, I didn't see Fuzzy again, until I made a trip back down South after my second season in the NBA. On that trip I drive up to Fuzzy's house, and there he is, sitting on the porch, whittling away at something.

"Hey, Fuzzy," I say. "How you doin? It's Jayson, Stinker's cousin on his mom's side."

Fuzzy says "Hey," but he doesn't look at me.

"What's up, Fuzz?" I say. "What's goin' on?"

Then one of Fuzzy's sisters sticks her head out the door.

"He can't see you," she says. "He went blind a month ago."

Turns out Fuzzy stayed sober for about eleven years, then he took his first drink, and just a few weeks later he was blind. Later on doctors told his family it was because of diabetes, but still, it happened just a few weeks after that first drink. Makes you wonder about those Methodist preachers.

Owls and Eagles, Boys and Men

When Butch Beard first came in as Nets coach for the '94–'95 season, I remember having a rough week, going out drinking and missing shootaround. And I called Butch and I told him, "Butch, it's ten o'clock and I'm feeling sick." I told him the truth, said I was out drinking, I didn't get home until 7:30 in the morning. And we had a nine o'clock shootaround.

He says, "Jay, if you're just getting in, don't go out, don't leave, stay in. I'll take the heat for you. But I'm going to come to your house to see you afterwards."

And then he didn't come to my house until noon. I was crying, because I'd been trying to cut down on my drinking and I'd screwed up. I never had a problem with drinking every day. My problem was when I did drink, I'd go to the extreme, I'd drink a whole lot. And he came over and said, "Jay, yeah, you screwed up. We all have done it. You come on back tonight and play hard, and don't worry about it. I love you, kid. I'm going to make sure you're straight." And that was it, and he left. And I said, "I love that man. I love him."

My mother sat me down then, too, and she said, "Jay, the good life, the party life, the wild life has to stop. You have to grow up and be a man, boy." About that same time, Willis Reed told me, "If you're not going to quit drinking completely, then start drinking responsibly." His line to me was, "You can't hang out with the owls at night and soar with the eagles in the morning." And he was correct about that, too. What Willis told me, and what Chuck Daly told me, too, is to pick and choose my days.

At first I used to pick five days every week. That was a mistake. What I know now is that drinking was affecting my work. I used to say I didn't have a drinking problem because I didn't drink every day. Now I know better. So now I figure all week you stay clean, right? And then on a Saturday night if you've got Sunday off, if you want to go out and have a couple of cocktails, you can. But the things I used to do all night, back in the days, I can't do it anymore.

Joker's Wild

A few years back, when the Nets were flying back from a game, I was sitting next to P. J. Brown, and I was worrying like I usually do about flying, mostly because of my claustrophobia. And P. J. sees me all scared, and he does what he usually does: He laughs and grabs my wrist and says, "Don't worry about it." That always makes me feel better. But this time, right after he said it, the plane dropped two thousand feet in about half a second.

This time he didn't grab anything. P. J. looks kind of like the Joker, from *Batman,* but with this plane dropping so fast, he looked like the guy in *G Force*. The g-force had his face and it was pulling it back and I was looking at him, thinking, Wow. Because for that one split second I was still thinking funny, thinking, Wait until I tell somebody about this and relive how I seen P. J.'s face. And then, real quick, I'm not feeling so funny. You know where I ended up? Under P. J.'s seat. That was a tight squeeze, but I somehow made it under there.

When the plane levels off, P. J. is shaking me, saying, "Boy, come on out of there."

And when he finally got me out, I was still shook up. I was so shook up that after Chuck Daly looked to see how everyone was, and saw me, he sent a flight attendant up to me with half a bottle of Absolut. We weren't allowed to drink on the plane then, but Chuck Daly, who'd been telling me about moderation and all, he said, "Go ahead and finish it." And I don't know if I was flying with the eagles or the owls or the friggin' crows, but I don't want to do it again.

A Matter of Taste

It wasn't that I ever said I need to stop. You just wake up one day and feel, man I'm getting old, I can't do this. My favorite dish in the morning was Cream of Wheat. My mom used to make it for me every morning. But I couldn't eat that anymore because once I got to about twenty-six, twenty-seven years, my body started rejecting milk for some reason. Maybe it was because the night before I might've went out and had twenty-five Absolut and cranberries. So that's another reason I cut back.

Social Lubricant

I don't think alcohol is bad by itself and I don't want anyone to think I think that. Sometimes I think it can help people. For example, I work out with the kids from Farleigh Dickinson University in the summer. Their gym is about forty-five minutes from where I live, so it's convenient. And a couple summers ago the coach told me there were eight new players on the squad, and he was a little worried, because they didn't know each other too well.

So I didn't tell the coach, but I invited the guys out to my house one weekend. Sent a couple vans to pick them up. I let them swim, ride bikes, stuff like that.

And I let them drink a couple beers. There's nothing like a pool table and a couple beers and a room full of guys. You know what? You have a room full of people, and you leave them for forty minutes with no alcohol, and you come back and the place'll be kind of quiet. You give them alcohol, and you come back in forty minutes, everyone is jumping up and down and people getting to know people. And that's what I did for these kids. They got to know each other, had a good time.

Monkey on Your Back

Cocaine will mess you up. And that's the main reason I don't use it. Another reason has to do with what happened to a friend of one of my relatives. My relative's friend—let's call him Spike—had a pet squirrel monkey, and Spike used to do a lot of cocaine. So Spike, because he loves his pet monkey, or because he's just stupid, he started coming home every day and giving his monkey a little taste of his stuff. So he did it for like three weeks, and then one day he comes home and he doesn't have any. Spike lets his little monkey out of the cage, and when that monkey sees he's not getting a taste, he jumps on Spike's back, grabs him around the neck with one arm and snatches a baseball bat with the other, and—*whop! whop! whop!*—he's beating the tar out of Spike. You have any idea how fast and how strong a monkey is? Even a little squirrel monkey like Spike's? A neighbor hears the commotion, hears Spike screaming and hollering, and calls the police. That cute little monkey had beat Spike into a pulp, put him into a coma. The cops had to shoot the monkey cold—they killed it—and Spike was in the hospital for almost a month.

I told my mom about Spike, and she said, "That's what you call a real monkey on your back." She thought it was kind of funny. But it helped to keep me away from cocaine.

Hot Times in the Old Days

A couple guys played for the Houston Rockets back some years ago, back in the days when you used to bring your uniform home and wash it yourself. They were back in the car smoking reefer before a game. They got so high, they fell asleep in the parking lot and they changed in the car. Then they smoked another joint, fell asleep again, and by the time they woke up, it was 7:30 and the game was about to start. They ran into the layup line with their uniforms and their warm-ups on, ran right through the stadium into the layup line. And one of the guys, let's call him Jim, noticed that the other guy—let's call him Jack—noticed that Jack's warm-up was on fire. So Jim was saying, "Jack, Jack, you're smokin'." And Jack kept shooting the ball and it was going in. So Jack was saying, "Whew, I know. I'm so damn hot tonight." And Jim was like, "No, no, no, you on fire." And Jim's like, "Who you tellin', boy? I ain't missed a shot yet." And Jim's like, "No, man, your warm-up is burning up."

They had to throw Gatorade on it.

What's in a Name?

The trainer gives you something when you're hurt, and one thing you never know is exactly what it is you're taking. What they always say is, "Oh, it's Tylenol Three." No matter what, no matter how bad you're hurt or how powerful what they give you is, they always say Tylenol Three. You take it and it don't feel like any Tylenol you've ever experienced, but you ask, and it's the same thing. "Just Tylenol, just Tylenol."

When I had a bad thumb in the play-offs in '98, I was taking so many painkillers against Chicago that when I went to the bathroom before the game, I was pissing blood. I looked and I saw blood pissing straight down, and when I saw that, I almost passed out.

Then when I went into the game, I had no feeling in my hands. When I went to grab a rebound, I could see the ball in my hand, but I couldn't feel it. When I shot, same thing. Through that whole series, I never once felt the ball. That was the strongest Tylenol ever invented.

In the Dark, They All Look Like Cindy Crawford

I've asked other players, "If you took a pill and it could make you another eighty-five million dollars because you'd be stronger and faster and a better player, and you would give ten years of your life to do it, would you?"

Of every player I've asked, I haven't heard one person say, "I wouldn't do that." Everybody said yeah, they'd do it. Because you come in diapers and you leave in diapers. And I don't know of anybody who wants to be here for the last ten years of their life, anyway.

I *do* want to be here on this earth as long as possible. So I wouldn't do a drug like that. But if there was a pill and you knew it would get you another $50 or $85 million by making you stronger and faster and more agile, don't you think you'd be tempted?

I'll tell you what I think is wrong—what kills me is, if you're going to do steroids, don't do it just to look good. You've got people who do steroids and don't make any money from their body, but they do it so they can look good when they go to the beach. And they're going to take ten years off their life just to go to the beach? They're going to take ten years off their life to get that gorgeous girl for two weeks?

If you give me ten years of my life or one night with Cindy Crawford, I'd have to go with the ten years. Not that I don't think Cindy's hot. But really, if you're with a woman and you cut the lights, then *she* can be Cindy Crawford. And you still got those last ten years of life. Otherwise, you take that pill and it's like the Black Widow, you know. You know how they do it. They demand it. It feels real good, and then they bite you and they kill you.

The Night I Made Jerry West Duck

With all the alcohol and drugs and sex available to us, the league not only wants its players to behave, it puts a lot of effort into making them behave. The NBA security people—if they think you're doing something wrong, they will come out and follow you.

A few years ago a player for the 76ers looked out his window at two in the morning and saw a car parked outside. At seven o'clock, five hours later, he hears a knock on the door and it's the two guys from the car. They say they're from the league and they want a urine test. So he gives it to them.

The NBA security folks are a suspicious bunch. Even when they don't need to be. I remember one game with the Nets, five years ago, there were about three seconds left in the game and we were up one and I had a free throw. I don't know what happened, but when I shot, the ball went in a straight line and hit the left-hand corner of the backboard. And then there was silence in the arena for about three seconds and then everybody just busted out laughing.

Then Chris Childs, our point guard then, he comes running up to me and says, "Oh, my God, Jay! You made Jerry West duck!"

Because there's that NBA sticker, that silhouette of Jerry West, on the left-hand corner of the backboard, right where my ball hit. And Chris is laughing, saying, "You made Jerry put his hands up and say, "Watch it!'"

Even the ref is laughing hysterically. He gives me the ball back for a second shot, says, "Here, Jay, try another one."

Funny, right? Not to the NBA. The next day I get a call from Rod Thorn, the NBA vice president who's in charge of things like game conduct and discipline. Rod wants to talk about that shot. He said, "Jay, when you shoot shots like that, it looks like you're shaving points."

I said, "Rod, I was trying my damnedest to make that shot." I said, "If you don't believe me, check it out. I'm only shooting 57 percent."

Look, Don't Touch

Every year the league tells its rookies about problems they might get into. But you know what? Some of the stuff the league says doesn't change any rookies' minds. Drugs? If you were doing drugs before you got in the NBA, you would continue doing them. You're definitely not going to stop using drugs because all of a sudden you got $30 million.

Not that the stuff they tell the rookies isn't good for them to hear. I did my training in 1990. They reenact different situations, with actors. They do one about a family member coming to you for money, another one about shaving points, another about date rape. The scariest one, they showed a tape of a guy going around slipping things into players' drinks after introducing him to a pretty woman, then taking embarrassing pictures later of the guy and the woman. That woke some of us up.

But when you're a rookie, you want to see what the world thinks of you. That's why the young guys are into the club scene. And that's trouble, because they're in there with a bunch of people and there's always someone with a Napoleon complex, someone who wants to build a reputation. The older guys, the veterans, they'll go to the topless joints. They'll pop a beer and look. Look but don't touch. Ain't nothing wrong with that.

Wild and Crazy Monks

What I'm proud of is that in the NBA, with 470 players in the league, such a small percentage get in trouble. How many people are in the headlines now? Probably about four. Only a small percentage of us ever get busted for drug use or get arrested. Three or four out of more than four hundred? That's less than the church. That's less than the monks. You put 470 monks in New York City for a night, I guarantee you'll have more than four of them being on the news the next day.

Chapter 4

Bathroom Brawls,

Cheating and Arguing

with Teammates

over Stats.

Why I Love

the College Game

Growing up in New York City, attending Christ the King High School, it's hard to believe that I would have considered any college other than St. John's, with its history, its games in Madison Square Garden, its famous coach, Lou Carnesecca, and its religious affiliation, which really made my mom happy. But I almost didn't go there.

Three other universities each offered me $50,000 to go to their schools. One of them was even throwing in a new Jaguar. And that's not uncommon for high-profile high school players, like I was.

I considered Seton Hall, because Seton Hall came up with the most ways to make money off the court. Nothing illegal, but cushy summer jobs, stuff like that. And my father was doing a lot of work in New Jersey then, spending a lot of time there, so it would have been perfect for me. One of Seton Hall's representatives was supposed to meet me and my dad in front of the Seton Hall gym one night at 8:00, and we were going to finalize the deal. So my dad drives me there, we get there at 8:00, we wait there till 12:30, and this guy never showed up. I was so pissed off I went and signed at St. John's the next day.

I never got an illegal dime from St. John's. I swear on my mother. St. John's gave me $1,000 a month legally, because they didn't have any dorms. That's one reason I didn't even want any more money. Plus, there was no booster club at St. John's. Coach Carnesecca never let alums get together and give players money, like they do other places. So even if you wanted more money, where were you going to get it from? The players at other places who were getting illegal money were getting like $600, $700 a month. And we were getting $1,000 a month legally, for "living expenses," because there weren't any dorms. So who was coming out ahead?

Another great thing about St. John's was the exposure. Coach Carnesecca told me, "When you play here, it's like you're in Macy's window, brother. Everybody sees you."

Making the Grade

I had some fairly well publicized troubles with tests at St. John's, and I had some problems with coaches there, too. But before I talk about those, I want to make clear that the problems I had weren't St. John's fault.

I was always what you might call a character. Pretty smart kid, but sometimes too smart for my own good. I had this one English teacher in high school, she didn't like me, I didn't like her. I was always cutting up in class, and maybe not paying quite as much attention to my schoolwork as I should have, and she flat out was not happy with me. She was also fat.

When it was time to take this teacher's final exam, I knew I wasn't in the best shape, so I went up to her the day before the test and I said, "What do I need on the final to pass the class?"

And she said, "You need a hundred and one to pass the class."

I said, "What if I get a hundred, I'll pass the class, right?"

She said, "No, you'll be one point shy."

I said, "Well, can I get some extra credit?"

She said, "No."

I said, "Well, I'm not going to take the final if I have no chance of passing the class."

She said, "If you don't take that final, you're going to fail all your classes."

Now I'm pissed. So when we get the final exam the next day, I just write one sentence on top of the test. That's it, just one sentence. I write, "Dear Miss C————, I need a hundred and one points to pass this class, and you need to lose a hundred and one pounds. Signed, "J. Motown Williams," because that's what I called myself sometimes back then.

So the teacher gives the note to the principal and the principal sends it to my dad. And my dad gave me a whipping.

A Man of Letters

To get a basketball scholarship to college, you have to be a damn good high school player. But I got cut from the junior high school team in the seventh and eighth grades. I just kept practicing, though. And toward the end of my year in eighth grade, the team needed some extra players. This was at Christ the King. And the dean of the school asked me to play on the team.

I said, "Uh-uh. You cut me last year. I'll never play for you. I'm going to Power Memorial next year. I'm not even staying here for the ninth grade." I was pretty good then, but I wasn't *that* good. It wasn't like I was going to make or break the team. They just thought I was crazy.

But I was embarrassed being cut in the seventh grade, because I was a pretty good athlete then. I was a better football player and baseball player than I was anything, but still, I was embarrassed.

So I went to Power Memorial, and I made the team and started playing. My sophomore year, everyone on the team was getting recruiting letters from colleges. But I wasn't getting any, and I was jealous. So I wrote a letter to Kansas, because I had seen them on TV.

A guy wrote me back, an assistant coach, telling me how I

should work hard, and he's going to be watching me, and I'm a little young right now, yada, yada, a bunch of slick stuff in it. Turns out that assistant was John Calipari, talking just as slick then as he does now.

I carried that letter around, in its envelope, and I'd show the envelope to all my friends, saying, "Look, Kansas wants me!" I would just show the guys the envelope with my name and the return address, because he started the letter off with "I'm responding to the letter that you wrote to me."

One of the guys, though, snuck it out of my bag one day on the F train and he showed it to all my other friends, and they made fun of me for writing to a college, just to get a return letter. But that made me work harder. Thank heavens for embarrassing situations, because I don't like to be in them. So I make sure I do everything not to be in them. (Which is why I work out so much today, so I won't be embarrassed on the court.)

Power Memorial closed after my sophomore year there, and I came back to Christ the King and I made the team there. My junior year, we had a stacked team. I came off the bench getting 10, 15 points a game. I got one hundred letters that season, and then, my senior season, when I finally got to start, I got a bunch more. And I didn't even have to write away for them.

For Whom the Bell Rings

My senior year, I decided on St. John's. But first I had to take the SATs. I had already taken the PSATs, and I hadn't done so well. I had heard that you got 200 points for just putting your name on the test, and I knew you only needed a 660 to be eligible to play, according to the NCAA. So I figured I'd put my name on it four times and get an 800. Didn't quite work out that way.

So when it was time to take the SAT, I didn't really want to take it. I knew I could have passed it. I'm an intelligent guy. But I went to school with some tough guys. They always had a scheme, and they loved me. And they said, "We'll take this test for you, Jayson. Don't worry about it."

So I gave them my student ID. And what they did was switch your picture for another guy's picture, then the other guy—who was a good test taker—he took the test for you.

The morning of the test my father drives me to Franklin K. Lane High School in Queens. He was so proud and so excited. Education means a lot to my dad. Every single one of his eight kids he's sent to college. I remember him watching me go in. He had bought three newspapers to read. "Good luck, son," he said. "I'll be right here when you get out."

I walked in, walked out the back door, went to the movies. Came back four hours later.

He said, "Jay, how did you do?"

I said, "Dad, I aced it."

When St. John's called me up, they said, "How do you think you did?"

I said, "I did well. I bet you I got 1,000."

The test came back a couple of months later. I got a 960.

The problem was these tough guys weren't only doing the test for me, they were doing it for a football player, too. And the guy who was taking it for that guy got caught. And the FBI came in and they shook him down. They put the light in his face and this kid told on us, ratted us out. Of course, when I saw him I beat him up.

But the damage was done. The FBI came into the school and they questioned me. And I swore that I took the test, and I was Mickey the Dunce. You learn, where I grew up, how to be Mickey the Dunce. Mickey keeps his mouth shut, you know? I kept my mouth shut.

Then St. John's wanted me to take the test again, because they were suspicious. They could have accepted the score, because they couldn't prove that I didn't take it. But they called me in one morning, we had a meeting, and they said, "Because of our ethics, we're not going to let you in the school with these scores. But we'll let you take it again."

And I said, "Well, I ain't taking it again."

They said, "Well, we're going to go talk to your father."

I said, "Oh, no." I said, "No, you're not." I was like, "No, you ain't. Don't do that, man. Don't bother him."

They told me they were going to be there at 7:30 that night, because they knew I was scared of my father. They knew that was the only thing in the world I was ever scared of.

So I contacted all my boys in the neighborhood. I told 'em, "Now look, guys, get out on the street about seven o'clock and keep your eyes out. You know who Lou Carnesecca is. Little funny-looking guy. Don't let him in this building. Tell him the elevator's broke. Tell him it's not working," I figure no way old Lou's going to walk up to the twenty-fourth floor.

But Lou's slick, he's street smart, and so is Ron Rutledge, who was one of his assistants.

They show up at 6:30, an hour earlier than they said. And they go in the back door, avoid my boys. They come upstairs and ring the bell. It's not even 7:00 yet.

I look through the keyhole, and I see Ron Rutledge's chest and the top of Lou's head. I'm thinking, Oh, God, they're here. How the hell did they get up? I'm wondering how my boys screwed up, and deciding I'll kick their asses when I see them. But while I'm thinking all this, the bell won't quit ringing. *Ding-dong, ding-dong, ding-dong, ding-dong.* And my father's yelling from his bedroom, "Who's at the door? Jay, answer the door."

I'm in trouble, so I say, "It's them Jehovah's Witnesses. They're wanting in."

Now my father comes out of the bedroom in his underwear. He's at the door, and he's kind of pissed off. "Dammit," he says (and my father was always mispronouncing words), "what the hell them Jebonah's Witnesses doin' knockin' on my door at this hour?" Then he opens the door and sees who's there. He sees it's Lou and Ron. And my dad's immediately polite. And I'm thinking, Uh-oh!

One thing you don't want to do with my father. When he comes home from work, he don't want to hear no bad news. He's been working for eighteen hours, laying bricks, digging trenches, building things, and it's best not to give him any bad news then. So when he goes back in his room to change into some clothes and Lou and Ron sit down, I'm sweating.

And now we're all in the living room and Lou says to my father, "Mr. Williams, your son has something to tell you."

I look at him, I say, "Dad, I've got nothing to tell you. Except how much I love you."

And Lou says, "Now, Jayson, tell him the truth."

My father says, "What is all this about, Lou? You can tell me."

And Lou says, "Your son didn't take his SAT test."

My father says, "You know, I can blame my son for a lot of stuff, Lou. And I love you and I believe you about most things. But let me tell you one thing. You're wrong on this one."

And I'm thinking, Yes! Way to go, Dad!

My dad keeps going. "I took my son to that high school," he says. "I watched him walk in the front door, right? While he took the test, I waited four hours out there, read three newspapers all the way through. And when I was done, he came out and got back in that car."

Then my dad looks at me. "Now, you took that test, didn't you, Jayson?"

And I say, "Sure did, Pop. Sure did."

Lou won't quit, though. He says, "Now, Jay, tell your father the truth."

I say, "I did take it."

And then my father looks at me real serious, because he knows Lou and Ron are looking real serious themselves. My dad says, "Jay, don't lie to me. You did take that test, didn't you?"

And I can't stand it. I say, "No, Dad."

My father gets up, real cool, real polite, says, "Okay, thank you, Lou. Thanks to everybody for coming. Appreciate it." He put everybody out. And I knew I was going to get a whipping. I was eighteen years old, but I still knew it.

My dad says, "Jay, go into your room. Take off everything but your underwear, and I'll be in there in a minute."

So I'm waiting in there, thinking about how much this is going to hurt, and then my dad comes in. He's holding his belt.

"Son," he says, "I ain't going to give you a whipping. But I'm gonna tell you something. All my kids went to college, and I'm proud of that. But you were going to be the only one who went to college who I got to watch on TV. The only one who would let me see the name Williams up there on the TV. That was going to make me the proudest of all. But you just disappointed me once again."

And he had tears in his eyes as he walked out. And that hurt me more than any other beating he ever gave me.

Beating the Bully

Because of the whole SAT mess, I had to sit out my freshman year. I was redshirted, a Prop 48 player. I was so mad at Coach Carnesecca for selling me out, I told him I'd never speak to him again. And that year, I didn't go into the gym one time. All I did was lift weights. And I put on sixty pounds of muscle. I went from 173 to 233.

So when I walk into the gym for the first time at St. John's, it was my sophomore year, and the first thing I see is the team bully, big muscle-bound guy from North Carolina named Matt Brust, picking on guys in a pickup game.

I was always aggressive, and I grew up getting into fights, but I was never a bully. I hated bullies, in fact, and that's the reason I was always getting into fights. I would not let people pick on me. And I hated seeing bullies pick on other people, especially little guys.

And here's Matt, who had played football and basketball at North Carolina, then transferred to St. John's. And every time he'd go to the hole, if he thought he got fouled, he'd take the ball and he'd hit the littlest kid on the court with the ball, right on the head.

My first pickup game at St. John's, and Matt's hitting this little kid with the ball.

I say, "Matt, don't hit that boy again."

He says, "What you going to do?"

The next time down he hits that little boy with the ball again, and this time Matt doesn't even get hacked. He does it just for fun. I say, "Matt, you hit that boy one more time, or you hit anybody on this court, I'm going to kick your ass."

Then there's a break between games. And I go talk to my boy upstairs, a friend who's been watching the games. Kaiser, my pal, a big guy with glasses. Big but soft.

I tell Kaiser to get my back, because if Matt hits that little boy again, I'm going to take care of him. I tell Kaiser that one of Matt's friends, another football player, is in the game, and I didn't know if I could handle both of 'em. So I tell Kaiser he'll have to take the football player, and I'll take care of Matt.

"Sure, Jay," Kaiser says. "No problem."

The next game starts, and sure enough, Matt takes the ball and starts pounding the kid on the head with it again. "Kaiser," I yell up to where he's standing, "come get him!"

Kaiser squints at me through his big old glasses, like he can't quite see what's going on. He cups one hand over his ear. "Huh?" he says. "What?"

I'm yelling, "C'mon! Come get him!"

He's squinting, holding his hand around his ear. "What? I can't hear you, Jay." Kaiser could hear fine when he wanted to. He just didn't *want* to at that particular moment.

So I walk over to Matt. "Didn't I tell you what I was going to do? Now, put your hands up." Matt put his hands up, I hit Matt three times, and Matt hit the floor. Now I'm on top of him, beating him. He's crying, "Stop, stop," crying and yelling. Finally I get off.

I get a call that night. Coach Carnesecca wants to see me in the morning. Now, I haven't spoken to Lou in a year, and my first day back in the gym I'm beating up his star player. So I figure I'm in big trouble.

I walk into his office the next morning and there's Lou. And he stands up from his desk. He says, "You shouldn't have beat up Matt Brust. But you're still one of us. Now, come here and give me a kiss, you big lug."

So I went over and gave Lou a kiss. And from that day on, me and Coach were tight. At least for a while.

Why College Coaches Deserve More Money

I quit the St. John's team twelve times. My second sister, Laura, had just contracted the AIDS virus, and I was an angry young man. I was lashing out at everyone. Especially the coaches at St. John's, who pissed me off all the time.

I love Lou now. And I love Ron Rutledge, too. Ron helped straighten me out, turned me from a tough kid into an NBA player. Lou and Ron both helped straighten me out. But at the time, I didn't want any straightening out.

Lou was the most amazing of the bunch, the biggest shock for me. When you sign up to play for St. John's, you and your family meet this guy, cute little Italian guy who likes to eat pasta, drink red wine, and give you big wet kisses.

Then I get on the court and this cute little guy's kicking me in the butt. I mean, literally kicking me in the butt. Taking his size $6^1/_2$s, or whatever they were, and kicking me straight in the butt. I couldn't believe it. That ticked me off.

One of Lou's assistants then was Al Labalbo. Coach Labalbo and I didn't get along so well. But you couldn't show that to Coach Carnesecca because as far as Coach Carnesecca was concerned, everything was family, and the family always had to get along.

Al Labalbo was an old guy, just about invented man-to-man defense, old gray-haired guy who always sat next to Lou.

One day we were scrimmaging, red team against blue team, and Lou was coaching one squad and Brian Mahoney, another assistant, was coaching the other. I was on Brian's team, the red team. And he says, "Jayson, go get Shelton Jones out of the game, take his place." So, just as a gag, I say to Brian, "Nah, Coach Carnesecca told me he wanted me to switch to the blue team."

And Al Labalbo hears me, and he says, "Jayson, Coach Carnesecca didn't say nothing about you switching teams."

And I say, "Don't tell on me, Al. C'mon, man, don't you tell on me." And Coach Carnesecca comes over.

"What's going on here?" he says.

I say, "Come on, man, just don't tell on me."

And Coach Carnasecca's going, "What? What's going on?"

And Al says, "I heard Jayson telling Brian that you told him to switch teams."

And now I'm busted. And Coach says, "Did you say that?"

"Yeah," I say, "but I was just joking." And Coach goes off on me, yelling and screaming.

I'm ticked off, so I say to Al Labalbo, "Didn't I tell you not to tell on me? Now I'm going to kick your old butt."

Coach Carnesecca hears that and he comes over and now he's grabbing me and punching me. He was a tough little guy.

Later that day, I found out, the coaches were all together, and Al is telling the other assistants, "Do you believe it? Did you hear what that guy said to me, how he was going to kick my butt after practice?"

Ron was always the voice of reason. Ron goes, "Al—Al, he's crazy, and he *will* kick your butt after practice."

The Last Time I Quit

Sometimes I quit because I got yelled at, sometimes because I wasn't playing enough, and a bunch of times because I was playing behind this Italian guy named Marco Baldi. A seven-footer who ran like he was stepping in crap. I used to complain all the time to Ron Rutledge about it. I didn't dislike Marco or anything; I just knew I was better than him. I always used to complain to Ron that it wasn't fair. I'd tell him it was embarrassing going home to my neighborhood, playing behind this stiff who ran like he stepped in crap. Ron always told me, "You do what you got to do in practice, show how good you are, and I'll see what I can do when it comes to the games." But a lot of times he couldn't do anything. So I quit a lot.

The last time I quit the team, I came home, where I was living with my parents, and I told my father, "I quit basketball." I said all I wanted to do was be a brick mason and work for him.

He said, "You're going to quit? You're going to give up your college scholarship, give up your television appearances, give up something that might get you a hundred thousand a year, a career in the NBA? You want to be a brick mason?"

Then he held out his hands to me, rough, workingman's hands. He said, "You want to be a brick mason? And you want hands like this? You want to go out and work twelve hours a day laying bricks in the cold, in the heat? You want to be that stupid?"

But you know what? I did want to be that stupid.

"Yeah, Dad," I said, "I want to be with you, I want to work with you."

He said, "Son, you've worked a lot of summers with me, and you're already a brick mason. You've already got your union card, so that's a good start. You're the man. You want to be a brick mason, go ahead, and I'll be behind you in your decision."

And when he said that, I was all happy.

"But you can't work for me," he said. "You've got to go out and get you a job. And you've got to pay four hundred a month for rent here, now that you're a workingman, and you got to go out and buy your own food."

"Okay," I said, because I was proud. Then I went into my bedroom and thought, Man! That's not what I had in mind.

I came back out and I said, "Dad, I'm sorry, man. I'll go back to school."

And he said, "Son, you make me proud. I see you on TV, and when I walk, I walk with my head high. And you know what? Your worst basketball day is my best day. Because that's when we get time to spend together. When you play well, you go with your buddies. But when you play bad, I get a chance to hold on to you."

And I never quit again after that.

Who's the Man?

By the end of my sophomore year, I was getting a lot of minutes, and Marco Baldi's butt was finally getting sat down. My junior year is when I was going to shine, to show the NBA scouts that I was definitely pro material. So the first home game that year, I come in with a brand-new suit, a nice hat, the works. And I only get 6 points. And a freshman, Malik Sealy, gets 17, and he takes a lot of shots. And I feel like a failure, because this was supposed to be my year, and because all my boys from the neighborhood are there, and everyone sees me play so bad.

After the game, Malik Sealy goes into the bathroom and I follow him in there and I throw him against the wall. Then I take him into one of them little stalls and beat the crap out of him.

I say, "Now, look here. You've got four more years here, and I'm a junior. I want you to understand one thing: This is my team. You got to understand who is the Man here. You're a freshman, so you act like a freshman."

And then I wait in the bathroom until Boo Harvey, our point guard, comes in. And I do the same thing to Boo. Well, not exactly the same thing. I don't hit Boo, I just shake him.

And I tell him, "Now, look here. When you're dribbling up on the break in the middle and I'm on one side and Malik is on the other, make sure you tip that ball off to me. 'Cause if you don't, when I'm getting those rebounds, you will never get another pass."

Those were the little pacts we made that day in the bathroom. That's how it went in college basketball. The freshmen didn't come in and take over at that time. And after that, I was the Man, and everyone treated me like the Man.

The Importance of Good Hygiene

One of my teammates at St. John's was Terrence Mullin, Chris' little brother. Terrence always used to do things that grossed me out. I'm a very hygienic guy, so it wasn't hard to gross me out. My house is immaculate, I take about five showers a day, and for passing gas, I've kicked friends out of my car in the winter with no money in their pockets when the temperature is three degrees. So even if Terrence hadn't been trying, he could have grossed me out. But Terrence was always trying. Terrence knew I was tight with his brother, Chris, but he also knew I'd kick his butt—Terrence's—if I had to, and that I'd have no trouble explaining it to Chris. Still, Terrence was always pushing the envelope with me. Then one day on a flight back from California, where we had just played UCLA, he opened the envelope and ripped it up.

Terrence was sitting by the window on the plane, and I was in the aisle, and there was a fat white lady in between us. Terrence goes and passes gas.

And I smell it and I'm disgusted. But you know what this old white lady is going to do—she's going to turn and look right at me. And she does. Now, I know Terrence did it, but I can't look at him, and I can't say nothing to him, because this lady's so big and fat. So I play it cool, you know, just look into space. Ho-hum. But all of a sudden, *boom*, he does it again, and this time he leans over and gives me a little smile, and then he leans back and I hear him giggling. Then he's talking to the lady and I can't hear them, but I'm pissed, because I can imagine what he's telling her. And he lets another one ride. And this lady looks over at me and she says, "Were you raised in a barn? Can't you control yourself?"

"It's not me," I say. "It's Terrence." But I can see she doesn't believe me. She just wrinkles her nose. So I lean over her, and I say, "Terrence, if you do that one more time . . ." and he starts giggling again. And leaning across that fat lady, it's like I'm listening to a sonogram for a baby's heartbeat, even though she wasn't pregnant, because she was just that big.

I say to Terrence, "One more time, and I'm going to kick your ass. I'm going to go to sleep now, so don't let me be smelling no more."

I lean back then, and before I even close my eyes, Terrence does it again. That boy must have been eating at Taco Bell or something. So now I jump across this lady and I'm beating up Terrence. We're on a 747, and I'm beating the hell out of him.

And this lady's catching a lot of elbows, and she's screaming. And here comes Coach Carnesecca from business class—he would never fly first-class—and he grabs me in a headlock, pulls me off. And I tell him what Terrence was doing. And Coach says, "You're kicking the kid's ass just for passing wind a couple times? Are you crazy?"

"But, Coach," I say, "she thought it was me!"

Coach makes Terrence switch seats with him. So now Coach is sitting by the window and Terrence is about seven rows up from me. And he keeps looking back at me and smiling, then lifting his ass up, like, "Here I go again." And I can't leave because Coach is there with me, right on the other side of the fat lady.

Man, that was one of the longest flights of my life.

A Sandwich to Go

We had another strange guy on our team named Billy Singleton. Billy was a big orange-looking guy—he had a crazy complexion. And he would wear this ugly orange wool outfit, and Billy wouldn't even put on a T-shirt underneath, so he was always itching and scratching.

If there was one thing Billy hated, it was away games.

"Why?" I'd ask him.

"'Cause I've got to put on that same itchy outfit."

I would room with Billy on the road and he used to wake me up in the middle of the night, rubbing lotion on his feet, moaning and groaning and saying, "Man, go get the trainer."

Billy had a size $14^1/_2$ foot, but his only shoes were size 13. That's how damn cheap Billy was—wouldn't even buy himself a new pair of shoes. And he wouldn't buy another outfit, either.

One day we're flying to Oklahoma, and we're grabbing some sandwiches at Roy Rogers in La Guardia Airport, and the team manager comes in, yelling, "You guys are late, c'mon!"

Billy had just bought a roast beef sandwich, and he's at the restaurant sandwich bar, getting ready to put pickles and stuff on, and he doesn't want to leave his free condiments. So I'm screaming at him to hurry up and he's piling the pickles on, and finally he's ready, so we make a run for it and we barely make the plane.

I sit down, but Billy's standing in the aisle, wrestling with his goose down coat that's about two sizes too small for him. There's an old black lady sitting next to him, and she's a big woman, just about as big as the white lady who was sitting between me and Terrence before. So Billy's struggling with his coat, beating hell out of this lady by accident.

Now we're getting ready to take off and the flight attendants are yelling at Billy to sit down. So he does, then he gets back up to grab something out of his coat pocket from the overhead bin. It's his roast beef sandwich. He pulls the tray down and starts unwrapping his sandwich. The old black lady has had enough. "Oh, Lordy!" she says. "Put that tray up and put that sandwich back in your pocket."

And he does, because she scares him. It's about a four-hour flight and when we get there, it's like springtime. A nice, warm Oklahoma day. We get to the hotel and find our room, and when I come out of the shower, Billy's got the damned heat on. The radiator is on. I say, "Billy, what the hell you puttin' the heat on for?"

"Don't you worry about that," Billy says.

I go back in the bathroom to dry off. I come back out, it's burning up. Billy's got a barbecue going. He has his roast beef sandwich on the heater, and it's sizzling away. The only $1.89 roast beef sandwich that ever made it halfway across the country. And Billy is getting set to eat it. It and every damn pickle.

Radio Days

I said before that I never got any illegal money from St. John's. Which is true, but I had some little side activities going to *make* some money. My brother, he was good at getting radios. We were just getting them off the street. My freshman year I sold Mark Jackson, who was a senior then, a radio. I told him I could get him a radio worth $700 for only $100.

Mark pays $50 to get it installed, and says he's going to come up with the other half once it's in. My brother puts the radio in Mark's car, a '78 Nova as I recall. But Mark doesn't come up with the other $50. I wait for my money for a month. Then when I don't get it, I have my brother come take the radio out of that Nova, right in front of Mark. He was so ticked off he didn't speak to me my whole college career. His first four years in the pros, he didn't speak to me.

Another guy we sell a radio to is Shelton Jones, another player on the team. With Shelton, we get him nice speakers and an amplifier and everything, and the price comes out to $800. Shelton gives me $450, says he'll give me the rest in a week or so. Week comes and goes, then another week. And now Shelton is telling people the same stuff Mark Jackson was telling people. "I ain't paying him."

So my brother and I do the same thing, except this time not in front of Shelton. We take a hanger, go in his car, take the radio, the amplifier, and the speakers back out, and also grab his four hubcaps.

The next day we see Shelton, he's all excited. "Man," he says, "somebody robbed me yesterday."

"What?" I say, all concerned.

"Yeah," he says, "got my radio. Can you get me another one?"

"Yeah," I say, "I think I can get you the exact same model. And I might be able to find you some hubcaps, too."

So my brother and I bring the same stuff back to Shelton's car and this time he says to my brother, "Hook up the amplifier somewhere robbers can't find it." So my brother puts it under the passenger seat. Then we steal it again and the next time we put it under the backseat.

We ended up selling Shelton the same radio and the same hubcaps four times. I would have left him alone if he would have just paid me the full price the first time. But after that, I made him pay the full amount each time.

About ten years later Shelton came to my bar, and I told him that I'd sold him the same radio four times. Oooh, was he pissed! He wanted to fight right there. But I talked him out of it.

Here's Your Seat

We were playing Providence one night, in Providence, and I got into it with one of the players. And as I'm walking to the bench, a guy in the stands spits on me. A thirty-year-old lawyer. Spits on me! So I grabbed one of the metal chairs on the sideline and I hit him over the head, twice. *Bam! Bam!*

And they *arrest* me! Now, it's against the law to spit on the subway—you can go to jail if you spit on the subway—let alone spit on a human being. So I could never understand them arresting me.

The next day I'm out of jail, I'm back home, and it's Sunday. Every Sunday in my father's house—it's a rule—you don't go outside until after four o'clock. You spend family time with your parents. Most Sundays I'd watch *Tarzan*, or a Clint Eastwood movie on Channel 5, because that's what was showing every Sunday. But this day Georgetown is playing Syracuse on Channel 2, and I oversleep, and when I get up, my dad's watching the game.

"C'mon, Dad, put on Clint Eastwood," I say.

"Nah," he says. He keeps the game on. I know what might be coming, so I'm begging.

"C'mon, Pop, it's one of my favorites of Clint's movies. Let's watch it. Please."

But it's too late now. It's halftime, and here comes James Brown and he's talking about how after the commercial they're going to have a Big East update, all about how "Jayson Williams goes berserk in Providence and he hits a fan with a metal chair after the fan allegedly spits on him."

My father looks at me on the bed, because we're both lying on the bed, and he says, "They ain't talking about you, are they?"

"Nah, Dad, nah, that's someone else. Can we please watch Clint Eastwood now?"

Then they come back from commercial. Show the whole damn thing, along with the damned commentary.

"You was in jail?" my dad says.

He was pissed. And even more when he found out he had to pay that guy in the stands $18,500.

Big Man on Campus—Big but Not So Bright

Junior year we win the NIT, I'm named MVP. I figure I'm hot stuff. I figure I'm king of New York. So I'm over drinking at the White Horse Tavern in the Village one night, and I am getting a little drunk, so I call my friend Brian to come pick me up and take me home. I figure I'll leave my car in the street and pick it up the next day. It's my senior year, 2:00 A.M., and here comes Brian in his father's Cadillac. We're driving down Houston Street, and all of a sudden, *bam!,* somebody just cuts in front of him and hits him. Right on the side of his dad's Cadillac.

Brian chases the guy, drives right after him. And I see the guy's got a St. John's sticker on his back window.

I say, "Brian, don't worry about this, let me handle it. The guy's got a St. John's sticker. I'll take care of it."

"No!" Brian says. Brian's a hothead, he wants a piece of this guy. But I make him stay in the car. I'm going to be the cool head here, the peacemaker.

The guy sees me. "Jayson Williams!" he says. "Oh, man, I'm so sorry, I didn't know you was in that car. I'm so sorry!"

"All right, man," I say, "don't get all worried. Let me just see how much damage there is, then we'll straighten this out." Mr. Diplomat, you know.

I walk to the side of the car and I look, then I come back to the guy. "Hey, man, there ain't no damage. Just go ahead, keep going."

I hear Brian screaming from his car. "No, no, no!" But he's a hothead, so I ignore him.

"Shut up," I say. "Let me handle this. Just shut up before I whup you."

The guy drives off. I get in the car.

"See, Brian," I say. "We didn't have to fight the guy at all. Wasn't that better the way I handled it, rather than get into a whole big confrontation?"

Brian's just looking at me like he wants to kill me.

"You stupid lug!" he yells. "He hit me on the left side! And you were looking at the right side!"

So I got out and looked at the left side and sure enough, the door was hanging off the car, there was a scrape from bumper to bumper. Turns out he'd caused about $8,000 worth of damage, and I let the guy go.

Me and Brian didn't speak for about two years after that. And that night I had to walk home.

The Numbers Game

Even though I broke my foot my senior year at St. John's, I was still confident I'd be a high draft pick. Ron Rutledge told my dad and me I could go anywhere from the fifth to the twenty-fifth pick. Of course, my dad heard "fifth." I was praying to go to New Jersey, be-

cause my parents were living in Newark then and because my dad
did a lot of work out there. The Knicks would have been great, too.
The one place I didn't want to go, and I let all the teams know this,
was Phoenix. Because of the pickup trucks and the desert.

We got together in Coach Carnesecca's office to watch the
draft—Coach and Ron and my mom and dad and me and about ten
other people. They start, and my dad's not even listening to the first
four picks, but when it gets to number five, he's all agitated.

"Shut up, everybody," he says, "this is important."

Number 5 wasn't me. My mom and dad are sitting behind me
and my dad pats me on the shoulder. Says, "Don't worry, you're
gonna be next, son."

Then comes the sixth choice. Someone else. Now it's my mom's
turn. "Don't worry, baby," she says, "you're next."

By number 10 they're holding hands, they're so nervous. Then
number 15, and still they're saying, "Don't worry, boy, you're next,
you're next." Number 17 is the Knicks, and I'm thinking this is it,
and David Stern steps up there and he says, "The New York Knicks
pick . . . Jeeeeerod Mustaf." And when he says that *j* sound, I at first
think it's me.

My dad's wearing down now. I can hear it in his voice when he
says, "Don't worry, son, you're next, you're next." So after he says
it I turn around real fast and I see him whispering to my mother.

"Jiminy!" he's saying. "This boy always messing up. He's gonna
have me laying bricks for the rest of my life. I ain't gonna never be
able to retire."

The Phoenix Suns picked me twenty-first.

Chapter 5

Poverty, Wealth, My Plan for Making Every NBA Player Take a Nine-to-Five Job Laying Bricks for Two Years Before Entering the League & Why I'll Puke If I Hear Another Kid Say, "I'm Leaving College 'Cause My Mama Needs a New House"

You know what pisses players off? You know what pisses any professional athlete off? It's when people start saying, "Athletes make too much money. They're all overpaid."

Let me ask you a question. Does David Letterman deserve $14 million a year for sitting behind a desk and making corny jokes? Does Oprah Winfrey deserve the $175 million she makes? David Stern, the commissioner of the NBA, makes $10 million—and he's the *commissioner*. He hasn't scored one bucket.

These same people who are complaining about athletes' big salaries are the ones who are screaming about how this is a free country, how entrepreneurs are so great. You know the problem? A lot of people don't like the idea of a kid coming out of the streets of New York or coming out of the suburbs—or anywhere they're coming from, but *especially* coming from the inner cities—and making this kind of money. They think, He doesn't know what to do with it. He's going to blow it. He'll be broke in two years. Just watch him.

That's bull. I've never seen anybody making $100 million go broke, except maybe Donald Trump. Fifteen years ago, different story. Yeah, we had NBA players go broke then. That's when they were making $200,000 a year.

I don't bitch about what Bill Clinton makes and I don't bitch about what a little guy who looks like a Keebler elf, Ross Perot, makes. Or how much money he has. And he refers to us as "y'all." African Americans he calls "y'all." I don't ask him where the hell he got his money and I don't say he shouldn't make that much money. The guy from Heinz ketchup makes $75 million a year. It's either him or the guy from Walt Disney. But you don't hear people hollering about how either one of them is making too much money. And what's the difference between them and us? As much as that guy from Heinz did in the classroom, we had to bust our butts on the playground. We put in more time on the playground than any of those guys did in the classroom.

I understand why we piss people off. Especially when you've got guys who are working, busting their butts for $300 a week, and you got a guy coming in here making $10 million who doesn't want to give it up for two hours. You've got guys in this league, they whine and moan about this and that, and the biggest problem they have is which $2,000 suit they're going to wear to the game.

Schoolteachers trying to teach a six-year-old how to read, these are the people that should be making millions of dollars. Firemen who save lives, they should be making millions of dollars. I might make in one game what someone else might make in a lifetime and I feel guilty about that. That's why I'll sign a thousand autographs at one time. Because I do feel guilty.

You've got some guys in this league, they don't go to practice because they're sick. An NBA player has the flu, he doesn't even practice for three days. In the real world, you have the flu, your bosses don't want to hear that flu stuff, you have to go to work. We sprain our frigging toe, we don't have to go to work. Meanwhile, there's people out there watching us who worry how they're going to feed their families, how they're going to come up with tuition money for their kids. That's what pisses people off. It pisses *me* off. I know what it is to make $40 a day or $50 a day. I worked construction. A lot of guys in the NBA don't know what it is to make that.

They don't know how good it is. I know how good it is because I work with my father in his construction business. Most every summer of my life, I've worked with my dad. I'm out with my dad and we got thirty guys on the crew working with us. I'm out breaking rocks with them. I know what it is to make laborers' money and have to go out and bust your ass every day.

That's what the problem is. This is my solution: All you have to do is before some guy comes in to play in the NBA, he has to work one summer in construction or one summer somewhere where he has to wake up early five days a week, work from nine to five every day, has to buy his groceries, and man he will appreciate the NBA, and the NBA will be a better place.

Pay, Then Play

Here's the thing about money, and about the players in the NBA: You hear a lot of talk about "Well, he hasn't proven he's a winner yet, so we're not gonna pay him the big money." But *until* you pay him the money, he ain't going to *be* a winner. You give a great player the money, get him where he's feeling like he's taken care of, his family's taken care of, he ain't got to worry too much about providing for people, then he's going to start being a winner. Besides, you got some players, the way things are today, if they're not making the big money yet, they feel like they got to go for that spinning alley-oop dunk, they got to take that stupid fadeaway twenty-four footer, because that's what's going to get them the big contract, the big sneaker commercial.

First you get paid, then you get the championship. Nice as the championship is, it doesn't put food on the table. First you have to get financially secure, then the ring comes. Once a player's feeling secure, he'll make the extra pass, he'll hit the open man, he'll play D and do that dirty work, and then he's a winner. He'll pass to someone who's got a better shot, 'cause he's not worried about making his stats look good.

The Root of All Evil

If a player's making a lot of money, other players look at him in the
layup line, and they say, "He's a player." They respect you more.
Unless you're someone like Jon Koncak, whose big contract just
pissed other players off because they didn't respect his game. (I always thought he was a decent player, but at the time he got his big
money, that size contract was unheard-of, especially for a player
like him.)

But the flip side of increased respect is when you're making the
big dollars, you got guys who are hungrier, looking to get that same
kind of deal, and they go after you—you become a target. You become something like the Chicago Bulls used to be. Everybody's
going to come at you because they're going to try to make you look
bad so they can get paid.

And then there are players who genuinely resent you making big
money, even if they respect your game. Sometimes it's even your
own teammates. Those people we call player-haters. And that's
wrong. I never player-hated anybody. My attitude was always,
"God bless you if you can make more money." Like I told Jerry
Seinfeld once, I'm not mad at him that he made $200 million in one
year. God bless him.

Your Mama

If I hear one more rookie say, "I went hardship for my mother," I'll
puke, I swear to God. It ain't like their mother had a year to live.
And I'm sure most of those mothers wanted their boys to get the
education. Quit the bull, you know. Tell the truth. The truth is a lot
of them just can't handle the schoolwork and they want a
Mercedes. It doesn't have anything to do with anyone's mother.
Besides, most of the time if you play ball at some of those ACC
schools way down South, they buy your mother a house anyway.
I've seen kids from New York leave here and go down there, and
next thing you know, their mothers are driving Cadillacs.

Other guys tell me, "Oh, I was so poor I had to wrap pennies to go to the movies." Well, if you're going to the damn movies, you ain't poor. My former coach John Calipari wrote in his book that he had to put cardboard in his sneakers and shoes. Give me a frigging break. You know what percentage of NBA people came out of poor, really poor families? Most of these guys don't know what poor is. I mean, poor does not mean owning a pair of Nike sneakers that cost $150.

Freud Had It Right

The other thing you hear is, "Oh, these poor kids from single-parent homes, they really need the money." I'll admit that one parent is never as good as two. But one parent can do a pretty good job. I did a good job when I had to adopt my kids after both my sisters died. We don't all come from silver spoons, we don't all come from Beverly Hills, but we make do. And what do you think makes one kid good and one kid bad from the same single-parent family? Let me tell you something: A kid learns most of his morals before the age of four. That's what Sigmund Freud said, and he's one interesting dude. He's my favorite author. Sigmund Freud will tell you a kid learns all his values before the age of four. And that's the truth, because I remember my daughter—my daughter used to lie when she was three. She could barely talk, but she could lie. And to this day she still likes to stretch the truth some. She's twenty-three now. And my son always had a good heart, but he was always taking risks, getting himself into dangerous situations. And he still is the same way, at age twenty. You got to instill values in your kids at a young age. Because after four, you're stuck. If they're robbing at four, they're going to be robbing when they're forty.

Speak Softly, Laugh Loudly

A lot of people think players are stupid. Richard Pryor used to do a bit about Leon Spinks, the boxer. He would talk about what people thought of Leon Spinks, where they'd say, "Leon Spinks sure is dumb, ain't he?" They'd ask Leon what he did for a living, and he'd say, "I knock people the hell out." You know, he wasn't supposed to be a philosopher. His job was to knock people out.

Same way, a lot of people give Patrick Ewing a hard time because they say he's not articulate. His job is to play basketball, but everybody, especially a lot of white people, talks about how unintelligent Patrick Ewing might be, because he doesn't articulate as well as they would like. Patrick's one of the brightest individuals I know, and not only because he graduated from Georgetown in four years. It's like I tell my accountant, and I tell my lawyer and my manager, "If you guys are all smarter than me, then why do you all work for me? Why do I have more money than all of you put together?"

So regarding Patrick Ewing, if people don't think he articulates well, I know one thing he does very well. He laughs well. He laughs well all the way to the bank.

The Politics of Wealth

Some NBA players are funny about money, just like everyone else. They'll buy eight sports cars, a bunch of $3,000 suits. But we'll still try to save pennies. I used to rig the TV boxes in my hotel rooms so I didn't have to pay for the movies. You know, you come in there, you take your key, you put it between the box and the TV, and you don't have to pay for any of the movies. I'd say about 25 percent of the guys in the NBA rig the hotel TV boxes that way (especially the guys who came from the CBA). Why? I guess to show that we're not Republicans, that even though I'm rich now, I'm still like a Democrat, fighting for the poor. Having made all this money, you want to act like you've still got your sly off the street and you can still pull a scam. You're still from the neighborhood. I guess that's why guys do it, because the movie's only $7.95.

Wanna Bet?

Something else NBA players do with money is gamble it. I myself bet on golf matches. I like skins games better than regular golf, because once I get up in the 100s or so—golf's not really my game—I lose concentration. Skins games, where every ball counts—it helps me focus. Plus, I wanna kick the other guy's ass. I'm a professional athlete, and I'll give you odds that most other NBA players are like me. So we gamble sometimes. I can say that and not get in trouble because I'm not Michael Jordan.

That was unfair what the press did to Michael about his gambling. You tell me one person who goes on the damn golf course, who goes out with a foursome or goes out with somebody else, and *doesn't* bet on a golf course. That was ridiculous what they were doing to Michael Jordan.

The Best Things in Life Are Free

I figure money can buy me things. It can buy me a house, food, clothes, education for my children, cars. It can help buy some security. One thing it can't buy is sophistication. A lot of players don't know that. Some former players don't know that, either. Clifford Ray, a great coach, a funny guy, the man who liked to do the thunder, lightning, and rain thing in the hotel bathroom, he thought if you had money, you had to act a certain way. He was going to teach me about that when I first got to the NBA. That was going to be his mission.

So he takes me out to dinner and he's trying to be all fancy. We look over the menu and the waiter comes over, asks us what we're going to have. "I'm going to have some of the chicken soup," I say.

Clifford wrinkles his nose, like you shouldn't order something so simple in such a fancy place. "I'll have the mine strone," he says. And he pronounces it just like that. Mine, strone.

"Sir?" the waiter says.

"The mine strone soup, if you please," Clifford says.

Finally the waiter figures out he's asking for the minestrone soup.

Another time, Clifford and I have had a few cocktails, we're going up in the elevator, and Clifford presses the 6 button and the 7 button.

"What the hell you doin'?" I say. "You getting off on two floors?"

"I'm going to the thirteenth floor," he says.

"But, Clifford," I say.

He says, "I'm on the thirteenth floor and you got to press 7 and 6 because there's no thirteen."

I say, "No, Clifford, you couldn't have been on the thirteenth floor. They just don't have thirteenth floors in hotels because people think it's bad luck."

Turned out when he looked at his key he was supposed to be on the fourteenth floor. I told him not to press 7 and 7, that one button should do the trick.

Dead but Not Forgotten

Most players, before they get the big money, they get an agent. Because I broke my leg my senior year at St. John's, I wanted a guy who was outgoing, who was a live wire, because I wasn't as high-profile as I thought I should be. So I went with Bob Woolf, who represented Larry Bird. One of the first so-called superagents. It was one of the worst mistakes I ever made. The first time I met him, he had a limousine pick me up, all fancy. It picked me up, along with my St. John's assistant coach, Ron Rutledge, and my friend and lawyer, Oscar Holt. When we got to Bob Woolf's office, here was this cat, talking all slick, telling us about all the things he can do, bragging about all the people he had, and the way he started.

And that was the last time I ever saw Bob Woolf. I wasn't big-time enough. He signed me, but he didn't have time for me. I got an assistant, a guy named Tom. I never did find out his last name. I dealt with him almost every day, and I asked for Bob Woolf almost every day.

Always the same thing. "Bob's not in." "Bob's on vacation." "Bob's in a meeting."

I talked to Bob one time after that. I had heard he was dying, and I mentioned that to a guy who knew him. I said, "Jeez, I heard Bob Woolf is real sick, that he might be dying."

And this guy must have told him, because that afternoon I get a telephone call. It's Bob Woolf, and the guy's yelling at me.

"I'm not dying," he says. "I don't know where you get that from."

I'm starting to apologize, then he starts screaming at me some more. Me, who he hasn't even spoken to in about a year. So I yell back. "Hey, Bob, screw you. I ain't heard from you in all this time, and you're going to be yelling at me now? I'll kick your old sickly dying butt."

Two weeks later he was dead. And I'm sure he was a good guy and a good family man and all, but still, it was the worst deal I ever made, partly because Bob never had time for me.

What I know now is that some agents screw players in a number of ways. These days, because salaries are scaled, a player is going to get a certain top dollar no matter what, but some agents still charge 4 percent on that money, and the player doesn't even realize it. And other times, when an agent pays a player's bills, they'll pay some of their own bills at the same time. They'll be paying your cellular phone bill, and they're taking care of their own cellular phone bill at the same time.

I've been with my agent now for nine years, Sal DiFazio. He's one of my best friends. I signed with him when I was barely making any money, especially compared to what I'm making now. I drive his son to school sometimes; we live two miles apart. But other agents still come up to me. I had one of the highest-profile of all the agents come up to me, saying he could get me more money, he could get me better deals, why don't I come with him?

Even if he could have got me more money, how could I leave this guy who helped make me all this money, who's one of my best friends? He has to make a living, too. How can I mess his livelihood up?

Hard Bargaining

I've signed my last contract and I'm set for life, so a lot of people might not be too sympathetic when I tell them how ugly negotiating can be. But take my word, it can be.

I remember the second contract I signed with the Nets. My father and I went up to meet the owners and I told my friend who had driven us to wait downstairs, it'd be about twenty minutes. It took nine hours.

They had these sheets of paper in front of 'em. They'd read from the papers. December 16: "Jayson went out." December 18: "Yeah, I seen him with three girls on his shoulder leaving the game." December 20: "I smelled alcohol on his breath."

My father says, "Boy, they talking about you? With all these lists?"

"Well, Dad," I say, "that's just the way they negotiate. I didn't do all that stuff."

But they're not done with those damned lists. January 1: "Jayson was late to practice." January 15: "He was late for the bus."

My father says, "Man, that's a whole lot of stuff you did wrong."

When that session is over, I get in the car with my dad, and he looks over at me. "Is that why you wear your hair so high?" he asks me. "Because you must have horns coming out of your head, the way they were talking about you."

Father Knows Best

When I first met Ray Chambers—one of the principal owners of the Nets—he just listened, and then he asked if he could spend a little time alone with me. Ray's worth more money than anyone I know, but he listens a lot, and he watches, and when he talks, he doesn't say much. He'll say one word, or when he's really going, maybe one sentence, but that one word or one sentence will make complete sense. Like Gandhi. One word, one sentence, and it all makes sense.

When Ray and I were alone, he told me about his philosophy of life. Here's a guy who gives about $100 million a year to charity. That doesn't fascinate me as much as the fact that he doesn't let anybody know where the money comes from. People wake up in the morning in the projects, and they might have a new stove, or an air conditioner, and never know where it came from. It's from Ray Chambers.

Ray's telling me his philosophy, and I'm impressed, but I grew up in New York, so I'm always a little suspicious, at least at first. So I say, "Now, Raymond, ask yourself, even though it's great that you're buying stoves and stuff, you ain't just trying to get into heaven because of all the things you've done to *make* these billions of dollars?"

And he looked at me and he never changed his expression. Ray's the kind of guy, he never loses his cool. Very calm and collected. He reminds me of Mr. Peterman from Seinfeld. Elaine's boss.

We talk for three hours. And when I get home I call my dad.

"Dad," I say, "I'm going to give back my money to the community. I want to give something back. If I make a hundred million, I want to give about ten million back and—"

"Hold on," my dad says. "Calm down now." It's after midnight and I woke him up, so he's already a little cranky. But I'm all excited.

"Dad," I say, "I'm going to do this."

"Yeah," he says. "Now, hold on. Calm down. Don't give away all your money."

"Nah, Dad," I say. "It's not giving *away* money. It's giving *back* money. And it's not just money, it's being part of the community."

I tell my dad about what me and Ray have been talking about, about cleaning up Newark, about putting air conditioners in the high-rises, about letting people own things, so they feel responsible for things, so they act responsible, so they all share in the life of a community.

"Dad, you know how the state cleaned up Highway 78, all the way from Pennsylvania to Newark," I say. "But then you get to Newark, you look out the car window and all you see is garbage, old mattresses, junk. No one's cleaning that road, and that's where a lot of the misery starts."

I tell my father, "You know what I want you to do? I want you to take your company's trucks and about fifteen guys from your work crews. I want you to get some paper bags and stuff and I want you to clean that highway in Newark."

There's quiet on the phone. I wonder if my father is back asleep. But after a couple seconds, he says, "What were Mr. Chambers and you drinking?"

"Huh?" I say.

"I know you, but is that man an alcoholic?"

"But, Dad . . ."

"It's two in the morning, I'm sixty-six years old, you're about to sign a contract for one hundred million, and you're going to have me on the side of the highway cleaning up what other people are throwing out their window? Now, son, what the hell's wrong with that picture?"

The next morning, my dad and I are drinking coffee. I tell him I'm changing my life, that I'm committed to really giving something back to the community. And he's proud of me. He tells me that I'm a good man. Then I tell him, "Dad, I used to want to grow up to be a brick mason, or a construction worker, like you. But I don't want to do that anymore. I want to be a philanthropist, like Mr. Chambers."

And when I say that, I see my dad give me a funny look, kind of like he's disappointed in me, or his feelings are hurt or something. I tell him no matter what, he'll always be my dad.

"Son," he says, "you can be a philanthropist or anything you want. I'm not going to force my beliefs on anyone. But I want you to know, I was raised a Methodist, and I'm going to stay a Methodist."

That's when I realized why he had looked at me funny. When I said "philanthropist," my dad thought I was talking about taking a new religion—becoming a Buddhist or something.

Workers Unite!

Most people hear "union," and they think of Norma Rae and coal miners and Jimmy Hoffa. They don't think of a bunch of good-looking young black guys with nice sports cars. So it's no wonder we didn't get a lot of public sympathy during the lockout of '98–'99. But I'll tell you what: The owners aren't exactly hurting, either.

What happened was we had all summer to start talking, and both sides could have sat down without lawyers and got it done. But both sides brought in their ten lawyers, and then what do the lawyers do? Well, they're lawyers. So they go back and they appeal this, they do this, then they appeal that, then they turn in these papers and say, "Oh, we have to meet again next week." They want to meet three and four times and ten times.

Why did we meet only once over the summer with the owners and then like ten times right before we reached a settlement? Because those lawyers get paid by the hour, that's why. And now that we're back to work, the lawyers will bill us again for another outrageous amount. So the lawyers of course didn't want this thing to be over in one day. If you were a lawyer, would you want it to be over in one day?

Only one lawyer could have settled the NBA lockout in one day. You know who would do that? Matlock. He was the only one who would have taken this case and done it right. The only one.

I said some of this stuff when the players' union and the owners were still sniping at each other. I said there's a lot of basketball players who want to get back to work; maybe we should take a vote on the owners' proposal. People criticized me for that. Spike Lee even got on me.

A lot of players also took shots at me for that. Newspapers said Patrick Ewing was pissed off, because he was head of the union. But you know what happened? Three days later we had a vote.

I had to put *my* head on the chopping block to make it go through. And Keith Van Horn put his head out there and said he supported me. I said what 290 people were scared to say. I think a lot of David Falk's superstar players probably had strike funds, but a lot of the other players didn't, and I was speaking for them.

When I came to that union meeting in New York for the vote, I didn't know what to expect. I had already spoken to about sixty players and I knew they were going to vote to accept the owners' proposal, but I also thought some other players might be pissed off for what I had said publicly. So I had recruited Charles Oakley, Shaquille O'Neal, Hakeem, and Anthony Mason to be on my side. With those guys, I *knew* I wasn't going to have to take any bull.

We had a vote that day, a union vote that was never publicized. But we voted. It was 216–4 to play, to get back to work. And ever since that day, I've been treated a little bit different by some of the players. Larry Johnson, who had never seemed to like me before, after the start of the '98–'99 season would always make a point to say a few words before the games.

"Yo, Jay, God bless. Have a good season." Stuff like that. I think he felt good about me saying what a lot of players were thinking.

A Dog's Life

I got a 31,000-square-foot house now, with a little golf course I built, and horses and a skeet shooting range. And I love it. But I also have to worry some about security now. That's why I bought myself a 150-pound rottweiler. A friend told me about this company in Atlantic City. They'd train these dogs for you and drop 'em off at your house, tell you the magic words that would make the dogs grab someone by the throat, and the other magic words that would get the dog to let the guy go. So I call Atlantic City and order one. And then I forget all about it. And one night I come home from dinner, and I've had a few cocktails. I open my door and turn on the light and just after I flick on the switch and take a few steps, I hear "*rrrrrr.*" And there, in the middle of my room, snarling and slobbering and growling at me, is this monster dog. And of course I can't remember any passwords at all. He's growling at me, and I'm moving backward, smiling, saying "nice doggy," stuff like that. It takes me two hours to move backward two and a half steps. And as soon as I get to that doorknob—*boom*—I'm out the door and into my car. I spend the night at the Holiday Inn in town, and of course a lot of people there recognize me.

"Aren't you Mr. Williams?" they say. "Don't you live in that nice new white house down the road? Is everything okay?"

So what am I going to tell them, that I'm scared of my own damn guard dog?

"Yeah," I tell the people, "the power went out."

The next day I call the guy in Atlantic City, get the magic words again, and I can go home. Now Zeus, the rottweiler, is my friend. But he still scares some visitors. I had Darryl Dawkins out to my house for a barbecue last summer, and Chocolate Thunder, he thinks he knows animals. I'm telling him about what a good guard dog Zeus is, and Darryl says, "Hell, Jay, you just rub a dog like this under his mouth, and he'll do whatever you say."

"Uh-huh," I say, "show me what you mean." Then I watch while Darryl rubs Zeus on his chin. Then I say the magic word and Zeus jumps up and grabs Darryl by the throat. He got that same look in his eye as when he first broke that backboard, kind of like he didn't know what was going to happen next.

Taste Test

Things change when you make a lot of money. For a long time I was ready to settle down. Now that I'm rich, I'm going to take a step back and look at whether I'm going to get married or not. When I was barely beating the dog to the garbage can, that was a different story. Then I was set to walk down the aisle. Now I don't know who to trust. My mom makes my food now. I make her taste it first. She's in the will for 33 percent, so I'm very careful.

Chapter 6

Race, Racism & the Night Tom Gugliotta Told Keith (the Great White Hope) Van Horn, "There's One Sheriff in Town, and I'm It," Then Proceeded to Light Him Up for 35 Points

My mom's white—Italian and Polish—and my dad's black. And I got white family who don't like blacks, and black family who don't like whites, and some family who don't like nobody. When I was growing up, all the Irish and all the Italians in my neighborhood—we lived on New York's Lower East Side and I went to Catholic school in Queens, New York—were Boston Celtics fans, and all the brothers liked Julius Erving. I not only was born in the Deep South—Ritter, South Carolina—but I spent three years of my childhood there, from the time I was six till I was nine, and I saw things my friends don't believe when I tell them. And my father and his parents grew up there and put up with things *I* can hardly believe. I'm telling you this so you'll understand my perspective when I talk about racism in the NBA. My perspective is the NBA is the least racist of any sport in the country, but that doesn't mean there's not racism.

This is America, and America's always looking for the next Great White Hope. We got a player on our team, Keith Van Horn, and in addition to everything else, he has to deal with being white. Keith is the real thing, he's a great player, but if you're white in the league, the brothers will think you're soft. Same if you're good-looking in this league.

Or if you're smart. Tim Duncan used to write articles for *USA Today,* and he's intelligent, and Grant Hill is intelligent, so other players at first thought both those guys were soft. Players would say to them, "You're soft." Well, they're not.

Another player who got tested a lot was Christian Laettner, because he was white and good-looking. When he came into this league, he was already being billed as a superstar. So a lot of the black players, they thought, Here goes the league trying to build up another Great White Hope. And when people played against him, they played a little harder against him because of that. Keith Van Horn had to deal with that, too, big-time. I told Keith when he was a rookie, he was going to have veterans come up to him and hit him, *boom!* They were going to try him. And they were going to go at him not just because he's white, but because he was the number two pick in the draft. And I told him he was going to have to take the first hit. But I wouldn't let him take the second. Other players were always coming up to me before games, saying, "I'm going to kick your boy's butt tonight." "Your boy," that's what they called him. And I'd say, "Yeah? Well, you better be talking about trying to outplay him. Because if you're talking about a fight, I'm going to have to whip *your* butt."

Everybody was looking for Keith to be Larry Bird, which wasn't fair. And I'll tell you who was harder on Keith than anyone, and that was Tom Gugliotta. Tom went to school at South Carolina, so he already has some major issues. I never met anyone from South Carolina who didn't have issues. But when we played the Timberwolves, in Minnesota, Tom went at Keith Van Horn like nobody else. He was saying to me, "Jay, your boy? Your boy? I'm gonna take care of him tonight." Tom went at Keith to let him know *Tom* was the sheriff. He went at him *hard.* And Tom had about 35 that game, and he was the sheriff that night.

Keeping It Real

What I hate is African Americans using the n-word so much, even to each other. I can never understand how we can use it toward each other and then as soon as somebody else uses it we're ready to crack them in the head. What it shows is how ignorant we are to the fact of how far we have come. Players use it on the court sometimes. And what bothers me is 95 percent of the people coming to see us are not African Americans. So even if an NBA player uses the n-word, thinking "that's a word we all understand among ourselves," how many people in the stands are going to understand it? Five percent of the crowd? And I'll guarantee that most of that 5 percent ain't sitting courtside. To me it's a word that shows ignorance about race and history and a lot of other things.

I don't like for people to come up to me and say, "Oh, my n——, what's happening?" If I was your n——, that means what? Your ignorant person. And there are well-paid athletes using that word. I take heat because people say I don't go to enough black clubs. I don't give a damn if a club's black or white or yellow. I don't go to violent clubs. I go to all-black clubs that aren't violent.

I'm not going to clubs with a bunch of rappers who are wearing sweatshirts, hoods, and pistols. What do I want to go in there for? So I have to take one of their pistols and hit them over the head with it and end up with the cops there and me in trouble? Some people call stuff like that "keeping it real." A lot of players think that, too. These are the guys who aren't as intelligent, or are afraid to explore the world they aren't familiar with.

To them, I'm not "keeping it real." Because I made a million dollars I'm supposed to act and dress silly, like I'm ignorant and poor? I was never ignorant and poor all my life. I wasn't the richest person, but I know one thing: I have never been ignorant and disrespectful of others. I've never been like some of these idiots, wearing my pants hanging down my butt with no belt. If that's keeping it real, I'll be fake.

I'll tell you what: Those guys can keep it real. I'll keep it alive. And I'll keep out of trouble. As soon as you hit one of those clowns

over the head with his pistol, you'll definitely be keeping it real—
real in court.

The Universal Language

Whatever color a rookie is these days, chances are he listens to rap
music. Keith Van Horn, he'll drive in with rap music on in his car.
Keith grew up in California, but I think it's a safe bet it wasn't
Compton or Watts or one of those neighborhoods. He tells me,
"Hey, Jay, I grew up with Mexican people," but I tell him he's *not*
from the ghetto. Then you got Armen Gilliam, and Armen is a
Mozart man, but he'd knock your block off if you looked at him
funny. Myself, I don't listen to rap. I listen to Al Green, Luther
Vandross, Ray Charles, and B. B. King. I don't like music that de-
grades women and curses every two seconds. I just don't like people who need so much attention that they act ignorant, be they
rappers, hard rockers, or Liberace and the Three Tenors.

Say What?

The first week that Stephon Marbury joined the Nets, when we
were flying home from a game, he walks up to where I'm sitting
on the plane, next to Keith Van Horn. Stephon's more hip than an
old guy like me. He's younger. I'm listening to Luther Vandross, and
Stephon's talking.

He's saying, "Yo, man, I'm twinking about your crib, and I want
to come out and check out the little pheasants out there, and word
is you got a dope vehicle and its music be germing."

And I don't know what he's talking about. Stephon's a smart guy.
But people his age, no matter what walk of life they come from,
they talk in a language people my age don't always understand.

So I look over at Keith, who's typing away on his computer.
Keith's always typing on his computer during flights. Dude's been
working on his degree for as long as I've known him. Back when
I was in college, we got our degrees in four years. Not Keith. He's

still working on his. He's on page eight. Every time I look at that damn computer, it's always page eight. Been on page eight for about two years now.

Anyway, Keith looks up from his computer for a second, says, "What Stephon was trying to tell you, Jay, is that he's heard you have a nice new house and he'd like to visit sometime and meet some of the pretty women he has heard you often invite over. And he's also heard about your new car and it's nice new sound system."

Then he goes back to typing on page eight.

And I say to Keith, who's as white as Opie, "How do you understand that lingo? How do *you* know what he's talking about?"

And this time Keith doesn't even look up.

"Buy the CDs, baby," he says. "Buy the CDs."

The Case Against Affirmative Action

These days, you still got your redneck fans in the NBA, but you're not going to hear any white person in the stands call nobody a nigger, because the league is 90 percent black. It's not like this is hockey. Someone might go to a hockey game and say, "Look at that nigger letting this goal go through," right? But you can't say that stuff at an NBA game. It wouldn't be wise.

As for trash talk, it gets intense, sure, but I haven't met anybody white in the NBA who says something about black people. They'd have to be crazy.

And blacks sure aren't going to say anything about white players. Because, think about it, who owns all the teams? All the players know who they're working for. The fact of the matter is I have never met a racist player, of any color, in the NBA.

Are there some players who are on NBA teams *because* they're white, and they might not be if they weren't white? Well, it's like affirmative action. You know what I'm saying? My dad's in the construction business, and I've worked a lot with him and I see so many people getting highway jobs they don't deserve, some black and some minority owners at construction companies who get jobs, and they screw it up. I don't believe in affirmative action, but that's the way the world is. So, yeah, maybe there might be some white kids in the league who aren't the greatest players, but the owners want them there for fan support, but then again there are maybe some black players on other kinds of teams that aren't so great. Some black hockey players, for instance.

The Mouth That Roars

This is America, so people think all kinds of things about race. Some of the players think the more pro-black they seem, the tougher people will think they are. Like Charles Barkley. People are always saying, "He's so pro-black" or "He hates whites." Charlie's got a white wife, Maureen, one of the prettiest wives in the league. He's got white friends. He lives in Phoenix, surrounded by white people. Charlie's the funniest guy in the world, but he isn't pro-anything or anti-anything. Charlie doesn't have one racist bone in his body, but he just says stuff to get attention. Or sometimes he says stuff just because he's Charlie.

Rough Justice

My father is a proud man, and he's the son of a proud man. My grandfather Ned Williams never worked a day in his life for any man, and back in the thirties and forties and fifties, in Ritter, South Carolina, where the Williamses lived, that was unheard-of. By the time my dad was a young man, my grandfather owned his own logging company, owned two logging trucks himself, and was a respected man in the community. And that might be what saved my father's life one night. That or my granddad's shotgun.

My dad loved cars, and he was driving outside of town one summer night with his first wife, Anna Lee, in his brand-new 1953 Chevy. They parked on a little dirt road and were talking and kissing, and suddenly three of the white boys from town come up on the car.

"Hey, nigger," one of 'em, a boy I'll call Sammy Jones, says, "What you doin' with that fancy car?"

Now, Sammy Jones knew my father and knew he owned that car, but that was the South.

So my father tells Sammy and his friends that he and his wife aren't causing anyone any trouble. But Sammy and his friends—those boys are telling my dad that black people shouldn't be in cars like that, and then they open the passenger door and pull Anna Lee out. Then they open my dad's side of the car and they start pulling him out. And on the way out, my dad grabs the banana knife he always kept under his seat, and he cuts Sammy Jones. Tears him from his groin to his sternum, then he grabs Anna Lee and they drive out of there, straight to my grandfather's.

About forty minutes later Sammy Jones' father shows up at my grandfather's house, and he's got about forty white folks with him. And they're yelling for my father. A young black man had just cut up a white boy—not killed him, Sammy survived—but still, you know what they were going to do to the black guy. But my grandfather goes out on the porch, and he cocks his shotgun.

"I'll make sure justice is done here," Granddad says, "but ain't nothing happening till tomorrow morning. So you all come back then and we'll get the police and the judge and work this out."

And maybe because of the gun, or because of Ned Williams' reputation, they left and came back in the morning.

And here's the "justice" they worked out: My grandfather had to give Sammy Jones' father his two logging trucks. Just *give* them to him, outright, in order to keep his son—my father—from getting lynched. So Ned Williams gave up those trucks. And it broke his spirit. He was a proud man, but after he lost those trucks, he started drinking, and he died some years later, a broken man. A broken man who saved his son's life.

And the weirdest part of the story, because you have to remember this is still the Deep South, is to this day my dad and Sammy Jones are kind of friendly. They've even been partners on some business deals together.

With Relatives Like These, Who Needs Enemies?

I experienced racism long before I got to the NBA. In Ritter, naturally, and from my own family, some of the time. My father used to drive one of my mom's sisters home from work sometimes. And she would make him drop her off a block before her job because she didn't want people to see her getting out of the car with a black man.

That same aunt had a son, my cousin, and this cousin told me one day that his grandfather, who was my grandfather, too, "hated all niggers. And he hates Jews, too. And I hate niggers and Jews, too." This was my own cousin. I beat him up for that.

Another time we came out of a club and my cousin was dawdling. We were running late, and it was past my curfew, so I said, "C'mon." I was eighteen years old then. He said, "Look, I'm white. Black people don't tell white people what to do." He started again with the grandfather stuff. "My grandfather always hated niggers and he hated your family, too." I asked him to please hurry up, I was going to miss my curfew, but he wouldn't shut up about niggers and his grandfather, so I beat him up again. That cousin and I haven't spoken in twelve years. And I haven't spoken to his mom, either.

I'm Not an Animal

My mother and my father had each been married before they met each other, and they each had kids—it was my mom's two daughters who died of AIDS—and they both had problems with each other's family, and I caught it from both sides. And I wasn't the only one who had a hard time. When we all lived in Ritter, my mother was the only white woman in the whole town. She was also the only white woman within fifty miles who was married to a black man, so she took a lot of heat. From some of the black folks and from her own sisters.

When I went down South to that little town, the people had

never really seen a black and white kid mixed like me. They'd say, "What is he, yellow? What color is that? What kind of hair is that? Is he Mexican?" I had curly hair, so I was like the devil to a lot of those people. And I spoke a little Spanish I had picked up in New York City, and when I did that, they thought I was speaking in tongues. And my dad's seven kids by his first wife, even they thought I was kind of weird. The girls were a lot more sensitive than the guys. And the guys, even though they thought I looked funny, they loved me.

I'm not saying all families are like this, but I got treated worse by the white side of my family than the black side. I remember going to an aunt's house, another one of my mom's sisters, and she put me outside on the screened-in porch—and it was a dirty house— outside on the porch in the cold, and she told me I had to sleep on the old couch out there. It was an *old* couch. There were fishhooks in it and smelly blankets and I had to sleep on that couch. My only company out there was the dog, named Duchess. I remember crying. I was seven years old. I'll never forget it. I was crying because I thought that I must stink—that that was why they put me out there on the porch. I was cold and I was on this porch by myself. The dog was the only thing that gave me any comfort. I was crying and petting the dog when the door opened and my aunt stuck her head out. I was so happy. I thought I'd get to come in out of the cold. But then my aunt said, "Come on inside, Duchess." The dog got to sleep inside, and I slept outside, by myself. And I didn't have much to do with that aunt after that.

The Man on the Porch

Racism exists everywhere, but I don't think it's quite the same anywhere in the world as it was in Ritter, South Carolina, some years ago. Ned Williams' wife—my Grandmother Elvira—used to work as a maid and cook for a rich man, a white man I'll call John Smith, who lived in a big old house with thick white columns on a big wraparound porch. A plantation house. He used to sit on that porch in his rocking chair.

John Smith was one of the meanest, nastiest people in Ritter, but jobs weren't exactly plentiful back then, especially for black people, so not only Grandma Elvira worked for John Smith but her daughters did, too. My aunts.

Just two years after my grandfather gave his trucks away, my dad opened a club outside Ritter, a juke joint called the Flamingo Lounge. He'd get big acts to come play. James Brown, people like that, would come down. It was the best place in town for black people to go. And everything was great until one day John Smith called my dad to his house and he said, "I don't want all those niggers on the road late at night. They might kill my wife coming home from bingo." This was 1955, and John Smith told my dad he had to sell him the club.

But my dad was a proud man, so he refused. Then somebody hired a boy to burn the Flamingo Lounge down, and that's what he did.

John Smith might sound like some character out of *Gone With the Wind* or one of those other Old South books, but I knew the man myself. When we moved down there, when I was just a little boy, I used to fish off a bridge over the river outside town. And one day here comes this big old nasty white man, swinging his cane at me.

"Get your nigger ass off that bridge," he says, "or I'm gonna kill you." That was John Smith.

Fame Has No Color

Success has a funny way of making people forget things. I'll tell you when I started being treated differently is when I started becoming well known as a basketball player. I have a friend whose mother is Jewish and she was prejudiced. Every time I'd come by to pick him up, his mother would make me wait outside. Every time I'd call, she'd pick up the phone and say, "No, he's not here," then she'd yell at me. This happened my first three years in college. And me and this kid were best friends. But his mom never let me inside their house.

Then my junior year at St. John's, I'm starting for the team, we win the NIT championship, I'm Most Valuable Player, on TV every day. After that, whenever I come by my friend's house, his mom says, "Yeah, come on in, sit down, and wait." I call, and she gets on the phone and wants to have a long conversation.

I'm glad I had a white parent and a black parent so I could see both sides of the coin and how ridiculous it is and how ignorant it is to be racist. I'm really glad of that.

Got Milk?

The Nets take a yearly trip to downtown Newark to help feed the homeless. Now, I own some homes in Newark, my uncle and my sister live in Newark, so I spend a lot of time there. I see that these people are a lot less fortunate, don't make as much money, and a lot of them are unemployed.

But you get people down there for the first time, and they make immediate assumptions. You get the news media there, most of whom are white, and everybody they see is black or Puerto Rican. And the first thing they say as soon as they see a bunch of black people, Puerto Ricans, or minorities, the media says, "Look at them. These guys are on drugs. Don't give them more than one juice." We were handing out food and juice. The Nets had all chipped in and bought all this food and juice. So some of the people wanted more than one juice; the juice was only four ounces. We're giving them all this turkey, and it's like one of those milk commercials. You know, the guy dying for some milk. He's squawking, "Got milk? Got milk?" So these people with the turkey, their mouths are dried out and they want some more juice. So I give it to them, and then some of the reporters—and some of the other people—they're saying, "No, you can't give them more than one. They'll go out, they'll sell it, they'll put them in their pockets."

Now, how they going to sell a four-ounce juice? I say give the man what the hell he wants to drink, he's thirsty.

Some people will drive through Newark or a minority neighborhood like the Lower East Side, where I grew up, and they'll be in their Volvo—a husband and wife—and the wife will look over and go, "Look at this. This is a shame. All these people on drugs. Where do these drugs come from? These people are animals."

And then they go home and they find their fourteen-year-old son doped out on heroin and they go, "Oh my! It's an epidemic!" The only difference is in the bad neighborhoods the people don't have money, or a home to go to, or a nice car. These people don't have choices that people with good jobs do. But they're no different. They're just people.

Who's Your Daddy?

Racial perception cuts all ways, and sometimes it's totally innocent. Gheorghe Muresan, the Romanian giant we signed in 1999, came to my house in the springtime for one of my weekend barbecues. Gheorghe is looking at my house, built by my dad and me, and he's working on his three plates full of food. He's got three steaks and five hot dogs, and he's shoveling it down, patting his stomach, just looking around at everything, like, "Ain't this a great country."

And Gheorghe is having such a good time, he decides he wants a house like mine, and he wants to hire my dad to build it. So every time an older black guy walks by, and I got about thirty of my friends out there, Gheorghe grabs him and says, "Are you Jayson's daddy?"

I guess to Romanians we all look alike.

The I-Man Cometh

I joke about race sometimes, because I joke about everything. And when it comes to race, I think that if you don't laugh at some people's stupid ideas, you'd cry. But what I've learned is, not everyone gets the joke.

I'm on the Don Imus radio show a lot, and Don's an equal-opportunity hater. He'll get on you no matter who you are—black, white, president or garbage collector. One time I was late to his show because I got hung up in traffic. I'm listening to him on my car radio, and he's going off on me.

"Here's this basketball player," he's saying, "and you give him some money, and you put him in front of a bunch of people, and now this nappy-headed kid is late all the time."

I'm thinking, Did he say "nappy-headed"? Nah, he couldn't have. Even the I-Man isn't big enough to say "nappy-headed" on the radio.

Then he says it again. "This is what I'm talking about with these high-paid athletes. These nappy-headed guys."

And my car phone starts ringing. My friends are calling.

"Did you hear what he said about you? How you gonna let that man say that? Jay, you gotta do something." That kind of stuff. Then I get a call from a prominent public figure who's also a minister. I mean, *very* prominent. He says, "You do not do this show. You do *not* do this show."

Of course I do the show. I have a relationship with Don. I like the guy.

But the next day I have to do a conference call, with all my friends and the prominent minister. Had to calm all of them down.

I'm saying, "I know Imus. He's not a racist. He hates everybody. Or at least he pretends to hate everybody. It's his facade. In real life he gives a lot of his money to charity, more than most anyone I know. He's really a good guy."

So now, even though I haven't really satisfied these guys, no one's bothering me.

No one's bothering me, that is, until Imus has one of his guys, right after I sign my big contract, on the air, impersonating me.

He says, in my voice, "Now that I've got a hundred million dollars, I can finally move my mama out of the projects."

He says, "Now that I'm making this kind of money, I'm gonna get to shoot more, get to take over the offense."

He says, "And I want to say one thing about Patrick Ewing. Patrick Ewing's just dumb."

The morning of the show, my father knocks on my door, wakes me up. He says, "Are you drinking again? What the hell's the matter with you?"

I say, "Dad, I was sleeping. You just woke me up."

"Bull," he says, "I just heard you talking on the radio. What the hell you talking about getting your mama out of the projects? Your mama doesn't live in the damn projects."

"Dad, that wasn't me. That was someone impersonating me."

"Don't lie to me," my dad's yelling. "I heard you on the radio."

Finally I convince him, but then I got to hear about the show in practice. The Nets' guys are saying, "What the hell you doing? You really think you're gonna get to shoot more this year?" Stuff like that. People are even coming up to me on the street, laughing. "Man," they say, "you were really loose on Imus this morning."

And then I'm thinking about Patrick. Patrick's got a temper, you know. And I'm thinking, if Patrick believes that was me saying that stuff about him being dumb, then I know who he's going to express that temper on. So I'm hoping somebody tells Patrick that wasn't really me.

Lost in Translation

Another time I got in trouble on Imus, I couldn't blame him, or anyone impersonating me. I was on his show during one of my earlier contract negotiations, when Jimmy Gerstein and Allan Offstein were the Nets' owners.

I say, doing a little shtick, on the show:

"I was telling Gerstein and Offstein I wanted fifteen million for three years, and they said they needed to go in the next room, and they did, to talk it over between themselves. And I put my ear to the wall and listened, and what I heard was one of 'em saying to the other, "Holy bar mitzvah, Jimmy, do you believe this guy?"

"And then I hear another voice saying, 'That's what eating all that fried food does to those guys, Allan, makes 'em crazy, makes 'em think they can get five million a year! How many Cadillacs can one guy drive?'"

We caught some flak for that, Imus and me. And it made me realize how many damn people listen to his show, and that not all of 'em share my sense of humor. Because we heard from a lot of them. Didn't hear much about the fried food and the Cadillac remarks, but that "Holy bar mitzvah" joke I heard a lot about.

So even though I thought it was funny, I was sorry I offended some people.

The Man on the Porch, Part II

I only spent a few years of my life in Ritter, South Carolina, but those years shaped me. They shaped me in good ways and bad, and in some ways I probably don't even realize. And I've spent a lot of time in my adult life trying to unshape some of the things that happened down there. After my second year in the NBA, the first summer in my life I could actually say I had money to spare, the first thing I did was drive down to Ritter. Drove down in a brand-new green BMW. And I took my Grandma Elvira, who had spent all those years working for the man I call John Smith, to the nicest clothing store in town. I called ahead and told 'em I'd be bringing her in, and could they close the store to everyone else, because I was going to be buying her thousands of dollars' worth of clothes. This was a store that would not even let her walk through the front door for most of her life, because she was black. But now that an NBA player was calling, and time had passed, they were happy to oblige.

So me and Grandma Elvira walked into that store that was closed to all its regular customers, one Saturday afternoon, and we walked up and down the aisles. And I looked at a lot of the dresses, and touched some, and pretended to be thinking. And then I said, "Nah, there's nothing here I like," and then we walked across the street to another store, a place that had never treated my grandma bad, and I bought her sixty-two outfits. Spent $7,000. Outfits don't cost a whole lot in Ritter, South Carolina.

And after I dropped Grandma Elvira off, I drove straight out to John Smith's house. And there he is, at sunset, rocking in his chair next to his big fat columns on that wraparound porch. I come squealing up his driveway, and I say, "John Smith, John Smith! I'm Jayson Williams and I come to talk to you."

"You Vira's grandboy?" the old man says.

"Yeah."

"Well, what can I do for you?"

"You can tell me how much you want for this old plantation house. Because I'm gonna give you however much you say, then I'm gonna burn it down, to make up for all the pain you caused my family."

He doesn't say anything, so I keep talking. And then I'm yelling at this old racist. And one of his workers—because he still employs a lot of black folks in the town—he says, "Hey, Jayson, let it go. It's all in the past." I remember the worker from when I was a boy. We used to play together.

But I can't let it go. After what John Smith did to my dad and my grandmother and my aunts. I can't let it go. So I'm yelling and screaming and I'm right up in John Smith's face when I feel the worker's hand on my arm. He's speaking real soft.

"Jayson, ol' John Smith don't understand a word you're saying. He's been senile the past ten years. His mind quit working a long time ago."

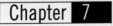

Chapter 7	**Dirty Tricks,**
	Hidden Fouls,
	Head Games &
	Other Tools of an
	NBA Veteran's Trade

Telling your opponent that his point guard can't get him the ball is just one way a veteran tries to get an edge. Another trick is you talk about a player's coach. This works especially well on the young guys. You take a rookie, his team's just played five games in seven nights, and you go up to him before the game, all buddy-buddy.

"Man," you say, "you didn't get a day off? And I hear you had to practice yesterday? You know, we never practice when we have that many games in a row. That's one great thing about playing here. They're probably making you practice because the coach thinks you're behind the other teams and he's worried about you."

It's not hard to put a player against his coach. People put me against John Calipari the first year we were together with the Nets. Charles Oakley and them, they played their games on me. Oak would come up to me before a game and he'd say, "You play for a guy like that and you ain't never going to get ahead. You got to get out of there. That guy's holding you back. That guy is going to make you *kill* him, then no one's gonna want you, and you can kiss your money good-bye."

I gotta say, it worked pretty good for a while till I figured it out. Now I do it to other players.

Raging Bulls & Stinging Bees

Head games are just part of an NBA veteran's strategy. There are physical tricks players use, too. At least players like me.

The first physical trick is just *being* physical. The first thing I do is I try to send a message at the very beginning of a game. I come out hard, sweat popping, eyes bulging, diving all over the place, going crazy.

I start the game like a raging bull, like a bull who just got stung on its nose by a bee. I'm coming out kicking, scratching, and hollering, like Tarzan. Other guys come out and they're too cool—they run cool, they look cool, they don't want to dive on the floor, they don't want to get physical. Not me. I know exactly how much talent I have. I can say that now that I have a big, long-range contract. I know that deep down, I have to outwork some guys with maybe more talent than me. So I don't come into the game and wait for my talent to take me through the game.

What Larry King and I Have in Common

Before each game, I jump rope and I do drills with three balls. I have assistants throw balls every which way, and I run and catch them and throw them back. And I get my heart up to capacity. I get it up to 175 beats a minute. Also, I drink two or three quarts of coffee—about twelve to fourteen cups—and take some ginseng to get me going. This is what gets me more alert, makes me start sweating, on the edge. Mark McGwire took andro, Jayson Williams takes ginseng. And it works.

When John Calipari found out what I was taking before the games, he called my dad to come in and talk to me with the coaching staff.

So my dad comes in, and he says to me, "Oh, man, you're on ginseng? Oh, gee whiz! What is that? Is that stuff you shoot up? Is that the new stuff on the street?"

I say, "Come on, Dad. Ginseng is just a natural herb."

"Herb?" he says. "Why didn't you tell me about smoking that stuff? That stuff, it will kill you."

He was going crazy. I say, "Dad, I just drink coffee to get me edgy. You drink coffee. And that other stuff is stuff I drink, too. It's an herb; it comes out of the earth."

"All drugs come out of the earth!" my dad says. "Hell, heroin starts somewhere in the earth before it's heroin."

And then Don Casey, one of our assistant coaches at the time, who's sitting there, he chimes in, trying to help.

Don says, "Yeah, it's natural, and some people drink it because it gets you an erection and stuff."

Now my dad looks at me all worried and he says, "Son, you got a problem with yourself down there?"

Fat Boy

I start the game banging people. I let them know this is the kind of game it's going to be. I learned it in poker. When people go to play poker and you've got a good hand, if you've got a pair of eights, and a guy's got a jack showing, you don't want that guy to get more cards, because most likely he's going to get them. So you don't let him get the fourth card. You bet a lot of money right there and make him fold. So that's what I do. In the first eight minutes I bang a guy, I try to make him fold. I don't play dirty, I just bang him. And bang him. And bang him.

So when a guy sees me like this, all banging and jabbing and worked up and all, if a guy didn't want to play that night, he would definitely not want to play now. So he'll pick a fight with the point guard or he'll pick a fight with the coach and get thrown out. I've seen it happen a lot of times.

It's like Larry Holmes tells me about fighting. You gotta let the other guy know what kind of fight it's going to be. You jab at the start. You jab some more. You make him know that jab's going to be there all frigging night. You know, Joe Frazier used to go in the ring and say, "Which one is the referee? Because I'm going to kill the other guy." And that's how I come into the game. "Which one of you is the referee? Which one? Because everybody else, I'm going to kill them."

I'm not dirty. I don't believe in playing dirty. And I talk to people at the tip-off. I'm friendly, a nice guy. But when that game starts, it's like, "You've got to feed your children, and I've got to feed mine. Let's see which one is going to be the fattest at the end of the game." And I'll tell you what. My son is going to be 400 pounds, I guarantee you. At the end of the game, I'm going to have to roll his fat butt out of the arena.

The $100-Million Duck, or How I Learned to Rebound

I got a big contract in 1998 because I'm a good citizen, and a good teammate, and because I don't do some of the wild stuff I used to. But mostly I got that money because I rebound, because when that ball goes up, I go up too, and I get it. By the time I retire, I plan to be the greatest offensive rebounder in the history of basketball. Which is saying something, because I'm only about six foot ten, though at contract time I always grow to seven feet.

Now, I'm not going to tell you all my rebounding secrets, because that might help put me out of a job. There was a contractor once, a guy my father was working for, and we were building him a hotel, and I was teaching him how to lay bricks, and my father came over and he called me off the wall and he said, "Now, if you teach him how to lay bricks, then what does he need us for?" And I want the Nets to need me. But I will tell you *some* of my secrets.

I didn't grow up wanting to be a great rebounder. I used to have a pretty deadly jump shot, believe it or not. But when I first joined the Nets, back in 1992, I was on the floor with Derrick Coleman and Armen Gilliam and Kenny Anderson. Derrick and Armen weren't really much about assists, and Kenny wasn't much better. So when Kenny would throw it in to Derrick or Armen, it didn't take me long to figure out that that ball was not coming back out, and if it did, it definitely wasn't coming back out to me. And sometimes Kenny would just take that ball to the hole himself. I mean no offense to Kenny, but when he was dribbling, he wasn't thinking, Now, how am I gonna get the rock to Jay?

So there's Kenny and Derrick and Armen, the Black Hole himself. And me and P. J. Brown used to stand up at the top of the key. We'd be the decoys. We were like those decoy ducks. During practice, sometimes even during the game, we'd be standing up by the top of the key, P. J. and me, and we'd be ducking our heads, waddling, going "quack-quack."

I'd say, "P. J., you the Man, quack-quack, quack-quack."

And he'd laugh and say, "No, Jay, man, you the Man, quack-quack, quack-quack."

Paul Silas, an assistant coach then, he takes me aside one day and he says, "Jayson, Derrick Coleman and Kenny Anderson are not going to pass you the ball. They're All-Stars. But they only shoot 40 percent, so they're going to miss six out of ten shots."

He told me if I wanted the ball, I'd better learn to rebound. "You go up there and get the offensive rebound and do what I've been doing for a lifetime"—Paul was one of the greatest offensive rebounders who ever played—"and you'll be just fine." And that's how I got started concentrating on rebounding.

Now, when I see a ball go up, I start out far from the basket, maybe about ten feet farther out than other players. I learned this from watching Lawrence Taylor playing linebacker for the New York Giants. He always created space between him and his opponent, because the closer you are to your opponent, the less you can go. Since I'm in better shape and I'm so much quicker than most of the guys I play against, I can go three feet to the right or left of him. When he goes three feet, I go another three feet and then shake him. And I just try to keep off from them as far as I can. So I take two steps this way, then four steps this way, and then, because I have good timing, I just jump. Most players don't do what I do because it takes too much energy. The day I lose my conditioning is the day I go from being an All-Star to being the 350th best player in the league.

I'll tell you the other things I do. And not just me, but all the good rebounders. You learn to hold people's hands down. Especially the young guys. You usually use all these tricks on the young guys. You know, soon as a guy goes up for a rebound, you grab him by the wrist so he can't get up very high. When you hold a guy's hands down, believe me, he can jump as high as he wants, he's coming straight back down. The other thing is, as soon as the ball goes up, I push somebody. It doesn't matter where or how, you just push 'em anywhere you can. Throws their timing off and you get better position.

And finally what I learned about rebounding is in the last twenty-five seconds of the game you can stay in the paint as long as you want, and you can go over a guy's back as much as you want, because the refs are not going to call that.

I'll guarantee you, the end of a game, ten seconds left, we have the ball, I'm not leaving the paint. I know they'll never make that call. Can you imagine, me tipping one in at the buzzer against the Lakers, maybe going over someone's back, and them calling something? Over the back, or three seconds? It ain't going to happen. Especially at home. Refs are human, too. They're not coming in with earplugs on, and they want to get out of the building without hearing that their mother's so fat she has to iron her pants in the driveway.

One Is the Loneliest Number

There's nobody one-on-one who is going to stop me from getting to the offensive boards. NBA coaches know that and they devise strategies to stop me. A lot of them used to send their point guard over to double-team me on the box-out. When teams start throwing their point guards at me, I'll mess with them. I remember playing against Phoenix, and Hot Rod Williams was guarding me, and every time one of the Nets shot, Hot Rod would try boxing me out, and here would come little Steve Nash, their point guard, to block me, too. Well, I didn't try any two-steps-this-way-two-steps-that-away moves. I just ran as hard as I could, as fast as I could, smashed straight into Steve Nash. I do that a few times, now he's flopping, now he's faking, now he's backing off boxing me out.

See, it makes sense for their coach to send the point guard to dou-ble-team me on the box-out. But that's their quarterback, the point guard. And if I have to take out the quarterback, I'm going to take out the quarterback. And the quarterback and his coach figure that out pretty quick. Then there aren't so many double-teams.

How to Make the Worm Turn

The only recent rebounder better than me was Dennis Rodman. Dennis Rodman was the greatest rebounder that ever played the game. Sometimes I get caught up in defense, or in scoring some points when points need to be scored. But Dennis never lost focus on rebounding. That's what he did. He was tenacious; he went after everything. There were only two ways to beat Dennis Rodman. The first was you beat him to the first six or seven rebounds. Then he got bored. The other way you beat him was you didn't give Dennis any attention on the court. You act like he's not there. Act like you don't even know Dennis was on the court, and he'd get bored. Even if he did something crazy like elbow you or something, you just acted like you don't even know he's there. And then if you kept ignoring him, he'd just go away. When he was with the Bulls and when people started paying too much attention to Mike and Scottie, Dennis didn't feel like he was part of things, and he'd get bored and give up some games.

Handy, Weighty Matters

I didn't come into the league knowing all these head games and dirty tricks. I learned. And I had some great teachers. I learned from Charles Barkley how to stop a great jump shooter. You watch Charles on defense sometimes against someone with a good J.

What Charles will do is fake that he's going to punch you in the stomach. That makes a lot of people flinch. You know, you flinch, that ball goes halfway. Or if the guy he's guarding doesn't flinch, Charlie will actually hit him hard the next time. Like the poker game again. You let him see you have a strong hand. With Charlie, literally a strong hand. Charlie would take his fingers and drive 'em straight into the shooter's abs while he was running by. That hurts, I'll guarantee you. That knocks your wind out. All Charlie would have to do it is once, and then they'd be flinching the whole game. Especially the inexperienced guys.

Something else I learned when I first came into the league was how to guard a big man who didn't have the ball. Rick Mahorn taught me how to lean all your weight on somebody while they don't have the ball. And as soon as they receive the ball, you release all your weight and watch them travel and fall down. Rick Mahorn did that to me the first three times we practiced together with the 76ers. And I swear to God, all I wanted to do was punch Rick right in his face. Now I do the same trick all the time.

Getting the Hook

Three out of four NBA players can score anytime they want one-on-one. If you put a guy in the box with the ball, you're going to foul him or he's going to score. Play someone outside straight up and guess what? He'll drive by you or shoot over you. He'll score. NBA players are big, we're strong, we're the best basketball players in the world. You watch a one-on-one game at an NBA practice sometime, I guarantee you the score won't be 15–3. It'll be 15–13, every time. These guys all were the number one player in their conferences. Not just their teams, their conferences. Except for maybe a couple guys on each team, everyone can score. First thing I told Keith Van Horn was he'd be amazed how much easier it was to score in this league that it was in college. That's because the league says you have to play man-to-man defense. So when one player gets double-teamed, someone else is wide open for that athletic, flying-through-the-air dunk shot. I told him he'd get some of those.

He didn't believe me till we played our first game against the Knicks. He got 19 points, real fast. After, his eyes were like saucers. "Man," he says, "you were *riiiiiight.*"

But the reason no team is scoring 300 points a game or something is because coaches figured out ways to double-team and switch and concentrate on a player's weakness. Especially now, with videotape, when we can watch what every team and every player does.

So you can study a guy's moves, you know which way he likes to turn 90 percent of the time. I can tell you what spots Charles Oakley likes to shoot from, what shoulder he likes to shoot over. Ninety-five percent of the time if he gets the ball fifteen feet from the basket on the right-hand side, he's going to shoot a jumper.

That's why smart NBA players are always working on new shots, and when other players figure out how to stop those shots, they invent even newer ones. Jordan, a player who could score at will any way, anytime, invented that little fadeaway about halfway through his career. Bird kept taking his jumper farther and farther out, till he could hit from about nine thousand feet. And Magic, he was known for taking the weakest part of his game each summer and trying to improve it. Like that goofy little hook shot he hit over McHale to beat the Celtics in the play-offs. He didn't just think of that at the moment.

So when I was with the Nets a few years, before I was really concentrating on rebounding, I tried to develop a new shot.

Assistant Coach Clifford Ray was trying to teach me to shoot a left-handed hook shot. One dribble left, then hook, right? I work with Clifford on it some, and then we're playing against the Knicks, and Patrick Ewing doesn't jump for every shot, and he doesn't always move side to side well, so even though he's a great shot blocker, I figured I'd get him with my new slick move, my left-handed hook shot. I faked right and went hard left and I beat him. But when I shot the hook, I missed everything. I mean everything. The basket, the backboard, everything, by about eight feet. My left-handed hook went right into the fifth row. I looked over at the bench and I saw Clifford Ray just throw his head down and start shaking his head, and when he picked his head up he had tears coming out of his eyes because he was laughing so hard, right? I was pissed off that he was laughing at this shot, the one he'd been teaching me. Because I didn't want to shoot it anyway. So when I got back to the time-out, I said, "Cliff, you sold me that old dumb frigging shot."

He couldn't stop laughing.

And then I said, "And then you have the audacity to stand there and laugh?"

He said, "Hey, bro, bro, bro. I didn't teach you how to shoot *that* shot."

He says, "Now do me a favor. Scratch that one from your repertoire."

And Butch Beard, the head coach, looked over at us. Butch said, "If he shoots another shot like that, Clifford Ray, you're fired!"

So right before I'm walking out, Cliff tells me, "Yo, Jay, please, please don't shoot a left-handed hook no more!"

But I'm pissed. He taught me the damn shot, then he laughed at me. So two plays later I get the ball on the post. I whirl right, shoot the hook. Same results. Fifth row. I look over at the bench and Clifford Ray was getting drilled out by Butch Beard. So I come back to the bench, Clifford says, "Motherf———, you're going to cost me my job! I told you not to shoot another hook."

I said, "No, no, you told me not to shoot a *left-handed* hook. You didn't say nothing about right-handed hooks."

Nowadays, my best move is a right-handed hook where I come swooping across the middle. I still shoot left-handed hooks occasionally. If Clifford Ray ever sees 'em on TV, he probably has little heart attacks.

Style over Substance

A shot not many players use, and it's one of the most effective shots in the game, is the jump hook. Kind of half jumper, half hook, and if you shoot it fast, you get it over a bigger guy, he's so surprised. But it's clumsy-looking, especially if you miss.

You know why not many players shoot it? Because it doesn't

look cool. Yeah, players don't like to shoot it 'cause it doesn't look cool, especially when you miss. Armen Gilliam still shoots it, and I shoot it sometimes, and Hakeem Olajuwon shoots it, but that's about it. Everyone else is too worried about looking cool.

Higher and Higher

So how do you stop an NBA player who can jump out of the building and who has all sorts of trick shots? One thing you do is you forget all the stuff you've learned since high school about never giving up the baseline. In fact, you *want* players to drive the baseline on you.

Why you give up the baseline is because you got people there who can block shots. Most players, unless they're stars, they go baseline and you push 'em a little, nothing's going to happen. Nothing's going to be called. Because most of the times the referee's going to say, "Well, he knows he couldn't get nothin' off there anyway, throwin' up a Hail Mary like that." You see rookies do that sometimes. They jump up in the air, figure they'll figure out what to do, whether to pass or shoot, when they're up there, like Michael Jordan. What they find out is this isn't like high school or college where you could jump over a player. You leave your feet in the NBA, you got guys who are going to wait for you, and they're going to jump, and they're going to jump higher than you.

How to Look Good on the Free-Throw Line

Most players in the NBA eventually figure out new shots, and how to grab and push and get away with it. But only a few figure out the *really* subtle tricks of the trade. Looking cool when someone else is shooting a free throw, for example. Players talk about all kinds of things during free throws. If a team is staying over that night and the guys on that team like the guys on the home team, we'll talk about where to go that night. Other times, no one will say much. Especially if you're tired, you just want to rest during free throws. But you'll notice that the superstars, a lot of 'em you'll *always* see joking and laughing. I know superstars who, when they know a game's televised and they're tired on the free-throw line, they'll be talking and moving their mouth and nothing coming out. They're not saying anything. They're just moving their mouth to make it look like they're talking. They figure it'll make 'em look better for their next sneaker commercial.

How to Look Unselfish

One way to make sure you get shots is just to shoot the ball every time you touch it. But if you do that, you look selfish, and everyone knows you look selfish. So you got to be tricky. Tricky like the players who get the ball in the post and pass it out to another player, but *always* seem to get the ball back for another shot. Here's what those players do: They hold the ball until there's about eight seconds left on the shot clock, and then they pass it outside. That player outside knows he doesn't have a shot, so he's gotta give it right back to the post player. He's got to throw it back into the hole. Anthony Mason is good with that, and so is Charles Barkley.

It's even easier to look unselfish and to make *another* player look like a ball hog. It's a rotten thing to do, but some players do it. They're smart: They watch the shot clock, and then, if he's a player who doesn't like you, he gives you the ball with three seconds left on the shot clock, and you have to take a bad shot. There's no way you can create a shot with less than five seconds on the clock, so you look bad, and the average fan thinks you're the dope, not the guy who passed it to you with three seconds left.

How to End a Shooting Slump

Everyone misses sometimes. For someone like me, who bases so much of his game on rebounding and putbacks, it's no big deal. For a shooter, which I at one time was, it can be bad. Keith Van Horn's a great shooter, but his rookie year, he hits his first big slump. I tell him what I used to do when I was in a slump was go out and get plastered. Get drunk, get a couple of cocktails and then go back home, and then the next day come back. I say, " 'Cause you know what? You'll be so sick in the morning you won't even be worrying about your slump, and you'll come back and you'll play well."

And Keith, who doesn't drink, says, "Do you think that will work?"

"Yeah," I say. "Trust me."

Keith had shot about 20 percent for the whole month, gone about eight for sixty or something when we were having that conversation. The last game before we talked, I don't know if he hit a single jumper. We're in Philadelphia, and we have a game the next day. And Keith doesn't drink. But he also doesn't want to stay in that shooting slump. So that night we go out, we have a couple of cocktails. Get plastered together. I take the complete blame for that. Or credit, depending how you look at it. 'Cause the next day he goes out and scores 30 points. Hitting from all over. Afterward, in the locker room, he says, "Where are we going tonight?"

I say, "We're going home, boy. Slump's over. So is the party."

Talking the Talk

You can be able to jump to the moon, shoot from Mars, and basically kick everyone's butt on the court from here to Saturn, and unless you can talk to the press, no one's going to know who you are. I learned this from Charles Barkley. What Charles taught me is how to deal with the media. That they have a job to do, and you can't just shut them down. It isn't fair for you to shut them down. You've got to give them an opinion one way or another. "No comment" is never going to work.

If anyone was ever a candidate for having bad things written and said about him, it was me. History of drinking, fighting with coaches, all that stuff. Then I sign a big contract and get hurt, which really makes me a target.

But for the most part, no one goes out of their way to rip me. And that's because I figured out a long time ago that the reporters are *not* out to get you. For the most part they just write what they see and what they hear. And the columnists, they write what they see and hear and what their opinion is about what they see and hear. And what most players never seem to realize is that you as a player are in control of what those reporters see and hear. You play like crap, then say something stupid or angry, what do you expect them to write? So even if you play like crap some night—and everybody does sometimes—at least have the good sense to not say something stupid afterward. Tell the truth, maybe give 'em a joke or two.

A few of my buddies from the other side of the Hudson are infamous for never figuring out reporters. They do something, then the media writes about it, then a bunch of those players get mad about it and whine and moan all over. No wonder people write bad things about them.

There are guys in the league who figure that their job is done after the buzzer sounds. That talking's not a part of their contract. You know, there are those guys who just come in, they do their job, and they leave. Nothing against them, but that's not helping them any, with the fans, with the press, even with their next contract.

I feel like there's only about 10 percent of the people in this league who are good with the media. And 45 percent don't talk to the media. And then the other 45 percent when they do talk, you know, they're so boring and dishonest probably a lot of folks wish they *wouldn't* talk. Everyone knows the boring ones. "Well, this was a big game." "Well, we have to execute." "You know, this team really wanted this one." I mean, people out there listening to those players can stop buying Sominex.

Worse than the boring ones are the really slick talkers, though. Now, Derrick Coleman is someone I've known a long time, but when I first got to the Nets, he said, "That Williams runs up and down the court one or two times and then he's tired." And then he told reporters he never hung out with me, which in fact he did. You know, those two things bothered me. And I went up to him and I asked him, I said, "Derrick, did you say those things?" And he said, "No, I didn't say them."

But Derrick's like a few guys in the NBA. You know what the

most commonly used phrase by a player in the NBA is? "I was mis-quoted."

What usually happens is a lot of reporters are always trying to make people go against each other. Players on the same team. A reporter will say, "Don't you think so-and-so should pass more?" Or "Shouldn't such-and-such quit shooting those dumb fallaways so much?" Those are like big chunks of meat dangling in front of you and you're a big great white, you know? You just want to take a big old chunk of that question and chew it up. But what I do is I don't talk to the reporters about that until I talk to the players. I'll go over to someone and say, "Well, look, man, I was open that time. You didn't pass me the ball." And then, if he's a jerk about it, I'll tell him about it again, but his time I'll make sure it's in front of a reporter. And you know what? Reporters might be a lot of things—they might be sneaky sometimes and a little weaselly—but they're just guys trying to do their jobs, and most of the time they get stuff right. And especially for me, who most of the time what I say is honest, I don't ever have to go back to a reporter and complain and try to take something back.

Nuts

I can tell you one thing you don't want to do with a reporter, and that's get in some kind of feud with him. You might be a big tough professional basketball player, but I got news for you: When that reporter stands on his little laptop, or satellite hookup, or whatever the hell they're using these days, he's about twenty-five feet tall. In his own way, he's going to kick your butt.

We had a local reporter a few years ago in New Jersey covering the Nets, named Dan Garcia. Good guy, good reporter, but Dan would push and push with his questions, and he would try to get something out of you. Then he'd take the little nut he got and he'd make a pecan pie out of it. You know, he'd blow everything up. So everybody knew you had to be careful with Dan Garcia. Even me, who is not exactly the most careful guy in the world.

Well, we also had a new coach at the time, John Calipari, who, if you were a pecan pie maker, he'd be your primary nut-supplier, if you know what I mean.

So Dan writes something Cal doesn't like, and Cal complains, and Dan writes something else and Cal bitches some more, and what ends up happening is Cal sees Dan in the parking lot one day, and he calls him a "Mexican idiot." (Cal's not a racist, but sometimes you think you can talk to people any which way you want to.) Garcia is five foot nothin', and with three cinder blocks in his back pocket, he might weigh a hundred pounds. And another reporter saw and heard the whole thing.

That was a really bad move on Cal's part. But still, nobody believed how much that escalated. He tried to ignore it, but there was no way to ignore it once it got rolling. And just when it was dying down, these four guys started coming to all the games, sat right across from our bench, wearing Mexican hats and playing big ol' bongos. Not even a good beat, as I remember. What ended up happening was Cal apologized. He learned that even little Mexican reporters stand tall when they got those laptops.

The NBA's Biggest Bargain

I heard a TV guy once say that if you think too much, you have problems shooting free throws. Then I must be the Einstein of the NBA, because I have had problems, especially early in my career. I'll tell you, I was struggling. And I was looking everywhere for help. I had this guy, they call him the shot doctor, he comes in, works with you, charges you about a zillion dollars, teaches you to relax, works on your mechanics, blahzee blahzee. I had Buzz Peterson, an old friend, work with me. I had psychologists, you name it. I spent about $30,000 in eight years to shoot free throws better, and I'll tell you what—these guys are full of it. They're like golf pros. You give 'em money, they tell you stuff, you still stink.

Then I call Chris Mullin, good friend, fellow St. John's alum, great free-throw shooter. He came over to my house in the summer— made 440 in a row. He looks at my free-throw shooting, says,

"Dribble three times, bend your knees, bounce it hard so it's at your face, then release it."

He tells me to shoot three hundred free throws a day for three weeks, then muscle memory will take over. I'll be like a secretary who's been typing for a hundred years.

Chris told me the only reason I'm a bad free-throw shooter is I don't put in the time, and he was right.

You've got to shoot a hundred free throws a day in the morning and a hundred before or after practice. If you do that, you'll shoot 75 percent. If you don't, you just don't *want* to shoot well from the free-throw line.

That's what I learned from Chris Mullin. Now I shoot over 75 percent.

That summer I barbecued him a steak and gave him a Coke. That retails at about $17.95. A bargain.

How to Win in the Postseason

The play-offs are a life-or-death situation. During the season, a lot of players have the attitude of "All right, I didn't set that pick, so I didn't get Kerry Kittles open to hit the jump shot. That's all right. We'll play it again tomorrow and I'll make sure I set it tomorrow."

There is no tomorrow in the play-offs. That's the theme of everything on a good postseason team. You know when you die? You die in the summer. That's what Paul Silas used to tell us when we had our play-off run a few years ago with the Nets and he was the assistant coach. Guys would say, "Man, I'm tired," and he'd say, "Hey, boy, die, but die in the summer. We got to win this now. You can die next week. But right now, you got to give it up." Play as hard as you can, every second. That's how great players win in the play-offs. That's how great teams win championships.

My sisters Linda *(left)* and Laura help celebrate my very first Christmas. Not a day goes by that I don't miss them.
BARBARA WILLIAMS

Graduation from nursery school. I was always big for my age.
BARBARA WILLIAMS

I wish I could say I was a sharp dresser ever since the first grade. In fact, at St. Joseph's School, we had to wear coats and ties. BARBARA WILLIAMS

First Communion. Eight years old. How could anyone ever accuse someone like this of grabbing, or pushing, or shoving on the court? BARBARA WILLIAMS

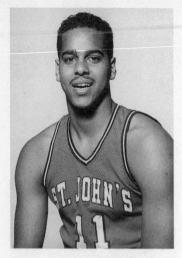

A lot of schools offered me money to play for them. St. John's offered me a chance to stay close to my family and my friends from the neighborhood.
ST. JOHN'S UNIVERSITY

My college coach was also my teacher, father figure, confessor, and guardian. Lou Carnesecca is still one of my best friends.
NBA PHOTOS

After meeting Charles Barkley in Philadelphia, he and I had a lot of fun. I think that's one reason I didn't get much playing time. NBA PHOTOS

Charles Barkley taught me a lot—about life on and off the court. Luckily for me, I've ignored some of his lessons—otherwise my liver would be the size of two footballs. NBA PHOTOS

When you're playing against the best, you do whatever you can to win. Here I am, doing whatever I can. It didn't work. NBA PHOTOS

Michael Jordan is the greatest basketball player ever to step on a court. He's also the meanest. He was so tough, he scared his own teammates. NBA PHOTOS

The first time I saw Larry Bird, I begged my coach to let me guard him. No way a slow, skinny guy like him could beat me. He lit me up for 14 points in six minutes. NBA PHOTOS

Some people say Patrick Ewing, one of the best players in the league, isn't smart, because he's so quiet. It's those people who aren't very smart. Patrick might not talk much, but he sure laughs a lot—all the way to the bank. NBA PHOTOS

Arvydas Sabonis has the biggest head in the entire NBA. I don't mean ego. I mean head. Check it out. The thing must weigh eighty pounds. He lays that thing on you, you can't move. NBA PHOTOS

When I first played with the Nets, our two All-Stars were Kenny Anderson and Derrick Coleman. Their attitude toward assists is a big reason I became such a good rebounder. I knew it was the only way I'd get my hands on the ball. NBA PHOTOS

There are two ways to beat Dennis Rodman. The first way is to beat him to the first six or seven rebounds, then he goes away. The second way is to ignore him, then he gets bored. As you can see, he's hard to ignore. NBA PHOTOS

There are tough guys in the
league, and strong guys, and
trash-talking guys. Vernon
Maxwell scares all of them.
NBA PHOTOS

The cheapest, funniest, toughest,
most music-loving son of a
preacher I ever met is Armen
Gilliam. He's another guy who
doesn't pass that much. We call
him "The Black Hole" because
once the ball went in to him, it
wasn't coming out. NBA PHOTOS

People say Michael Jordan and
Scottie Pippen didn't like Toni
Kukoc because of his big contract. But the real reason they
didn't like Toni sometimes is
because he'd do stupid things
on the court, then when they
yelled at him, he'd pretend that
he didn't understand English.
NBA PHOTOS

Charles Shackleford is sensitive.
He also chopped sugarcane with
a machete when he was a little
boy. As Armen Gilliam found
out one day, that's a dangerous
combination. NBA PHOTOS

Without Butch Beard and Paul Silas, I might never have developed into a solid NBA player. I can guarantee I never would have become an All-Star or signed such a good contract. I owe these men much of my success. NBA PHOTOS

John Calipari was a master motivator. He also yelled more than any man I ever met.
NBA PHOTOS

The ultimate coach is Phil Jackson. That's because he understands it's not a coach's game. That's why so many players respect Phil. NBA PHOTOS

After the first time I saw Keith Van Horn practice, I went to the Nets owners and the coach and apologized for every bad thing I'd ever done or said. With Keith, I knew I wanted to play for New Jersey for the rest of my career. NBA PHOTOS

There aren't a lot of guys in the NBA who you'd trust with your life. Kendall Gill is one of them. A true warrior. NBA PHOTOS

With a $100 million contract, All-Star status, and a great team, I didn't think anything could go wrong. Then I found out otherwise. NBA PHOTOS

Not everyone sticks with you through bad times and good times. Here are three who did. My adoptive son, Ejay, my dad, E.J., and my mom, Barbara.

BARBARA WILLIAMS

Going up strong with nothing between you and the rim is one of the greatest feelings in the world . . . NBA PHOTOS

. . . but it doesn't even compare to touching a child's life.

NBA PHOTOS

Sure, I want to be remembered as a good basketball player. Even more, I want to be remembered as a good son, a good father, a good citizen. I want to be remembered as someone who gave something back. NBA PHOTOS

**On the Road, at the Bars & in the Backwoods. L.A. Has the Best Cheerleaders, There Are Some Real Animals in New York City, and Milwaukee Is Strictly *Laverne & Shirley*. Plus, Why Utah Fans Are Crazy but Nice**

Growing up in New York, like I did, and hearing all the jokes I heard about New Jersey, if someone would have told me I'd end up playing with the Nets, I'd have laughed. Or cried. Or punched the guy telling me. Being from the city, with Madison Square Garden and all those great Knicks teams and all, all I knew was that New Jersey was supposed to be some kind of joke.

But now I'm the one laughing, because I love it where I am— we got a great team, I got a great house, my family's out here, and the fans are terrific. I love playing in New Jersey.

Which just goes to show, you can't always judge a place by what you hear.

And I don't care how much you've heard about various cities, or how much you've traveled, you haven't seen some of the cities in the United States like an NBA player has seen them. Now you will.

The Wild, Wild, Wild West

Take Utah. Please. Before I first played there, I figured it'd be a nice, quiet place to play some hard basketball. I knew they had that temple, or tabernacle, or whatever it's called, and a lot of people who went to church all the time, even though their grandparents had about ten wives apiece. So if the fans were going to be polite anywhere, I'm figuring it'll be Salt Lake City.

But all I see and hear when I go there is a bunch of crazy people. They are the most cursing and yelling and rudest fans in the whole league. And any player will tell you that. My second year in the league, when I was with Philadelphia, we're playing in Utah, and I look over at Hersey Hawkins and I say, "Look at them, hollerin' and yellin' at everybody. Look at all these crazy people, they're all drunk."

And he says, "Naw, Mormons don't drink."

And I say, "You mean, they're just this rude?"

Now I see why they can't drink. If they're this rude when they're sober, man, can you imagine? But then you meet them on the street twenty minutes after the game, they're the nicest people in the world.

But during that game, they're the worst.

They're screaming all kinds of stuff, mostly "Don't touch Karl, don't touch Karl," every time I get near Karl Malone, which is kind of funny, since he's supposed to be the strongest guy in the league, and they're acting like I'm going to knock him down when I blow on him or something. You think Karl Malone needs a fan to help him against me? But they're also yelling personal things. There's one guy right behind the basket, he will just not let up. "You're no good." "You're ugly." Stuff like that. I don't mind fans yelling, but this guy will not shut up, and it's all yelling at *me*. So I go up to the guy during an out-of-bounds play in the third quarter—he's still yelling, cutting me up really bad—and I look at his girlfriend, who's not bad-looking, and I say, "You got too much makeup on, lady," and that shuts him up. So now every time before a game, I go down to him and I say, "Now, keep it easy, because if you start bothering me, I'm gonna snap on her again."

That guy doesn't give me any trouble anymore. But some of the other Mormons do.

One game in Utah, I hit Karl Malone with an elbow. You know, you got a guy like Michael Jordan, who'll come up to you and say, "How you doing? How's the family? How's everything going?" And then you got a guy like Karl Malone, who's not exactly known for being friendly before a game. He don't say much, and then he goes crying and complaining about a call here and a call there, and you'd think a guy with all those muscles would just go out and play ball. So after I hit him, I got called for a flagrant foul and he said, "My son hits harder than that." So I'm jawing back at him, saying, "Right, after the game let's you and me fight."

Then the owner from Utah stands up, Larry something, and he says something and I say, "You don't know who you're messing with. Sit your fat ass down before I put my fist through your brain." I'm never going to play for Utah, so I didn't lose a lot of sleep over that. Unless Mormons can start sinning, I'm not going to Utah.

Laverne & Shirley

A Milwaukee Bucks game on a Monday night in the middle of December is about as exciting as going to your ex-girlfriend's third cousin's funeral. On a Sunday morning. Christmas Day.

And for nightlife, it's nothing but *Laverne & Shirley*. That's all that happens, ever, in Milwaukee. I don't see how they're ever going to get good free agents. Not many people are ever going to go to Milwaukee. What are you going to do? How many times can you tour the beer vats?

Never Trouble Trouble

The way I figure, I never go out when I'm on the road. In New York and New Jersey, I know I'm safe. I know everybody in New York. I know where you can go, where you can't go, and I only travel with a few of my boys—a few of them are cops, the others are my old pals from the neighborhood. Plus, I've been known to knock a troublemaker through a brick wall myself, so when I'm home, in New York, I don't have to worry too much.

But if you're on the road, and you get in trouble and start running from somebody, if you have to make a breakaway, a lot of times you're just running into more trouble. There's nothing more frustrating, believe me, than getting caught up somewhere, in trouble, not knowing where you are. Imagine somebody chasing you and you having to stop someone else and ask how to get back to the Four Seasons. So that's why I stay in my hotel these days. I've even slowed down in New York. Now if people want to get wild and throw a party, get crazy, they have to come do it at my house. I'm not always an angel. But if I'm a devil at home, no one gets hurt.

Peanuts

Being a well-known professional athlete is great, and if anyone tells you different, they've taken too much Prozac, or some other medication. But it also comes with some problems, and I'm not just talking about screaming Utah fans and their girlfriends. Not too far from where I live, which is in the woods near the New Jersey/Pennsylvania border, there's a little bar which shall remain nameless. This bar gets its redneck clientele, and used to be every time I walked in there I had a problem. First time I walked in there, I was wearing a sweat suit, and a jacket over it. There was this guy kept looking over at me and saying real loud, "Yeah, I don't watch basketball anymore. I don't like the kind of people they got playing the game."

I drank my beer, ignored the guy. Then I went into the bathroom, and as I walked by, the guy kept making dumb comments. I kept ignoring him. The idiot followed me in the bathroom and he says, "You know, someone like you, I think you've got a gun under your jacket. I think you should take it off. Why don't you take it off?"

Well, of course I didn't have a gun. But I looked at this guy—

one of my good old country neighbors—and I said, "Nah, I'm not gonna take it off yet. But wait here for me, because now I'm going to go back out to the bar and shoot about three or four rednecks. And then I'm gonna come back in here and I'm gonna shoot you, and then I'll take my jacket off and put it over your face and prop you up against the toilet."

He left me alone after that.

The next time I went in that bar, I met Ron Rutledge, my former assistant coach at St. John's and a good friend. Ron's black, so me and him were the only two brothers in this place. But I figured we wouldn't have any problems, especially after the incident I had in the bathroom. Shows what I know.

We're sitting at the bar, and there's little bowls of popcorn all over the place. So Ron reaches his hand into a bowl to get some popcorn and this guy—must have come out of the woods or something—he walks up and says, "Hey, dude, get your dirty paws out of my popcorn." There were like twenty bowls of popcorn on the bar, so it wasn't anybody's individual bowl, of course. It was like peanuts on a bar.

Have you ever been walking, minding your own business, maybe daydreaming about something, and somebody blew the horn and just scared you in the middle of the street and made you look like an idiot? That's what hit Ron. He was like a deer caught in the headlights. I looked at him and I was trying not to laugh. I wasn't too worried, because I have dealt with guys like this clown from the woods my whole life.

Here's a guy with cowboy boots on, a bald head and big stomach and a goatee. I said, "Is this your popcorn?" He looks at me with these narrow little pig eyes. He must have learned that look studying some Steven Seagal movie. I can tell you for sure he didn't get it from Clint Eastwood movies, 'cause I'm a fan of Clint's movies and Clint's squinty-eyed look was a hundred times scarier-looking than this pig-eyed idiot (who I later found out was *always* trying to start fights at this bar). I threw the popcorn on the floor. I said, "Now that's your popcorn down there. Now let's go outside so I can kick your ass. He didn't know it was your popcorn. This popcorn's on the bar for everybody."

I went outside and I waited for him. And of course he didn't come out. He was just a big redneck, and he thought all his buddies were going to jump in behind him. And of course they didn't come out, either. Ron's the only one who came out with me.

When we went back inside, no one bothered us. Ron didn't eat any popcorn, though.

Trouble in Paradise

Redneck bars aren't the only place a guy can get in trouble. Sometimes it's like that Alfred Hitchcock movie, where Cary Grant's standing in the middle of nowhere, minding his own business, just ho-humming and waiting for a bus, when all of a sudden a damn crop duster starts attacking him.

Here's what happened: My lawyer, Oscar Holt, and some of our friends and I went down to Grand Cayman Island in the summer of 1999 to do a commercial for the tourism board. We're on a boat with Miss Grand Cayman, and we're supposed to be filming some tropical paradise stuff, when the sea gets rough and everybody starts puking. Everybody except Oscar, that is. I don't know if it's because Oscar has such a strong stomach, or because he's been concentrating so hard on stalking Miss Grand Cayman the whole damn boat trip, but he's watching the rest of us with our little vomit baskets the tourism board gave us, and he's laughing and laughing. And keeping his eye on Miss Grand Cayman, of course.

And while he's laughing, Miss Grand Cayman drops her vomit basket, and I swear to God, Oscar sprints over there to pick it up. Now, I don't care how pretty somebody is—and Miss Grand Cayman was very pretty—*nobody* should be in a rush to go pick up a vomit basket. But that's Oscar. He sprints over there, and right when he reaches it, a big wave hits the boat and Oscar hits the right side of the boat's railing. *Bam!* The boat rocks back, and there goes Oscar sliding the other way and he hits the left side of the boat's railing. *Bam!* He's holding on to that vomit basket for dear life, and vomit is spilling all over him, and here comes another wave, and *Bam!*, Oscar flips over the railing, and he's hanging on with one hand. And of course he's got Miss Grand Cayman's vomit basket in the other hand.

Now, as sick as we are, we're all laughing, and the crew's yelling "Man Overboard! Man Overboard!" and pulling Oscar up. And Miss Grand Cayman is taking it all in, kind of horrified-looking. "I can't believe you guys are really friends, the way you were laughing," she says. "That man almost died."

Oscar lost his shoe in the ocean, and he's ticked off about that. And he's ticked off that we were all laughing at him. And he's ticked off that for all his jumping after that damn vomit bag, Miss Grand Cayman didn't seem too impressed.

So to cheer Oscar up afterward, when we get back to land, we go to the local Burger King. All except Miss Grand Cayman, who says she's going home.

We're about to walk in when I point out the sign to Oscar, the one on the door that says NO SHOES, NO SHIRT, NO SERVICE.

Oscar just scowls at me.

"The sign says, 'No shoes,'" he says. "I got on a shoe."

He was looking so sorrowful, and so angry, the Burger King people didn't say a word.

The Animals at Madison Square Garden

The best place to play in the league is also sometimes the worst. That's Madison Square Garden, where the fans love you one minute, hate you the next. A peacock one day, a feather duster the next. That's how New Yorkers are. But the Garden—that's where every little kid dreams of playing, especially a little kid like I was, growing up in the city.

The Knicks' locker room, which I got to check out when I played in the All-Star Game in '98, is big and nice. But the visitors' locker room at the Garden is without a doubt the dirtiest, ugliest locker room in the league. Towels lying everywhere. Dark and smelly.

Here's something else you might not know about the Garden: When I played for St. John's, we used to go to the Garden for shootarounds the mornings we had games there, and there'd be wild cats fighting on the floor. I don't mean like in Kentucky Wildcats, I mean cats that were wild. And they'd be chasing rats, and they'd all be hollering and screeching and skittering across the floor. I guess after all the people leave, they come out of their hiding places. Since I saw that, I don't ever eat any hot dogs at the Garden. I only drink the beer.

Something else I saw there was how the Barnum & Bailey Circus treated their animals when they came to New York. I thought it was cruel. They put these bears in these little cages, and the bears just take their tail and they bite it and they try to go around in circles and circles and circles, so they get dizzy and fall down. You know, like they're trying to commit suicide, ramming their head against the cages. Just a terrible life. If you ever came back reincarnated as something, you'd never want to come back as a circus animal.

I used to love the circus when I was a kid, but after what I saw at Madison Square Garden, I refuse to bring any of my grandchildren to the circus, or any kids. And when I get married and have kids, I won't bring 'em.

You should see the people who take care of the animals. Some of them are just as smelly as the animals, and a lot of 'em are just as big.

I asked this circus guy once, "How can you do this to these animals?" He says, "Animals love this, and they love this life. They love to perform in front of people."

If it were up to me, I'd put this guy's fat butt in a cage in the middle aisle of Madison Square Garden and ask him how he liked living there.

Benoit, Me & the LAPD

One of the nicest places to play in the league is Los Angeles. You got the nice arena, and all the movie stars sitting courtside and plenty to do after the game. Also, the Lakers have the prettiest cheerleaders in the league. But you can still get in trouble there. One day when the Nets were in L.A. to play the Lakers, I had to go to Western Union, and Benoit Benjamin says, "I'll drive you there."

He put me in this Porsche, and he drove me all around this

neighborhood, this ritzy neighborhood. He told me it was called the black Beverly Hills.

Benoit was with the Nets then but he had played in Los Angeles for a lot of years before that, for the Lakers and the Clippers. He had some big money. He's got his Porsche, and he's showing me that it can go sixty miles an hour in first gear. It's about three o'clock and kids are coming out of school and Benoit's going about ninety miles an hour and he kind of misses a stop sign while he's telling me about life in Los Angeles.

"Man, I'm *laaarge,*" he's telling me. "I played with the Clippers here. I played with the Lakers out here. They love me out here. Everybody knows my name."

As soon as he says that, *whoop-whoop! whoop-whoop!* Police pulls us over.

I say, "Aw, hell. We in trouble."

Benoit says, "Don't worry about it—*part*ner. I'm *laaaaarge.*"

Cop comes over, says, "License and registration."

Benoit says, "Don't you know who I am?"

Cop says, "Yes, I do, sir. License and registration."

Benoit says, "What did I do, then?"

Cop says, "There was a stop sign back there."

Benoit says, "Well, I slowed down."

Cop says, "But the sign says stop."

Benoit says, "Yeah, but I slowed down."

And the cop says, "Sir, but the sign says stop."

Benoit says, "Stop, slow down, it's all the same stuff, *part*ner."

And the cop takes out his blackjack and starts hitting Benoit over the head with it—that leather blackjack—and says, "Now, do you want me to stop or do you want me to slow down?"

East Meets West

At the beginning of the 1996–97 season with the Nets, we traveled to Japan to play some exhibition games against the Orlando Magic. They were crazy about electronics over there. They had these bidets in the hotel. You hit a button and water shoots up your butt, and then you hit another button and it has this dryer. But you know how big and tough NBA guys are, right? We all come down to breakfast the morning after we arrived. When someone brings up the bidets in the room, most of us are like, "What? You had a bidet? Oh, yeah, yeah, I hit that button. I didn't know what happened. Water was running out."

And then you get all the tougher guys, they said, "Naw, man, screw you. You know I didn't try that bidet." And then you get the kinky guys, the guys who are just all-out kinky. They're like, "Yeah, man, I had hot water shooting up my butt for twenty minutes." But the majority of everybody was, "Oh, yeah, I didn't know what that button was for. I hit it by accident. It was just an accident."

It was eye-opening to all of us to be in a place like Japan. I mean, they say all us brothers look alike? But these people are very honorable. They do something that could never work in my neighborhood. They have 12 million people in Tokyo, and they have about 10 million bicycles, and not one of them is locked up on the street. They don't chain them up or anything. I guess it's like in the Old West, if you stole somebody's horse, you got hung. Maybe they have the same method out in Japan. It got me thinking, though. If someone wanted to make some big money, he should go over to Japan and open up a bike shop.

If you pay attention, you can pick up a lot about a culture. Like in Japan, you learn that it's very impolite and very rude and a big insult to the Japanese people if you blow your nose in public. So what I did was wherever the team was eating, I'd look at one of the coaches or the team trainer, and I'd say, "Hey, your nose is running." And then the coach or the trainer or whoever reaches for his handkerchief and blows his nose and all the guys who are serving us give the guy a dirty look. Even the police guard outside can see inside and he gives the poor coach a dirty look. And I laugh, but no one knows why, because I'm the only one who's studied up on the customs of the country. One time one of the coaches falls for it and blows his nose on his napkin, then after the meal is over, he puts the napkin on his plate, and the server wouldn't move the plate, wouldn't even touch it. The coach gets all insulted, and he's hollering, "Hey, you, clean up this plate." Then the little Japanese guy gets pissed off. It was an international incident.

Another night in Japan, Gerald Wilkins, who played with Orlando then, was giving a press interview. He said, "Yeah, I played well last night. I'm adapting to this life. I shot eight out of ten, and I'd like to shoot eight out of ten every night. So for my pregame dinner I'm going to keep eating that Chinese food every night, even when I get home." Here we were in Japan, and he's talking about Chinese food.

What Really Bugs Me About Florida

Japan took some getting used to, but for overall weirdness, it didn't have anything on Florida. Actually rural Florida, where the Nets used to have their training camp. We're talking about country, deep country. And that's not always familiar to some of the players who come from the city.

The first day of training camp a few years ago, me and Khalid Reeves were driving back to our hotel, a real nice resort.

And Khalid looked over at me and said, "Jay, guess what, man? There was a roach in my room big as a small bird. It scared the hell outta me."

And I was laughing, because Khalid grew up in the projects in the Bronx and I grew up in the projects on the Lower East Side of Manhattan and I know, growing up in the projects, even if you don't have roaches because you're clean, that means that the guy who lived a two-by-four stud away from you, who wasn't clean, if he had roaches, then you had roaches. So I said, "What did you do?"

Now, this is a man who's six foot three and is 215 pounds of raw muscle. And he says he took a barstool and held the roach at bay, then got on the phone and called a maintenance man to come get it. So I was laughing and laughing, and as soon as I get back to my room, I picked up my phone and what ran from under it? A damn roach just as big as a damn sparrow. This was the Godzilla of cock-roaches. Scared the hell out of me. I hit this thing with a magazine.

I was hitting this monster with a newspaper. If I would have hit it with one more thing and that thing didn't die, I was going to go look for a golf club, a Big Bertha, and I was going to attack its huge ugly head. This thing was a big roach, no lie. And then, it's like when you're going hunting in the woods or you're going somewhere and one of your friends has a tick on them or something? And then he starts scratching, then you start scratching. Well, everything that touched up against me on the bed that night I thought was one of them damn roaches. I was sleepy at practice that next day.

Coach Calipari always worked us hard, but he also took care of us. And I think he knew some of us were feeling a little strange in rural Florida. So one day we didn't have practice, he decided to give us a little treat. So Coach Calipari took fifteen National Basketball Association players bowling. You should've seen people's faces in Tampa when they saw fifteen big guys like us walk into a bowling alley. I didn't see one other black person in the bowling alley. One old lady just about gave Yinka Dare her purse. She thought it was a stickup.

On our last night of training camp—our first one with Calipari—I decided I was going to go down and get a Budweiser. I hadn't had a drink in sixteen days, because I wanted to be in great shape for the season. So I figured I'd treat myself. But I didn't want to drink alone. And then I thought about it. None of my boys were around. Should I go down to a Florida bar and drink with one of these rednecks, and the next thing I know, I'd be like the pig at a Klan meeting, tied high to one of those tall Florida trees, out here, swinging? I decided not to drink that night.

Chapter 9

Friends, Hangers-on, Entourages & the Relative You Haven't Heard from in Ten Years Who Wants to Borrow Fifteen Grand— Yesterday

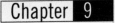 I don't have that many great friends in the league. P. J. Brown, Kendall Gill, Armen Gilliam, Keith Van Horn, Charles Oakley, and Charles Barkley are about it. And I consider Michael Jordan a friend. Otherwise, no. In this league—in the entertainment business in general—there's backstabbing that goes on, people starting rumors, anything to make themselves look better. I don't like people putting themselves on a plateau because they make a lot of money. A lot of that goes on in this league. And it goes on in all the sports today. It goes on in business, in many parts of society.

About the only time I'm *really* relaxed with friends is when I'm with my boys from the playground—the guys I grew up with, guys like Boogie and Marcus and my brother Victor. I know I can count on those guys.

Another guy I can count on is Danny Aiello, a good friend who shares some views with me about people.

Danny and me are the same, in that we're both two kids who

149

grew up tough. And Danny has all the same friends that he went to grammar school and junior high with. So when we all go out we all have the same friends. I've had them for twenty years, Danny has had them for forty-five years. And we're all comfortable with each other. Because we know everybody sitting at the table is loyal to each other.

How I judge a friend is somebody who's loyal. Somebody you can leave your kids with, somebody you can leave your family with, and when you come back, your friend won't be working on his tenth Budweiser and your kid's wandering around in some woods. Where every word out of your friend's mouth isn't "motherf——."

Yes-Men and Elephants

The problem with some NBA players is they get addicted to their entourages. They learn to love their twenty dudes always hanging around, doing things for 'em, telling 'em how great they are. But you know what happens when you go out with twenty dudes? The odds are against you. One of those twenty dudes is going to get into trash, he's going to say some junk to some musclehead idiot, and then *you've* got to fight, and if you don't fight, you know what your friends say? "Oh, man, you are false. You ain't keeping it real." That's one thing I learned a long time ago.

Another problem with entourages is they always tell you what you want to hear, even if you should be hearing something altogether different. A few years ago Derrick Coleman gained a bunch of weight in the off-season. Well, some of the clowns in his entourage wouldn't be making any money if it weren't for Derrick. They do errands for him, and he pays them. Nothing wrong with that; honest dollar for honest work and all. But these dudes start thinking that they'd better make sure Derrick is happy all the time, or he *won't* be paying them. So when Derrick is all ballooned up, pieces of fat hanging off his ass, what do these guys in his entourage tell him?

"You lookin' good, Derrick," they tell him. Or " 'Bout time you bulked up, man; that extra weight is gonna help you battle under the boards," or "You a strong mother now, man; you gonna hurt some people this year." Not one of them says, "Hey, man, you look like a fat old elephant. Why don't you start workin' out and lose some of that blubber?" And that's what a real friend should have said, because that extra weight didn't help Derrick any.

My friends are people who are secure with themselves. They have wives, families, they've had jobs for twenty years, and they don't need me. I'll take them on vacation with me, but they tell me what it is, what I'm doing right and what I'm doing wrong. They don't have to worry about their missing a paycheck, because I'm not giving them one.

They ain't the kind of friends who stroke you. My friends, we'll be sitting on the beach in the summer, and we'll have some piña coladas, or some Bud Lights, and one of them will come up and say, "You know what, Jay? You said you were gonna have a great year, and you didn't produce."

And here I am, just having paid $40,000 for all these guys to come down here on vacation, and they're telling me I had a bad year. It's irritating sometimes, but those are the friends you need, not the kind of people, the kind of entourage, that goes around telling you, "You the best, you the best, you the best."

Little Rascals

My best friends today are the guys who were my best friends when I was twelve years old. We all played on a YMCA team downtown. And we were just kids, always getting into kid kind of trouble. One day after a practice, there was a locker open in the locker room, and everyone on the team took a look inside, and there was money and stuff in there. I was home sick that day, but I heard about it.

So the guys—Boogie, Marcus, all the guys—went in and divided it up. Everyone got five dollars. That next day they were all bragging about this big heist they pulled. You know, "We hit this locker, Terry got a watch, Danny got a new pair of sneakers, we all got five dollars."

Now, I know the right thing to do would have been to tell them to put it back. Or to tell them it was wrong and they should go to confession or something. But I was a kid, too. So I said, "Give me five dollars or I'm telling." They said, "You wasn't there, you don't get nothing." I told 'em again I was going to tell if I didn't get my money. They didn't think I was going to tell, but I did. The next day Mr. Moore from the YMCA called the team, kicked us all out of the tournament. We easily would have won that league. Afterward, the guys were really pissed off at me. I said, "All you guys had to do was give me fifty cents apiece." I felt bad about that for a long time. But our friendships survived.

Country Road, Take Me Home

Sometimes they were tested, though. Like the time I took some of my New York friends down to see where I had lived in South Carolina. I was still at St. John's, and my childhood buddies Marcus and Sean and I piled in Marcus' brand-new Maxima one day and headed south. We picked up a South Carolina local guy, Scott, along the way, and then we headed to Ritter, to see my Grandma Elvira.

By now it's nighttime, and Marcus and Scott and I have been drinking beer funnels—where you pour three beers in a funnel and drink the whole thing in about seven seconds. Sean's the only one not drinking, 'cause he's driving. But then Sean says he doesn't want to drive anymore, because the roads are so dark. These are country roads, and Sean's a city kid. And there's no way I'm gonna drive, 'cause I've been drinking beer since we left New York City. And Scott's been drinking since we met him at the Holiday Inn. That leaves Marcus. Which is a problem. Because Marcus has also been drinking. And maybe even worse, Marcus is just about blind. Dude can't see! But Marcus is too cool to wear glasses. And he didn't know anything about contacts back then, we were just kids.

So here's Marcus barreling down this little country road in his new Maxima, and I'm trying to tell him to be careful, but every time I say something, he turns up this song on the cassette player. It was a real popular song back then. "Top Billin'" was the name of it. The chorus was "Milk is chillin', Giz is chillin', what more can I say, top billin'!" Sometimes I can still hear that damn song. So every time I tell Marcus to slow down, or to watch the road, he turns up the music real loud and starts singing along, just to be funny.

"Slow down," I say.

"Milk is chillin'," Marcus yells.

"Man, I'm serious, watch the damn roa—"

"Giz is chillin'," Marcus yells.

"Marcus, man, I'm not playing, if you don't slow down—"

"What more can I say, top billin'!"

We get to a place called Saxby Hill, that I remember from when I was a kid, and I look at the speedometer, and it says 82, and I look out the window and I see a sign with an arrow pointing straight to the left, and that sign says 15.

I look over at Scott, next to me in the backseat. Scott knows the roads, 'cause he lives here, and he knows what's coming. Scott is already in the crash position, like he's in an airplane, with his head down and all.

Marcus never even turns the wheel. Just keeps going straight. We go about three quarters of a mile, Sean screaming in the front seat, one hand on the dashboard, one hand on the sunroof, trying to brace himself, partly 'cause he's such a big guy, weighs about 450 pounds. I'm just staring at these bushes going by, whacking the car, *whop, whop, whop, whop!* Scott's in his crash position. And Marcus' head is stuck between the steering wheel and the dashboard, blood squirting all over the place.

When we finally stop, Marcus yanks his head out and jumps from the car, his brand-new Maxima. He's yelling, "My car! My car!"

The rest of us jump out, too, and I say to Sean, "Careful now, you know what they call this place down here—Rattlesnake Cove."

So Sean jumps up on the top of Marcus' car, like an elephant scared of a mouse. He's on top of the car and Marcus is still yelling, "How's my car, how's my car?"

We realize he's delirious, in shock or something. And he still can't see. So we're lying to him. We're saying, "It'll be all right, Marcus, don't worry man, it'll be all right. The car's fine."

And just then, we hear this horrible sound, *"Creeeeeeek! Creeeeeeek!"*

It's the top of Marcus' car squashing down, 'cause of Sean's weight. Sean is crushing Marcus' car.

Now Marcus and Sean start fighting, and I tell Scott, "We gotta get out of here."

We break up Marcus and Sean and we tell 'em we got to walk and get help, someone to tow the car out. But Sean will not step on the ground, because he's so scared of snakes. The sonofabitch would not step on the ground. He's screaming like a woman. We can't just leave him there, so Scott and I finally carry him back to the road, and we almost break our backs doing it, he's that heavy. When we get to the road, Sean says, all scared, "Dog, do snakes go on concrete?"

I say, "Nah, nah."

He says, "Yeah, they do! I seen that on the Discovery Channel. Snakes do go across the road."

I say, "Yeah, okay, they do. But you know what? They're allergic to yellow."

He goes, "Yeah?"

Here's a kid who never left the Lower East Side. "Yeah," I say. "If you walk on the yellow line, they'll never get you."

Now, we're two miles from a farmer's house. Sean walks that yellow line like he's a high-wire guy in the circus. A 450-pound high-wire guy, with his hands straight out.

We get to the farmer's, he drives us back out to Rattlesnake Cove, and he tows that Maxima all the way to my Grandma Elvira's, where he drops us all off. And my grandmother, she's been expecting us.

She comes out on the porch, sweeping dirt. Down South, they sweep dirt. She's out there with a broom she made from some straw, sweeping dirt. She looks up and she sees Marcus' Maxima. Four flat tires, the windshield broken, with blood all over it, the top squashed down. And the front of that Maxima looks just like a sad face, all squashed up and frowning. My Grandma Elvira, she must have been eighty-four then, she looks at that car, and at me and

Marcus and Sean and Scott, then back at the car, all while she's sweeping some more dirt, and she says, "*Ooooooooooh, chile,* you drive that car all the way from New York like that?"

What I Learned from Larry

One of my best friends is Larry Holmes, who lives just across the state line. He probably comes over to visit about twice a week, if I'm not already at his place. Larry is always telling me about money. Larry's one boxer who never had money problems. He made millions of dollars and he still has every dime of it. Plus he owns about all of Easton, Pennsylvania. "You might be richer than me," Larry's always telling me, "but I've been richer longer."

What he taught me is you have a few friends in the world, and everybody else is an associate. A couple summers ago I tried to make everybody my friend, and what happened was you go out a few times with someone, then when you can't go out with them one weekend, they say, "You've changed." They make up stuff on you because you don't hang out with them.

So you keep your real friends close to you, and you keep it tight-knit. That's what I've learned. You don't need an entourage. You see a celebrity with an entourage, chances are that celebrity is insecure, and he's being taken for a ride.

Family Feud

A man who makes the kind of money I do should take care of his family, and that's what I've tried to do. I bought my Grandma Elvira a new house. I paid for my sisters' children's—my adopted kids—education. And I paid for the education of my nephews and nieces on my father's side, because it wouldn't be right to pay for the kids on my mom's side and not on the other. But even with all that, there have been some hard feelings in my family about money. And some of those hard feelings have involved the people closest to me.

I had an aunt come up to me—she had a thirty-foot boat—and she wanted to borrow $15,000 from me a week before the draft. This is before I had received a single NBA paycheck.

I still got people in my family who are eighteen, nineteen years old asking me for money, and they're family—you got to give it to them, but Jeez, when I was making $2.5 million a year, my adopted son was thinking, By golly, I should be getting a check for fifty grand a year. I set him straight about that.

Then you got the associates—they say they're your friends, but if you're smart, you know they're just associates—who think you're the dumb athlete and they want you to invest in something. Do *they* have anything to invest? Sure, they have time. But they want *your* money. And when stuff goes wrong, you're stuck with the bills.

The Breaks of the Game

If you're a professional athlete, you find out who your true friends are when you're hurt. The people who like hanging around when you're getting all the rebounds and the headlines, they disappear when you can't even put on your uniform. The guys who stick around are people like Danny Aiello. Right after I tore the ligaments in my thumb in 1999, I was having dinner with Danny and my agent and some other guys. Danny was the only one telling me to rest it. My own agent was saying, "If you don't play, you're gonna take a hit in the media, that's for sure. They'll say you're the highest-paid player, and now you're quitting on the team."

But Danny says, "Screw the media. The kid's hurt, the season's basically over, no way they're making the play-offs. It's his body, let him rest it up."

So I go out and play, and then I break my damn leg. Danny stayed with me all that night in the hospital, along with my dad, and when I woke up from surgery, there's my dad again, and Danny and his two sons.

Danny stayed with me and my dad the whole time. And on the day I got out of the hospital and went home, there's Danny waiting for me on the porch. And he's got a big sandwich for me. Pepperoni and cheese on a big roll. Danny drove all the way to New York to get the bread. Drove to Hoboken to get the cheese. The pastrami he had to drive to Lindenhurst to get. Danny's old-school Italian. And here he is with this giant-sized crazy sandwich for me, fresh out of the hospital. Must have been half a pound of cheese on that sandwich, and I'm just done with surgery. But I eat it, because Danny's been driving like half a day to make the sandwich.

So the next day, when Danny's leaving, I'm sitting on the toilet bowl, cursing him. I was so constipated. And I was so beat up that I couldn't move, so I had had one of those special handles installed in the bathroom. And I'm gripping it so hard, I break it off the wall.

I'm sitting there, cursing Danny Aiello and that damned sandwich, holding a broken metal handle in one hand, in the worst pain in my life, too embarrassed to call somebody.

That was the one time in my life I got angry at Danny Aiello.

Chapter 10

What's Love Got to Do with it? Or Why Guys Who Really Can't Stand Each Other Can Be Great Teammates, Why Good Friends Occasionally Almost Kill Each Other & Who Hates Who

There are running feuds in this game. There are players who just flat out don't like each other. There are some players in the league I don't like, because I think *they* think they're bigger than the game, when they haven't even won nothing yet and they're always talking smack. It's no secret that Shaq and I don't exactly get along. And Larry Johnson and I once had a falling-out. But playing against someone I don't like just makes me play harder. And in the NBA you need that. You need every three or four games to go against a guy you just can't stand who's overrated and you think can't play. You need that for incentive, to get you going, to get some fire under you.

When Bulls Bicker

There are teammates who don't really get along with teammates, which surprisingly doesn't always hurt the team. On the championship Bulls, Michael Jordan and Scottie Pippen and Toni Kukoc weren't so tight. Now, a lot of people thought Michael and Scottie didn't like Toni because he got such a big contract, and some people even said it was racial. But it was none of that.

They were pissed off at Toni because he was hardheaded. They weren't mad about him being white or making big money; they were mad because when they would tell him something, he wouldn't listen to them.

I mean, they would yell at him, "Don't pass there" or "Don't shoot there," and he would just give them a crazy look and act like he didn't understand English. I think they thought he was a little lazy, too. He got yelled at by Scottie Pippen all the time, and by Phil Jackson, and by Michael Jordan at least twice daily. And I'm talking about some serious stepfather stuff. Once during a game when Phil was yelling at Kukoc, I said to him, "Damn, Toni, how in the hell you going to let Phil Jackson talk to you like that?"

And he says, "Man, I know. I know. All they do is yell at me on this team."

And I think he deserved it, because he never acknowledged them; he kept doing the same stupid stuff. And that's what pissed them off. If he would have just said "Okay" once, they might have quit yelling. But he never did, just gave that crazy, me-no-understandum-English look.

You can't argue with the results, though. They yelled, and I think it drove him. And it sure didn't hurt the team.

The Play's the Thing

Sometimes you see those stories at halftime on TV about some veteran taking a rookie under his wing and helping him out. Heartwarming but not always true. Around the league, a lot of the older players only want bad things for the young guys. When I was a rookie with the Philadelphia 76ers, Rick Mahorn, a guy who taught me a lot, a guy who I respect a lot, used to tell me the wrong plays. He'd tell me I was supposed to run one place, and I would, then the coach would yell at me and there'd be Mahorn staring up at the ceiling. A few years later, when we both ended up with the Nets, and I was a lot better player, and we were friends, I asked him, "Why did you tell me the wrong plays when I was a rookie?" He said, "Jay, I was always that way. Do you think I was going to tell you where to go and get the right plays, and then you take my job and I'm out of work?" Now that I'm one of the older guys in the league, I understand. I'm not sure *I* wouldn't give some hard-charging young guy a few bad tips. Especially if I thought he might take my job.

Share and Share Alike

On a losing team everybody blames each other. They blame everybody from the guy picking up the jockstraps to the guy who owns the team. On a winning team it's a lot better, unless you've got bad people around you. If you have bad people around you, then these are the people who will take all the credit for winning. The real winners are the most unselfish people. You know why the Bulls were so successful? Because everyone knew Michael Jordan was the Man, but everyone also knew he was unselfish. Michael Jordan would always pass that last shot off to someone else if they were open.

That's been one of the problems with the Lakers the last few years. There are a few inflated egos in Los Angeles, but no one agrees on who's the Man. If you ask people on that team who's the Man, they couldn't tell you. Some would say Kobe, some would have said Eddie Jones, when he was there, some would say Shaq. That's what caused them some problems. I think that's why the most successful teams have one declared superstar, or in the case of Utah, two. That way you know who's who.

Now, if you would have asked Charles Barkley who was the superstar in Houston, him or Dream or Scottie Pippen, he'd probably have said it's the Dream's team. A few years ago, he would have said it was his, but even though Charlie is a very, very good player in this league, he is no longer a great player and he knows it.

Table Manners

Rebounding's important. Defense is critical. And you hear all the time about how you've got to have good athletes to win games, or a go-to guy, or a low post presence. I don't disagree with any of that. But what a lot of people forget is in order for a team to win, there has to be leadership.

We had a player like that on the Nets, Michael Cage. He hardly ever played, but the owners offered him $1.3 million to come back, just because of his experience, his heart, what he said in the locker room. He's the one guy who would get on Keith Van Horn, tell him he was playing soft, to "toughen the hell up." He'd give it straight to anyone, Don Casey, John Calipari, Keith, me. That's what a team leader does.

Here's what I mean: After Calipari's first exhibition game with the Nets in 1996, we're flying back home and he and his staff are up there eating before we get our food. Before Cal showed up, the players would always eat first. Michael Cage is sitting behind me, and he taps me on the shoulder.

"Jay," he says, "they getting their food first? The coaches are eating? We just got through playing this exhibition game, we're hungry as hell, and they're up there eating?"

Michael goes up there and he tells Cal what he thinks about the coaches eating first.

Cal goes, "Oh, yeah. Oh, yeah, yeah, yeah, yeah. You know, I just wanted to get this food out of the way, you know, eat so I could watch tapes."

But he says he understands, and he promises it'll be different in the future.

So the next day we're flying again, and damn if Cal hasn't got his food first again. So Cage runs up there, and now he's like Reverend Al Sharpton.

"I told you about eating first," he yells, and he puts his hand on Cal's tray like he's going to snatch it away. "Didn't we discuss this?"

Cal says it's all a mistake, blames it on the stewardesses. But from that day on we always ate first.

The Sins of the Fathers

A few years ago a former player named Rick Barry—a Hall of Famer—said something about me. What he said was, "If you want a part-time player and a full-time party animal, Jayson Williams is your guy."

Three days after I heard that, I was playing against Rick's son, Brent, who was with the Los Angeles Clippers then. I'm kicking Brent's butt, knocking him on the ground every chance I get. One time I knock him on the ground, and when I run back down the court he's still lying there, so I kick him in the head. Next free throw, he comes over to me on the free-throw line.

He says, "Jay, why you knocking me around so much, man?"

I say, " 'Cause I don't like your pop. All that stuff he's saying about me."

He says, "Jay, *I* don't like him either."

"Wow," I say. "I'm sorry, man."

Eat or Be Eaten

My theory on how you know if you have a good basketball team is this: which team would survive in a plane crash in the middle of the mountains, in the winter. I watched *Alive* thirty times, the movie about when the soccer team crashes and they have to eat the dead bodies to stay alive, and it got me to thinking.

What it got me to thinking was what would happen to different teams that crashed? Who would help each other, and who would be selfish enough to drink that last bit of bourbon on the plane? Who would eat that last Snickers bar?

The team that would have been most likely to make it out of those mountains alive would have been the championship Bulls. You know why? Because everybody would have had a role. Michael Jordan would have taken charge. Steve Kerr would have known what he was supposed to do. Phil Jackson would have known what he was supposed to do.

With the Nets a couple years ago, it would have been a little different. First, Sam Cassell would have stood up and said to our former coach, John Calipari, "Okay, Cal, all that coach business is out the window now. We in charge. Who we gonna eat next?"

Keith Van Horn's favorite word is "maaaaaaaan." That's all he would be saying, he'd be like, "maaaaaaaaan," because he'd have been freezing. If Kendall Gill had his headache medicine, we'd have been all right. But if Kendall lost his migraine medicine, he'd have killed everybody in there. He would have survived, because he'd have eaten every one of us.

Kerry Kittles, he's so skinny, he would have been like a Popsicle. I'll tell you the only one who would be in good shape up in those mountains would be Rony Seikaly. Rony would have been all right, because Rony's a big hairy mother. Plus, it would have been good for Rony, because he's always spraining his ankle, and he could have just kept it in the snow.

At least we'd stand a better chance than the Nets of ten years ago. Then we would have all been fighting over the bourbon. We would have been like, "Hey, you don't need that for no cuts. Gimme a drink."

Another team that would have a problem in those snowy mountains would be the Knicks. They would all fight over the sunlight. Who's going to sit in that little patch of sunlight? Will it be Larry Johnson or Patrick Ewing or Allan Houston? And don't forget Chris Childs, he wants a little sunlight, too. If the Knicks had more food and stuff than we had, and their plane went down near ours, they definitely would not have made it, because I would have raided their stuff and left. I would have had no problem leaving them for dead.

Biting the Big Dog

For a long time I didn't like Glenn Robinson. It had to do with a misunderstanding with a girl at St. John's. When we played Purdue, I had a good game, and Glenn knew this girl, and he asked her where she was going after the game. She said, "I'm going with

Jayson Williams." He said, "Who's that?" And I had just played the guy! Had a pretty good game against him, too.

So after that I made it a practice whenever I played him to play him extra hard. Like if he ever tried to box me out, I'd make sure to go over his back and to put some pain on him.

Then about two years ago I found out I had misconstrued what she said. She said he said something, and it turns out he didn't really say it. But that's how feuds start, over stupid little things like that.

Every Day Is Mother's Day

We used to have a point guard on the Nets who was a little raw in his personal interactions. I'm not talking about Sam Cassell. Sam Cassell is a little loud, a little overfrank sometimes. But Sam has a good heart. I watch how he treats my mom and my dad, and he treats them well. That means a lot to me when I see how people treat other people's people.

But we used to have a point guard on the team, and I'm not going to name him, because I hope he's ashamed of the incident, but he was the opposite of Sam. I had a birthday party at the Hard Rock Cafe in New York City, and my mother was walking around the place. She grabbed this guy, this point guard, and said, "Hi, can you take a picture with me?" And this guy smacked her hand away from him and said, "Get your *damn* hands off me. Everybody frigging touches me."

My friends didn't tell me about it until about three days later. I asked why they waited so long. They said, "Jay, if we had told you inside that place, you would have killed this kid."

The next day I got to practice early and I said to this kid, "Now, why would you do this to my mother?"

He says, "Jay, man, I knew they were going to tell you—I didn't know that was your mom."

I said, "You ignoramus, if *any* lady, especially one sixty years old, comes up and asks you to take a picture, you could say no, but you don't smack her hand away from you and push her away.

And if I ever catch you putting your hand on any other lady, I'll beat the crap out of you."

You know, I really dislike "me me me" people. Everything is "me this, me that." There aren't a lot of really polite, well-mannered players in the NBA. But you know what? There aren't a lot of really polite, well-mannered athletes or entertainers in society. I'm talking about a problem that afflicts a lot of guys who are in the public eye. You see, once they get in the public eye, it's cooler to be rude. It's a cool thing to be rude. Some guys don't want to be rude; they just figure it will give them more privacy. Like, if they look mean and rude, people will be less likely to come up and bother them. Unfortunately they're right.

Chemistry

I really get along well with most of my teammates. Keith Van Horn and I have a great relationship. He's been married a long time, so he asks me a lot of questions about being wild and stuff. And he's got a great wife and great little kids. I play with his kids all the time, and his little girl, Sabrina, runs into my arms every time she sees me. That kind of friendship is rare on a team. It's rare in sports. Hell, it's rare in life.

Shaquille O'Neal and I have gone at it a couple times in games. Part of that had to do with Chris Gatling. A lot of people say I'm the strongest guy in the league, and I think that's true. But Chris would ride me on the bus, say things like, "We're playing Shaq tomorrow. We'll see if you're the strongest man in the league."

Now, I respect Shaquille's game, but I'm not scared of him, in a basketball game or in a fistfight. So I say, "Yeah, we're playing Shaq tomorrow. We'll see what happens."

And Chris is the kind of guy who'll run back to Shaq and tell him something like, "Hey, man, Jayson Williams says he's stronger than you, he ain't scared of you," just to egg him on. He did that, kind of joking like, but you would think your teammate *wouldn't* do something like that. But Shaquille is his friend. I'm just his teammate.

The Golden Rule

Three years ago, when the Nets were flying from Utah to Phoenix, we found out that Marcus Camby, who was then a rookie with Toronto, who had played for Calipari at UMass, passed out before a game. It ended up just being a muscle spasm in his back that caused it, but Cal came to the back of the plane where all the guys were, like he had to make an important announcement. He says, "I just got off the phone with the hospital . . . Marcus Camby's going to be all right."

It was funny. Cal came back all melodramatic about "Marcus Camby's gonna be all right; I just got off the phone." As soon as he turned around and left, all the players look at each other and say, "Marcus Camby? Who the hell cares?"

Why Can't We All Just Get Along?

Toughness is a necessary thing in the NBA, but sometimes it's taken too far. Tyrone Hill was in a bad accident a few years ago. I called him at the hospital when I found out. Called him every day for three days. No big deal. He's a colleague of mine, we work in the same business. I just wanted to express my concern. And you know what? He was shocked when I called him. Turned out I was the only player from another team who called him. Not one other player called him. That's not right.

Black Magic

Just when you think you're doing good with all your friends in the league, and even when you got your enemies where you want 'em, some player's friend or relative goes crazy on you. When I played with the Sixers, I was over at Manute Bol's one night—and I want to make clear that this was a long, *long* time ago, when I was wild and crazy, because if I don't make that clear, I'll never get another endorsement in my life—and his uncle was there. We're all drinking Heinekens, and Manute's uncle, who was from the Sudan, like Manute, was giving me a hard time.

He kept saying, "Yeah, you the one they call Mr. Al Capone? You go to school with all the Mafia guys and all of this? Hey, Mr. Al Capone, you not so tough."

When you're in somebody else's house, you just be nice, you laugh it off. So I laughed it off. My friend Franco was with me, and I looked over at him, because I'm thinking he's not appreciating the Al Capone cracks, but Franco's cool, he's laughing it off, too.

But this guy keeps coming on and on with the same stuff. "You think you're a tough guy? You're not so tough. Look, I put this stuff on."

And he puts on this necklace with crow's feet and rooster's feet and turtle heads. Then he says, "Look, you can shoot me, you can stab me, you can do anything you want, and it'll bounce right off me. You can hit me and it won't hurt me."

I think Manute will calm his uncle down, but he just lets him keep going and going. Now it's 3:00 A.M., and I'm pretty intoxicated, and Manute's uncle is still yammering about his magic necklace, and I turn to Franco, and I say, "If frigging Dr. Buzzard comes over here one more time with that old bull about 'Oh, bullets will bounce off of me,' he's going to have a problem." And as soon as I say that, here comes Dr. Buzzard, Manute's uncle. He gets right in my face.

"Hey, Mr. Al Capone, Mr. Tough Guy, c'mon, what are you going to do to me?"

So I run out to my 750 BMW and come back with my pistol, which naturally I make sure is empty, and I aim it at him, and he says, "No, no, no, Mr. Williams! It does not work! The necklace does not work after 2:30 A.M.!"

The next day at practice, Manute Bol goes and tells Harold Katz that I came in to stick up his whole family.

Wrong Number

Some of the worst stuff you hear isn't from the guys you hate or your teammates' nutty relatives. It's from your friends on other teams. When New Jersey was really struggling a few years ago, these guys were really riding me—in games, out at dinner, even on the phone. These guys were merciless. I had to hear Armen Gilliam's needling all the time. Chris Childs, who left New Jersey to go to New York, would call. He'd say, "You're an idiot for staying there, man. You need to get out of there. You know, that boat got a lot of holes in it, you're not going to be able to patch it back."

P. J. Brown was the worst. He'd call and leave a message on my answering machine. He'd say, "Hi, this is P. J. Brown calling from hot heaven—Miami. I'm calling Jayson Williams in hell."

Fore!

As long as you got one person on your team you know is a true professional, who's got true heart, is not scared, and goes out there and plays hard and practices hard every day, it makes the NBA a whole lot better. It takes a lot of burden off yourself. It's like going to a fight. If you had to fight four or five people, and you go in by yourself, it's going to be hard. With two people, your chances are a lot better, but only if the other person's the right guy. A lot of guys in the NBA would just be in your way if they were on your side in a fight. Not Kendall Gill, though. He's got heart. He's tough. He's a true professional. Which doesn't mean sometimes we don't want to kick each other's ass. Especially when we play golf.

When you go out to play golf with another professional athlete, you try to be courteous, because it's a gentleman's sport. So when I go out with Kendall, the first hole, Kendall hits the ball, I say, "Great shot." And if Kendall, or any other athlete, beats me on that hole, I say, "Yeah, you played that one really well."

By the time you get to that fourth hole, you ask your opponent what he got on that score and he says, "I got a five on that. I parred that."

Now you get to about the seventh hole, you ask him what he got. "I got a five," he says. And that's when problems start coming up. You say, "Maybe you count that again. One there, two into the water, three out, four into the trees, five out, then you three-putted."

Now you're counting every one of his strokes. By the time you get to the tenth hole, you're swearing at each other. You get to the thirteenth hole, you're throwing clubs at each other, and when you get to the eighteenth hole and you're coming back and everybody's there, you're bloody. And what happens tomorrow morning? You don't pass each other the ball. But I'm fortunate me and Kendall don't have that problem.

When we play, all he does is pass me a nice fat check.

Terror at 30,000 Feet

You know when somebody's going to get traded in the NBA, be-cause people start whispering, people start looking at you funny, and when other players start meeting with the coach, then you know you're gone.

Calipari's first year with the Nets, there were all sorts of trade rumors. So everyone was worried. We're in the airport one day, about to fly to Cleveland, and Cal pulls Kendall Gill aside to talk to him. So afterward I go up to Kendall and ask him, "What's going on?" and he lies to me and says, "Oh, nothin', nothin', nothin'," and we board the plane.

We're in the air and Shawn Bradley comes and sits near me— Shawn, who I had become very good friends with—and he sits down and he says, "I was with Cal two weeks ago, so I don't think it's me getting traded; I think it's you."

After a few minutes the PR director comes back and he says, "Shawn, Cal wants to see you." Shawn gets all googly-eyed and he was like, "Huh, he wants to see me?" And you know what? If the coach wants to see you at the front of the plane and it's only two days before the trading deadline: See ya!

Shawn goes up and he talks to Cal, and Shawn walks to the back of the plane where me and Tony Massenberg are sitting and Shawn goes, "God damn!"

And Tony Massenberg says, "Oh, my God, Shawn, I never heard you use the Lord's name in vain. You're a Mormon."

And Shawn says: "I can say a lot f———g worse than that."

Then Shawn sits down.

"Shit!" he says. "They just traded me."

Man Overboard

There was a player a few years ago, Luther Wright, never did much in the league. Big guy, about seven feet two inches, almost 400 pounds, sweet guy, but he had some problems with depression and never recovered enough to get back in the league. Never could get straightened out, but a helluva nice guy. So one summer we went down to Myrtle Beach, me and Luther and his dad and my pal Charles Shackleford, who had just bought this new boat.

Shack is proud as can be of this new thirty-foot boat, and he's cruising, and I'm asking him, "Are you on the right side of these buoys?"

"What the hell you think?" he says. "Of course I am."

A couple minutes later the Coast Guard comes over and yells at him because he's on the wrong side.

We keep going, Shack's driving about thirty knots, like a madman. We see a buoy way out, and he says, "Hmmm, I wonder what that's for. What could that be for?" He gets too close and *wwwoosh*. We're stuck on the bottom. The boat's not moving. We sit there for about two hours, and after a while, Luther says, "I'm sick of this. I'm going to jump off the boat into the water and I'm going to push us up out of the sand."

Luther hits the water and sprains his ankle. His father goes crazy. "Luther, Luther," his dad yells. "I'll save you."

Then his dad jumps in headfirst, hits the sand, sprains his neck bad. Knocks himself out. So now we're stuck, 103 degrees, Myrtle Beach, the boat's not working, Luther can't get in the boat with a sprained ankle, and his dad's floating like he's dead.

We pull in his dad and see he's alive, but Luther still can't make it up into the boat. He's like one of those beluga whales or something, who get themselves beached somewhere and all the tourists come and try to drag him out to deep water but they can't and the beluga ends up dying with all the little kids crying around it. The Discovery Channel shows that sometimes. Anyway, now the tide starts coming back in. Now the water's getting up to Luther's chest, then his neck, and now Luther's getting scared.

And every time Luther tries to pull himself up, he about sinks the boat, because he's so fat. And he's getting weaker and weaker. Now he's holding on to my arm and I'm getting weaker and weaker too. And now Luther's carrying on about sharks. We're drifting now and I'm getting seasick. I throw up over the side of the boat, all over Luther, but he doesn't care, he's so scared about sharks and drowning and trying to get his life saved.

Now the sun's coming down and it's still about 103 degrees and I'm dead tired. I've been holding on to Luther for three hours. Charles Shackleford looks over—and you have to remember that Shack is from South Carolina—he says, real loud, "Jay, we got to cut him loose."

He says, "He's going to kill us. We can't hold him no more."

I say, *"What?!?"*

Shack's like, "We'll cut him loose. We'll just tell people he drowned. We'll say we did everything we could."

I'm going, "Are you kidding me?"

He says, "Jay, we can't hold that boy no more."

I'm going, "Shack, are you crazy?"

He says, "I'm telling you, man, it'll work. We just tell people he fell off the boat. They'll find him."

Now, the father is unconscious, but Luther's not. So we hear Luther yelling, "What you all talking about up there? You ain't talking about leaving me, are you?"

So I look down at Luther. I say, "Luther, you been floating there for three hours." I say, "My hand can't hold you no longer." I say, "Shack's talking about just speeding off and leaving you." I say, "You better get your butt in the boat."

He jumps right in the boat then. Puts his leg up and climbs in.

I say, "What happened? You been floating there for three hours and now you just jump right in?"

He says, "You all weren't talking about leaving me before."

Shack would have left Luther in the middle of the ocean. Some sharks would have had a nice big dinner, with leftovers for their baby sharks.

Pass on the Pie

When we get back, we all go down to Luther's house, right on Myrtle Beach. Luther had bought his mother a condo on the beach. And his mother's a big woman, about 500 pounds, about six foot four, with a size 14 foot. When we get there she's sitting on the beach and a bunch of little kids are looking at her. Just staring at her in amazement. I walk up, and she's got a banana knife in her hand. She's carving all the corns and stuff off her foot. And she looks up at me and she says, "Oooh, baby, I'm going to make you a sweet potato pie that's going to knock you out tonight."

Later that night, Luther comes knocking on my door. It's about 7:30. I'm staying upstairs with my girlfriend. He says, "Here's my mom's sweet potato pie she made for you."

When Luther leaves, I look over at my girlfriend, who I had told all about my day. She says, "Are you crazy? You saw this woman peeling her feet on the beach with a banana knife? And now you think I'm going to eat a pie she made?"

That pie beat Luther downstairs. Right into the ocean, like a Frisbee.

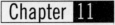**Riches, Fame, Celebrity,**

and the Night George Bush

and I Put Our Heads Together

to Figure Out What Was Up

with UFOs, Aliens & Area 51

Ninety percent of basketball players act like movie stars, which is cool, I guess, because they are. We're on TV more than Seinfeld, even counting reruns.

I like people and I'll sit down with anybody and chat. But a lot of basketball players won't do that. And that's what causes confrontations, when basketball players look over people like they're not even there. That pisses people off, and then they want to fight. I understand why some players ignore fans, because when you're a famous pro basketball player everybody wants your autograph, everybody wants your time. And you can sign 1,000 autographs, and if you don't sign that 1,001st piece of paper, suddenly you're a jerk. People talk about Princess Di and how tough she had it, but the paparazzi are in the NBA now. They're everywhere.

It comes with the territory. If you're going to get $10 million a year, or whatever, seems to me you learn to put up with all aspects of the job. You learn to deal with it. Because where would you rather be: doing a nine-to-five job, taking home $250 a week, or making $250 every fifteen minutes, and dealing with a few snap-shots, a few rumors, getting harassed some? I know what I'd choose.

The Magic Word

I have never turned down an autograph, especially if someone asks the right way. But you got some kids from the inner cities and you get some spoiled rich kids from the suburbs who come up and act like it's your *job* to give them an autograph. I've done bar mitzvahs before, birthday parties, stuff like that. I've had a spoiled kid come up to me and say, "My mother says sign this." "My father said you better sign this."

So I'll say, "You go get your father." And they bring their father back and I say, "Is this the way you teach your kid to come up and ask me?" One time one guy said, "Look, I paid you to come to this party." I said, "I don't give a damn. Here's your money back. Now, you teach your kid some manners."

It feels great to sign an autograph and watch the smile on a kid's face, but if someone doesn't know how to ask nice, doesn't know how to say please, I won't sign anything for them.

I treat everybody like I want to be treated. First thing, they're not allowed to put their hands on me. Second thing, if they say some-thing negative to me, I say something about them. Then, if they put their hands on me, I get the chance to peel their cap. But most of the time, 99 percent of the time, I never have a problem, because people know I'm real. What you see is what you get.

Lessons from the Gridiron

If you spend any time with football players, like I do, you learn that a lot of them are more humble than basketball players. Not because they're better people, but a lot of times because they're not as rec-ognizable as you, with all the equipment they wear.

I like hanging out with Jason Sehorn from the New York Giants and Wayne Chrebet from the New York Jets. I like to hear their insights on what they have to do to prepare for big games. When I'm thinking how I have to prepare for the play-offs, I listen to them talk about how they prepared for their play-offs, and how they dealt with pressure. We share stories all season long. We watch each other play. And there's nothing better than to have someone from a different sport come to your game, all eyes on you, so you do a little showing-off for that guy; you play even harder.

Aliens Among Us

At one time, the most famous person I ever spent any time with was George Bush, when he was president. I had always said if I ever met a president, I always wanted to ask him one important question.

So one night some years ago, we were playing the Rockets in Houston and I walk over to where George Bush is sitting and say hello. The Secret Service lets me sit down, and me and George Bush shoot the breeze for five minutes. After, when I'm shooting layups again, I realize I had been so in awe of meeting the president of the United States that I forgot to ask my question. So I try to get to him after the game, but the Secret Service has about three minutes to get him out of there, so they won't let me near him. And that pisses me off. Because the question I wanted to ask him is the one question I want to ask any president: That question is, "Are there aliens?"

Not Cubans. Are there *aliens*—another life-form? I know he knows.

The Biggest Bopper

I had another chance to find out about the aliens in the summer of 1999 when the White House invited me to lunch. Me and my lawyer, Oscar Holt, and a bunch of big shots from entertainment. Guys like Harvey Weinstein from Miramax and Sumner Redstone from Viacom. I was the poorest guy at the table. Except for my lawyer, of course.

Before we go in to meet the president, we get briefed by the Secret Service. And these guys are serious. All about six feet three or bigger, none of 'em smiling. The head guy, he says, "Mr. Williams, the president is very happy to have you here, he's a big sports fan, a big Jayson Williams fan."

I'm thinking, All right, that's cool.

"But," the Secret Service guy says, "he is president of the United States. Now, we know you're a very funny guy. But don't be so funny today.

"Let me explain something to you," he says. "Around the president at all times are snipers. Everybody here is a trained marksman. And if there are any sudden lunges toward the president, if anyone makes any sudden moves toward the president, that person will be shot three times behind the head before he hits the ground."

I look over at Oscar, and I say to the Secret Service man, "But I have a clumsy lawyer. This guy falls or trips three or four times a day."

The Secret Service man doesn't crack a smile. He says, "Well, he better not fall in the next three hours."

So before we go in to meet the president, I put my arm around Oscar, who really *is* clumsy. I say, "Do me a favor, bro, just today, don't be around me. Go hang out around Sumner Redstone. Sumner's getting up there in age. You know, those three behind the head for Sumner, that's one thing, but I'm a young man, I got a whole life to live."

As it turned out, I got along real well with the president. He walked into the place with a real bop. Like some of the young black people walk, with a real bop in his step. He's a smooth guy. And he loves talking sports.

I told him at lunch, "When I came into the NBA, I was making five hundred thousand a year under George Bush. And I'm going to leave here making about twenty million a year, because of how well the economy's done under your terms."

Then I said, "I know it's the first time in the country's history we have a surplus. But I don't think we should lower the taxes on the rich, because I think there's so much more we can do to help the underprivileged." Everyone at our table stood up and clapped when I said that, even Sumner.

I liked the president, and I think he liked me. When I got home, there were two messages from him on my machine. It's great to hear "This is President Clinton." And at the end of his message, he says, "Give ol' Bill a call."

Pete Sampras and Me

Another famous guy I met was Pete Sampras. Calipari brought him down to our training camp in Florida the first year Cal was with the Nets. Sampras had just won the U.S. Open, in a big, dramatic finish, when he was getting sick all over the court.

So Cal tells us that Pete Sampras is going to come in to speak to us. Well, Pete Sampras is a nice guy, but how much can Pete Sampras tell a bunch of guys who make just as much money as he does and are professional athletes? That's one of the things that Cal brought with him from UMass that probably should have stayed at UMass: that motivational speech stuff. Most NBA guys really don't care what Pete Sampras has to say.

But we all give Pete a chance. Before he showed up, Calipari told us, "I wanna ask Pete Sampras what he thought about when he was puking on that court when he won the U.S. Open. What was driving him? What made him go on?"

So Pete Sampras comes in, and the first thing out of his mouth is, "Sheesh, you guys are really big." And you can tell he is nervous. He's such a little man, looks more like a terrorist than a tennis player. Coach Calipari gets into his thing; he says, "Pete, I just want to ask you one question. What made you go on when you were puking? You were puking your brains out, your stomach was hurting. What made you go on?" You know, he put it on so theatrically. He'd already gone over the questions with Pete so Pete would be prepared. So here's Cal waiting for a great response. It's all set up very dramatically.

And here goes Pete Sampras:

"What made me go on?" Pete Sampras says. "Shit, the match was almost over."

That was it. A great tennis player he is, a motivational speaker he's not. After that I had to rib Cal a little. About how he brought Vince Lombardi down to give us a talk. The Vince Lombardi of tennis.

Celebrity Tax

I think when anyone gets rich and famous, he should at least act rich. What I mean is more NBA players need to start being better tippers.

I used to invite players to my bar, and I'd give them the VIP treatment, hold about seven tables in the restaurant for them. I never charged them to eat. But they never once left the waitress a tip. They didn't feel they had to tip her. Here they are taking up seven of my tables, tables I could have been making money on, and they stiffed this poor waitress.

It's not just basketball players. You hear all the time that this actor's cheap, that celebrity's tight-fisted. I don't want people saying that about me, so I overtip everywhere I go. I go to a club, a bar, a restaurant, I'll always get the best tables, and not just because I'm famous. It's because I always tip 30 percent. I think all famous people should. Fifteen percent for the tip and another 15 percent for the celebrity tax.

The Cos on Saving the World

Bill Cosby is a good friend of mine, and he's helped me out a lot, especially when it comes to charity work.

One day I was telling him about some of the charity work I was doing and some of the foundations I was helping, and he said, "Jay, you'll go broke trying to save the whole world, and all your family will go broke, too. Take a little section that you think you can help, and that's all you can do in this world. Because people are always going to talk about you, they're always going to make up stuff on you, no matter what you do, and trying to do more isn't going to make those people stop. When you're on top, there's always going to be a million people looking to knock you off, no matter how many good things you do.

"So you just take a section, every summer when you're off, you just take a small part of the world you think you can make better, and you make it better."

That made sense, but I still find myself going from one thing to another, doing twelve foundations, being a spokesman for all of them, not having any time left in the summer. And still, people don't understand when you turn them down, and I don't blame them. They see a rich young guy, they think he's got all the time in the world on his hands.

Schoolteachers especially make me feel bad. I love schoolteachers. I think they should each get about $2 million a year, the nonsense they have to put up with. But every schoolteacher I meet, they all want the same thing. Sometimes they even drive by and see me and just yell at me. "Hey, Jay, P.S. 147, Newark, can you be there Thursday?"

One day three teachers came up to me—two in a gym I was working out in and another at a stoplight. And that's when I came up with my schoolteacher concept. My concept is I'm going to put together a tape, tell some stories, a few jokes for the kids, and I'm going to send it to any schoolteacher who wants it. That'll be my inspirational talk.

Bottoms Up

It's not just eager schoolteachers and rude little kids who can bother you. One night I went to Moomba in New York City. That's where all the stars hang out. Real celebrity zone. So I'm sitting at a table and this other couple that I don't know comes up and sits down. Never seen them before in my life. They just come to my table. So I don't say anything. I'm pouring champagne for myself and the couple friends I got at the table.

This lady who just took a seat at my table is drinking Pellegrino water. She looks at me and puts her glass up, right in my face. I say, "You want champagne?" She says no, and looks at the water, then at me, then at the water again.

I'm thinking, Who the hell does this woman think she is? But I want to keep everything cool. So I pour the water for her.

Now it's five minutes later and I'm in the middle of a conversation, and she's hitting me on the shoulder with her glass.

Now I'm a little pissed off. I say, "Come on, babe, you think I work here? I ain't no damned waiter. Tell your husband to pour for you."

Then she looks at me and says, "Why don't you go back to the jungle and climb trees?"

Now, here's some rich old lady from another country. I think she was Swiss or something, and she's talking to me like that. So I take her water and I pour it on her seat. Not on her, just on her seat. She jumps back and runs to get her husband. Her husband comes back and he's trying to get in my face. So I say, "If you want to fight me, we can go downstairs, but if not, just argue here with my bodyguard."

Now, if I hadn't been a celebrity, I wouldn't have had a bodyguard, and chances are I wouldn't have been in Moomba. But if I had been there and not been a celebrity and someone got in my face like that, I wouldn't have done something as nice as just pouring water on that rich old lady's seat and talking nice to her husband.

That's the difference between being a famous athlete and a famous movie star. If I had been a movie star, I'd have done something really bad. Because you know what happens when a movie actor gets caught doing something really bad, gets in some serious trouble? More people come to their next movie and all their agents and accountants are happy as can be. But *we* get caught doing something, a professional basketball player steps out of line, and then it's like, "Oh, my God, we told you what happens when you give a lot of money to a kid from the ghetto." Or people say, "You can take the boy off of the street, but you can't take the street out of the boy," stuff like that. That's why I can't get as wild as my actor friends.

Fame's Rewards

The nicest thing about fame and celebrity—and I don't want to say I don't like the millions of dollars and beautiful women and the table at Moomba—is how much it lets me touch other people's lives.

I really believe I was put on this earth to help people, and that's why in the summer I go to three or four hospitals a week to visit sick kids, and why I help hand out food to homeless people. Nothing makes me feel better than seeing how I can cheer someone up. And I'll tell you, it's a funny thing, but my first year as an All-Star, people got cheered up a lot faster. I believe that God made me an All-Star not to make the Nets a championship team, which would be nice if God would give us a break, but to make other people feel better. I tell my friends who are pro athletes, "Brother, you have no idea how good it feels to give to someone else, to help someone out who needs help." I tell them charity ain't about bringing in TV cameras to a hospital to embarrass the kids and to show your ugly mug, which is what a lot of pro athletes do, and it definitely ain't about paying some big company to put up some backboards in some city park while you and your pals sit around and drink beer, which is what a lot of other pro athletes do. It's about helping people, about touching people. I'm no angel, and a lot of people who have known me over the years will back me up on that, but when you touch someone else, the person you're really helping more than anyone is yourself.

The Promised Land

I was on my way to do the *Chris Rock Show* a few years ago and I got a call from the Starlight Foundation, a charitable organization I do a lot of work for. They told me there was a girl in the hospital who had cancer, and that I'd given her an autograph once, and did I think I might be able to see her sometime? I said I'd drive over right after the show.

When I got to her room, the doctors told me she hadn't sat up for four weeks. Seventeen-year-old little girl. But she sat up, gave me a hug. We talked for a little while. I told her about the *Chris Rock Show*, just talked about life, and I think she cheered up a little. That was on a Thursday. I went to see her Friday, went to see her twice on Saturday. On Sunday I took four of the New Jersey Devils to meet her. She at first didn't want any of them in there—she thought she was ugly because she had a bald head—but it ended up being fun for her. When we left, she said she was feeling better, but I knew she was still sick.

Then I had to go to California for a few days. I spoke with her on the telephone the day I left, and I called her from my car the day I landed, but the nurse I got said she was no longer in the hospital. There I am, driving down the highway, crying, kicking myself for not having called her more. I called up her parents' house to offer my sympathy. But my friend picks up the phone. I've never been so happy.

I try to act all cool, like I hadn't just been crying on the highway. "Well, little sister, how are you doing?" She says, "I'm feeling so much better, I'm home."

The doctors told me they didn't know how she got better, but she just did. Right then I went out and did thirteen more visits to sick kids, went to six more hospitals. That was a point in my life I felt like Moses. Not Moses Malone. Moses.

We All Drink from the Same Cup

Kids are incredibly sensitive, always trying to make adults feel better. One little boy who was real sick—in and out of the hospital—I used to talk to every day. Then last summer he didn't call me for about three days, so I called him, and asked him why I hadn't heard from him.

And he said, "I'm feeling better and I call you a lot anyway, so I didn't want to bother you."

I said, "You know, I met you because you were sick, but I don't love you because you're sick. That's not the reason I talk to you and see you—because you're sick. I do it because we're friends."

There was another little boy I used to visit in the hospital all the time. Nine years old, he had AIDS. He liked Gatorade, and the doctors and nurses always used to make a big deal out of marking his cup. And then he would make sure to keep that cup right next to his bed, underneath a chair where no one else could get to it. I watched him, because I remember watching my sisters dying, and I remember the nurses and doctors doing the same stuff to them. They would take all my sisters' stuff and mark it up and it used to burn me up so much. Even to this day when I think about it, it burns me up.

One day I'm in this little boy's room and we're talking, and I say, "Man, I'm thirsty, gimme some of that Gatorade," and I reach for his cup.

And he says, "No, let me get you a fresh one."

"No, man," I say. "I'm thirsty. Gimme a sip of that one."

He says, "No, no, no, you can't have that one." And I don't know if he knows I know he has AIDS.

I say, "Give me that damn thing, because I don't care what kind of disease you got. Because when I get home I can walk off a curb and get hit by a bread truck and die right there. Right now I'm alive and you're alive."

I explain to him about the new drug therapies for his disease and I tell him he might outlive everyone in the hospital, doctors and nurses included. I think it made him feel better. It definitely made me feel better. Because if I don't at least try to make some kids feel better, I feel guilty, like I'm letting people down, like I'm letting myself down.

Chapter 12

Liars, Cheats,

Tramps & Thieves.

All About Coaches

(with a Few Words

on Refs)

 I've never seen a team win a title because they have a stacked coaching staff. They win because the team is stacked. The Chicago Bulls were stacked, the Lakers were stacked. Coaching played little or no role in it. A winning NBA team is determined by 80 percent personnel, 10 percent luck, and 10 percent coaching. As a result, you cannot win in this league without players. The jockey can't win without the horse. In this league you need thoroughbreds. A great coach helps—a lot—but even a great coach needs great players.

I don't think coaching in this league is that hard. The only hard thing is keeping unity. It's not like in college where you have to mold a man. You're not molding anybody in the NBA. Everybody makes outstanding money and just about everybody makes more than the coach. Because nobody comes to see the coach, I don't care how high he jumps around on the sidelines.

The Problem with Penny

Any NBA coach who thinks he's the Man is going to have problems. You see an example of that with what happened down in Orlando with Brian Hill and all the players who got him out of there.

The story was that Brian Hill and Penny Hardaway didn't get along, that Brian was saying Penny was tough to coach. Well, Penny's a superstar. You'll never meet a superstar who *isn't* tough to coach. Penny Hardaway is one of the top five players in the league. You have to learn to tolerate him if you're the coach. It's not about him tolerating the coaches, but the coach tolerating him. Someone who's going to get you a triple or a double every night, you *better* learn to tolerate.

Anyone who thinks coaches control players these days still believes in the two-handed set shot. A couple years ago we were trying to trade for Penny Hardaway. And Penny asked me, straight out, "What kind of guy is Calipari?" I had had some problems with Cal, but I looked Penny straight in the face, and I said, "You can tolerate him." Well, perhaps Penny heard different from some other players, because he decided not to come.

No-Brainer

Players talk. They talk like women in this league. I heard players talk about P. J. Carlesimo being a yeller, even before the thing with Latrell Sprewell. And not that it ever would have really happened, but Michael Jordan two years ago, he met with one of our owners, who said, kind of joking like, "What would it take to get you to come play for us next year?" And Michael said, "Number one, you don't have enough money in the whole organization to pay me. And number two, I'll never play for that man you all got coaching up there, yelling at the young kids like that. That ain't right."

Now, if it came down to a choice between a coach and Michael Jordan, who do you think the owner's going to pick? Unless he's the genius over at the Chicago Bulls, of course.

The Coaches I Like to Piss Off

Personally I don't want to say anything bad about anyone I'm play-ing for, but I can tell you that I enjoyed pissing off a couple coaches in the league, particularly the former coach in Washington, D.C., and the former coach in San Antonio. The coach in San Antonio wouldn't give up Will Perdue for me. Will Perdue! And the coach down in Washington could have given up Gheorghe Muresan for me. So every time we were on the free-throw line against the Wizards a few years ago, Rod Strickland would look over at me and say, "Do you believe those stupid idiots wouldn't trade him for you?" Then I would laugh and toss Muresan to the ground and get another rebound.

Sitting Pretty

A lot of the coaches in this game have big egos. And that's one rea-son you have some of the great rivalries in this league. People don't want to admit it, but most of the rivalries in this league are between the coaches instead of the players. Because each one of them thinks he invented the game.

When John Calipari had just come to the Nets, in 1996, the Bulls were still the *Bulls*. And Phil Jackson was Mr. Cool.

Cal couldn't stand it how cool Phil Jackson always was, how he always won. Before one game, Cal told us, "I just want to make that guy worry enough to uncross his legs. Just one time in one game I want that guy to uncross his legs."

A lot of coaches don't like other coaches, or are jealous of them. All of them are jealous of Pat Riley—they all want to be Pat Riley—even though Pat Riley isn't the winningest coach. Lenny Wilkens is. But Pat has that flair. Pat's bigger than the team. I don't think that should ever happen, but it's made a lot of money for Pat, so more power to him, I guess.

Lower the Volume

You watch TV enough, you get the idea that coaches spend most of their time devising brilliant strategies, and coming up with speeches that make us all run headfirst through brick walls, and telling us things that make us behave like choirboys sometimes and trained killers other times, depending on what the coach wants. I think some of the coaches believe that, too, especially considering some of the crazy things they come up with.

Take discipline. You really don't have a boss in the NBA. You're your own boss. Nobody can tell you what time to come in for a curfew. Nobody can tell you to get to a practice early or lift weights. Nobody can tell you anything. You have to be a man enough and a professional enough to do those things. But a lot of the coaches do think they can make you do things. That's why a lot of 'em yell so much. They do it even though you don't have to yell to win. Look at Rudy Tomjanovich. Everybody loves Rudy. *Everybody* loves him. He's easygoing and he wins. And if you can get results and be loved, what's better than that? But they still yell.

You ever see Phil Jackson yell? Lenny Wilkens? Those are two of the best coaches ever, and they won being quiet.

Keeping It Simple

You think coaches come up with brilliant theories all the time, revolutionary strategies? Then I got a bridge to sell you. To realize what deep thinkers most coaches are, just consider two things—play-offs and free throws.

Now, when we go into a play-off game—when any team goes into a play-off game—we have a week to prepare. We watch an hour and a half of tape a day, we know every play they're going to run, and they know every play we're going to run. So with everyone knowing everything, you would think the smart coaches would put in some surprises. And the best coaches do put in new stuff, new plays. The Rileys, the Fratellos, they will do this.

But 95 percent of the coaches are superstitious. They want to stay with what got them there, and they're afraid if they put in too much new stuff, it'll confuse guys. So they might start off a quarter with the new stuff, and as soon as it's not working, they'll go right back to the old stuff.

Or let's talk about free throws. There's one center, I don't want to use his name because me and him, we don't get along, but he plays for Los Angeles. Terrible free-throw shooter. Any smart coach would be making him shoot free throws in practice—during practice, not after. Coaches don't seem to understand this. You can't shoot free throws *after practice.* And yet on most NBA teams, that's exactly what happens—you shoot free throws at the end of practice, and that's a mistake. When you shoot at the end, the coach says, "Did you shoot fifty?" "Yeah, sure, I shot fifty." Bull. You're getting out of there *now.* Most of the time you're mad at one of your teammates for fouling you, or you're mad at your coach, and you don't want to be around. You're in a bad mood, so you don't shoot 'em. You just say you do. After practice, ain't nobody talking about sitting there and shooting no free throws. Everybody's in their car, top down, music blasting, getting the hell out.

To be a good free-throw-shooting team, you have to shoot free throws during practice. I don't know why coaches can't figure that out.

Chuck Daly

I liked Chuck Daly because he was a professional. Not necessarily fair, but a professional. Chuck used to say, "I'll take some crap from the stars, but I won't take any from guys who don't play." He was to the point. He didn't want any relationship with you, he didn't want to see your butt after the game. He'd tell you, "Go out, get drunk, do whatever you want as long as you show up to practice and to play." He'd say, "I don't want to meet your wife, I don't want to meet your girlfriend, I don't want to be your buddy. I just want you to show up."

When I was playing for Chuck, I wasn't one of the stars, so

maybe that was part of the problem I had with him. I had plenty. I remember one game with the Nets. It was 1992 and we had just got Rick Mahorn, who had been playing in Italy. Up until then I had been the backup to Sam Bowie, our center. Wasn't playing a lot, but I was getting in from time to time.

We're playing the Knicks in the Garden that night, and every coach I ever had would always go out of his way to give me playing time in the Garden, because they knew my boys were watching me, my friends from when I was a kid, and the coach knew I had a lot of pride and he knew I would play well. Even Jim Lynam at Philadelphia played me there, and he hardly ever played me.

So here we are in the third quarter against the Knicks, and Sam Bowie is messing up, and Chuck's getting ready to take him out, so I get up. Chuck looks at me, says, "You know what? You sit down." He looks at Mahorn and goes, "Rick, you go get Sam." So Rick, his first day here from Italy, and all of a sudden he's taking my job.

Later in the game, Chuck's been thrown out of the game for getting a couple technicals, and Sam has been out all game, and now Rick's messing up. So Brendan Suhr, Chuck's assistant, yells at me, "Go get Rick. Get him out of there."

So I go in, but Brendan Suhr sees I'm kind of unhappy, and he says something to me and I say something to him—nothing horrible—but the next day at practice I see Suhr talking to Chuck. Chuck is looking at me. Some of the guys are shooting around, others are stretching, but I'm just sitting there. Practice isn't officially started yet, so I figure if they're going to treat me like they did last night, I'll wait till practice starts to get up. When he blows the whistle, then I'll work, and when he blows the final whistle, I'll be going home. I look at him and he looks at me, and I can see it's going to be a long morning.

He blows the whistle and says, "Okay, now start warming up. Run the floor." So I'm running, just as fast as everybody else. He blows the whistle again and he says, "Jay, I said run the floor."

I say, "Okay."

He blows the whistle a third time, he says, "It's the one thing you can do is run. It's the *only* thing you can do. Now, run the floor."

So I look over at some of my teammates, who really don't want to get in the middle of this, and I say, "Am I running as fast as you people?" They say, "Yeah," because I *was* running as fast as them. I say to them, "If he blows that whistle at me one more time, I'm going to shove it—"

Before I can finish my sentence, *brggggg,* he blows it again. Before he can say anything I jump over to him. And before *I* can say anything he gets in my face. As mad as I am, I can see nothing good's gonna come of this, we're both so steamed, so I walk out, straight to my car. And that night I go to dinner with Willis Reed, one of the top guys at the Nets, and I explain how I feel about things and what happened. And Chuck and I never spoke about it after that. It was just business. And it was good like that, because I think we both liked each other deep down.

That might sound funny, but I believe it. I believe Chuck liked me, and at times I liked him okay. In truth, the problems with Chuck and me probably started before we even met. Chuck tried to stop the Nets from signing me. The Nets were trading to Philadelphia for me, and I heard Chuck arguing with my agent. Then Chuck came up to me after the meeting and said, "I don't want you on my team." But they made the trade anyway.

And my first practice, Willis Reed says, "You better be worth the draft pick we gave up, or it's gonna be my ass." So Willis overrode Chuck to get me. And maybe that's one reason Chuck always resented me. I resented him as soon as I heard he tried to keep me off the team. When I find out stuff like that, I'll hold it against you for a very, very long time.

Truth is, I think I was the only one on the team who ever really had a problem with Chuck. To everybody else he was tolerable. I don't think anybody loved him, but he ran a professional ship. Everything was first-class. He made the Nets pay for everything. He even made them pay for his Medicare. And whatever he got per diem, he had to get a dollar more than Pat Riley, who was with the Knicks then, was getting. We had lobster and steak on the plane every day. With Chuck, the Nets got their own plane for the first time. His practices were more professional than any other coach I ever played for. You came in, and even with the stretch and the workout, you're in and out in fifty minutes. And that's why his teams always win a lot of games, because guys have stuff left for the games.

Larry Bird

A lot of times you hear that the guys who were really great players don't make great coaches. That's bull. You know who's saying that stuff? The guys who never were great players, who never played on that level. In other words, the guys who think they invented the game, the guys who should be working on the sports radio.

What makes Larry Bird a great coach is what made him a great player. He *knows* he's great. (And he knows the game, of course.)

When Larry coached in the All-Star Game, he didn't say twenty words the whole game. He came in, he wrote on a board in the training room how many minutes you were going to play and when you were going in, and that was it. Michael Jordan—it was his last All-Star Game—he comes in and looks at the board and he says, to Larry and to everyone else, "Hey, man, you know, I ain't going to be out here all day playing."

And Larry looks at Michael, and Larry's not really joking around, and he says, "Oh, now you don't want to be out there? When you were playing me, you wanted to be out there all the time."

And Mike says, "Well, you know, it was easy then," or something like that.

And then Larry gives him a look like, "I'll still bust your ass." It was just a look, but everyone could see what he meant. Larry's got a lot of pride.

Pat Riley

Pat Riley's strength is his record. He gets it done. But I've heard that playing for Pat takes time off a player's career. Look at Patrick Ewing, Alonzo Mourning—look at all the wear and tear on their bodies. That's from Riley's practices. I heard Michael Cooper say a lot of the guys on those great Lakers teams of the eighties would have had another three or four years in their career if they had played for someone besides Riley. But Cooper also said he wouldn't have had those championships. So he wasn't complaining. Tell you the truth, I'd take a few championships in exchange for a shorter career. Most players would.

That's the word on Pat Riley. He's going to kill you, but he's going to get it done.

Phil Jackson

The guy who's the ultimate coach is Phil Jackson, and that's because he really takes a backseat to the players. He understands it's not a coach's game. That's why so many players respect Phil. And everybody loves Phil; they love playing for him.

He comes in, he gets the practice done, you work hard, you get your little sweat in one hour, you go home, you save your body, you've got a great facility. And how many times have you seen Phil Jackson get up and start yelling?

Even when he had teams without Michael, or when he had just Michael and Scottie and he wasn't winning, he still wasn't yelling too much. But every once in a while, even Phil would snap.

One game we were playing the Bulls, and Calipari was yelling at Keith Van Horn. It was his rookie year, and Cal was just drilling Keith.

I run past the Bulls' bench, and Phil says to me, "How are you going to let him talk to your boy like that? How are you going to let him yell at your boy?"

And then five seconds later Phil just drilled Kukoc. So even the Zen master himself, old Phil Jackson, still yells sometimes.

The one thing I didn't understand that Phil did was when he went to Kukoc in that game during the season that Michael wasn't playing. There were about three seconds left, and Phil called the play for Toni, and Scottie Pippen was so pissed off he wouldn't go into the game, and everyone got all pissed off at Scottie, especially after Toni hit the shot.

I understand why Scottie was mad. Scottie wants to win. He thought he was on the floor with a bunch of guys who weren't pulling their weight, and all the pressure was falling on him. And then someone else gets to take the last shot? What I would have done in that situation was I would have followed the coach's orders and then when the play was over I would've walked over and told Phil, "All right, we did it your way, and we lost."

The thing is they didn't lose. But I still don't understand how Phil could not have gone to Scottie Pippen. The only reason you wouldn't go to Scottie is if Michael Jordan was on the floor. And he wasn't. But Phil didn't go to Scottie, and they won that game. I guess that's why Phil is a genius.

P. J. Carlesimo

P. J. is loud, he will provoke you, he will definitely yell. And everybody knows he yells, because of what happened with him and Latrell Sprewell. But P. J. has always been a yeller. Since well before Latrell.

What happened with Latrell Sprewell—when Latrell got yelled at by P. J., then got pissed off and choked him—that was a fluke. I doubt something like that will ever happen to P. J. again. And as for Spree, every game he scores 20 points, people are going to forget all about what happened there. After the choking, everyone was writing about what a bad guy Spree was. Then he had a good year with the Knicks, and people are writing more about his shot selection than his choke hold. That's the way it works.

I should add that I like P. J. Carlesimo. He's got a sense of humor that a lot of people don't know about. When I was on TV for hitting the guy in the stands with a metal chair, in Providence, P. J. saw it. He was the coach of Seton Hall then. Ever since that incident, he's called me the Lion Tamer. Like, "Hey, Lion Tamer, how you doin'?" I like a guy who can see the humor in situations.

Rick Pitino

I don't know if I could ever play for Rick Pitino. Tony Massenburg, who I used to call the Brown Hornet, after the big muscle guy from *Fat Albert,* told me he had gone from 255 to 225 in one of Rick's training camps. He said the first practice, he passed out he was running so much.

When he woke up he said, "What am I on?" He was on an IV, and he looked over and there were six more of his teammates all lying down with the IVs. He said Pervis Ellison just fell out. They had to put two IVs in Never Nervous Pervis.

Tony told me, "Man, Rick Pitino's crazy. His training camp is no joke."

Lenny Wilkens

A lot of players would like to play for Lenny Wilkens. That's because he's a proven winner, he's professional, there's no favorites, and he has no ego. I think the guys who do less, who say less, are the guys who do best. And less is best in coaching an NBA team. You don't get any less than Lenny Wilkens.

But even someone like Lenny has players he doesn't get along with. He had one player, a power forward named Ken Norman, he and Lenny just rubbed each other the wrong way. And what Lenny would do, he wouldn't even say Ken Norman's name. He would just say, "Number 51, get in the game."

You know what I would do in a situation like that? I would just say, "Okay, Head Coach."

George Karl

A coach who's the opposite of Lenny Wilkens, in just about every way, is George Karl. Big guy, loud, gets into the faces of his players. Which not all his players appreciated too much.

What I know about George mostly is how much my friend Kendall Gill had hard feelings against him. That's natural for players who get traded; there's always a lot of hard feelings. Players who get traded have a tendency to come back and play extra hard against the team that traded them. But this was more. I mean, Kendall hated George Karl's guts. Kendall gets migraines and he has to take medication for them. I'm not sure George was real understanding about that. Kendall told me that he was so worked up about George that he ended up in the hospital for six days. He couldn't sleep. Kendall told some newspaper reporter, "If I ever see him in a dark alleyway . . ."

And when that came out, I told Kendall, "I'm putting my money on George."

Kendall was upset for a while, but George laughed it off—he made a joke out of it. So in a way I *like* George Karl. I like him because he's got a good sense of humor. People that make me laugh win me over.

John Calipari

The problem with John Calipari was that he was insecure, and he needed to prove he could run everything. He wouldn't give the rest of the coaching staff a chance to coach. Cal needed to do everything himself. At least he was honest about it, though. Or as honest as he could be. When he first took the job at the Nets, in the press conference he said, "I bet on me."

It was a risky bet. And he lost.

I didn't like Cal when he first came to the Nets in 1996, and that was my fault. I was pissed off that the Nets had fired our previous coach, Butch Beard. Butch got us to win thirty games the year before, even after we traded our two All-Stars, Kenny Anderson and Derrick Coleman. Then our best shooter, Kendall Gill, went down with an injury. That was a bad time, with all the injuries and trades, and I was contemplating retiring. And Butch gave me the opportunity to play, he counseled me, he set me straight. Basically, he gave me my career back. So what happens? They fired Butch.

His last season, with about three games left, he knew he was gone. He told a reporter, "I don't care who you bring here. If you bring in a John Calipari or you bring in Rick Pitino, let me see them try to win thirty games with this team."

So of course they bring in Cal. And I had that feeling like you get when you see an old girlfriend out with another person. Or when your father gets married—I don't know how that feels, but I can imagine—if your father was to get married again, and it's not your mother. Then your stepmother comes in, how you don't want to give her a chance. That's how I felt with John Calipari coming in. That's how it sometimes is with players when a coach they like gets fired and a new one comes in. So I started pissed off. I didn't want to cut Calipari any slack at all.

And before we even met, I got even more pissed off at him. That's because when he came in, he changed the whole Nets staff, even the administrative people who had worked with the Nets just about forever. Which is probably what I would've done too, canned the old squad and brought in my boys who have been watching my back my whole life. But I didn't like it when he did it. Especially what he did with the weight coach.

He wanted to bring in his own guy, named Ray Oliver. The weight coach we already had, named Richard Snedaker, had trained me for three years and he had whupped me down from 265 pounds and 18 percent body fat to 235 pounds and hardly any body fat. He had made me into the strongest guy in the league, got me to where I could bench-press over 400 pounds and clean, jerk, and snatch over my head right around 385 pounds. Nobody else in the league could do that, and Calipari wanted to fire him.

My first meeting with Cal, I complain about that. I know that Cal has the power to trade me, that I'm the most tradable player on this team. And Cal tells me at that meeting that fifteen teams in the NBA have called about trading for me as soon as he got the job. He says he had heard rumors that I didn't like to practice and that I was going to give him a hard time.

I do not like to practice during the NBA season for two hours a day. I like to go in and get it done and get out, so I can save my body for the games. People have to get in shape in the NBA on their own time. You can't make players do it in practice.

While Cal's talking about practice, I'm trying to keep the conversation focused on Richard Snedaker, who was not only a great trainer but who had become my good friend.

I tell Cal that he couldn't fire this man, that I would be very disappointed if he did fire him. And that if he did keep Richard on, I would make sure to go out and bust my butt for Cal every day, every practice, every game. He didn't want to be pressured in this situation, but he also didn't want to start off on the wrong foot with Jayson Williams. So he considers what I said, thinks about it for a little while, and then he says, "You know what? I'm going to keep my guy *and* your guy."

I thought that was a pretty good solution. But then Richard went down to a weight training convention in Atlanta, and he talked to some other coaches there, telling them about the arrangement, how Richard wasn't so sure he was going to get along with Cal. So of course Cal found out. And what happened was Cal called me into his office and told me what he had found out, then said, "Now, Jay, what would you do?" And I said, "I probably would fire him." And that's what Calipari did—he fired him. After that, I was a little wiser about how Cal operated.

The first meeting Cal ever had with the whole team, he sat us all down and had all his guys around him. He had his crew with him. An entourage of workers, guys who had been loyal to him, who he demands loyalty from. About four or five of his assistant coaches and the guys in his administration lived in his home with him then, with their kids and his kids. I had never been over to John's house, but it must have been a helluva big place. And it must have been damn noisy, with all those kids.

John's crew was mostly white, and almost all the players were black. They were the Gambinos and we were the Moonyans. John told us at that first meeting that he demanded excellence from his guys and that he would demand excellence from us. I came away from that meeting knowing that he had a big ego and also knowing that this was a man who knew how to maneuver things, a man who knew how to get what he wanted, a man who knew how to manipulate and motivate.

He was so good, I think Cal could have sold fried ice cream. If you were an atheist, when he finished talking to you, you'd definitely be Muslim or Mormon or whatever. You would believe in something. After he got done talking that first meeting, I believed in John Calipari. And even with the Pete Sampras bull and the four-hour practices, I believed in him.

Then the season started and we started losing.

No one's happy on a losing team. And I can't think of anyone who hates losing more than Cal. But the more we lost, the more Cal kept yelling and having meetings. Cal has a lot of meetings. This guy had more meetings than the damn Senate. And at first, it makes you feel good, to be included, to hear all the special things he has planned. But after a while, it was just another meeting.

As for the yelling, John Calipari might be the yellingest coach in the history of the league. But this isn't college, this is the NBA, and you can't be yelling at your own men like they're college kids. Constructive criticism is okay, but you can't yell at every play, you can't coach every play, because if nobody made any mistakes out there, every game would be 0–0. After a while, all Cal's yelling just fell on deaf ears, because he was yelling so much. We got used to it.

But that's his style. Cal used to take the pacifier out of his mouth to yell. He's been yelling since he's been eight months old. Tell you the truth, I kind of enjoyed some of his yelling. With some of the guys we have on the New Jersey Nets, I think he needed to yell. It helped some of the guys. Some of the things I wouldn't dare tell my teammates, he would go ahead and do it. So Cal and I played good cop/bad cop. He was the bad cop, I was the good cop. He'd wring out a player, like Kerry Kittles, and then I'd say, "Hey, don't worry about it, man. You come back and show him, you hit that three-pointer the next time."

On Monday, after our day off, Coach Calipari was yelling because we came out so slow. One thing about a coach. They give you a day off, you owe them the world. You gotta go in there tomorrow, after your big day off, and you gotta do everything a hundred miles an hour. But, sheesh, Jesus took a day off. He rested on Sunday. And I'm sure Joseph didn't tell him Monday morning, "Dang it, I gave you a day off. Get your butt up and down the floor, you lazy bum."

Our first training camp with Cal, we started with two a day, ten to twelve in the morning, then in the evening from four to six. So one day Cal tells us he's got a big treat for us, that we're switching to only one practice a day. And the guys are all happy and excited. So we get to the gym at ten. And what time do we get out of the gym? At three o'clock. An extra hour of practice, but the guys are still happy and excited! No one complained. It's not like there are a lot of brain surgeons in the NBA.

Cal wants to win, deep down in his heart he wants to win. He's obsessed with the game. I would look at him sometimes and I wouldn't understand how he had a family life. Sometimes, with all the time he put in, with all the yelling and the meetings, he looked like he didn't want to go home.

And we kept losing, and Cal kept yelling and having meetings, and everyone kept getting grumpier. Then things got personal with me and Cal.

Early in Cal's first season, two days before we were going to play the Dallas Mavericks, my agent called me and said that Cal said he had smelled liquor on my breath during practice. Now, this was the 1996–97 season, and I had made a concerted effort for the previous three years to pick and choose to only go out on the nights before a day off. If we had back-to-back Friday and Saturday games, then on Saturday night I'd go out with friends, because we had Sunday off. Once a week. And I had not had liquor on my breath since Cal had taken the coaching job.

I tried to call Cal. I was fuming. I didn't just want to talk to him; I had other things on my mind, too. First they told me John Nash, the Nets' general manager, said it. When I talked to John Nash, he told me that Cal said it. The next day at practice, before anybody did anything, I called all the troops around—all my teammates—and I said, "Which one of you guys smelled liquor on my breath? Tell me."

And everybody on my team said, "No, nobody smelled anything. You've been good." Then I asked Cal. And Cal passed the buck to John Nash, saying that John Nash said it. I don't know how John Nash would know anything about it; he wasn't at practice. That pissed me off: Cal and them coming up with a straight-out lie.

At that point in the season, I was top of the league in individual rebounding. But we were still losing. One game against Utah, we got blown out by Utah by 16 points. I had eleven rebounds, but Cal took me out. And I didn't appreciate that. Even though the team comes first, you still have to maintain your individual stats. Charles Barkley doesn't come out of a blowout, and neither does Dennis Rodman. Dennis Rodman and Charles Barkley had made a bet that season over who would win the rebounding title. Dennis bet that if Charles beat him, Dennis would wear a dress. And if Charles lost, Charles would have to wear a dress. I figured Dennis would throw it so he would have an excuse to put on a dress, the freak. But I would have hated to see Charles Barkley with a dress on and with lipstick, especially with that big lip he's got.

But they didn't even consider me in the rebound race. And at the time I though I could win it. So I was pissed off at Calipari for taking me out of the game. And I told him.

A few days later we played the Phoenix Suns, who were 0–13 then. This was going to be a big game for us. We were 2–7 and we were going to kick a worse team's ass. Well, after the game, the 0–13 Suns were 1–13. They beat us by 22 points. It was a tough night. We shot terribly, and after, some of the guys were talking about some of the other guys. That's how it goes when you lose, a lot of finger-pointing. So Cal hears some of the whining, then he starts yelling at us.

"*Now* who do you want to blame it on?" he said.

When he said that, I thought of the year before Cal came. We had Armen Gilliam, P. J. Brown, and Chris Childs. Kendall Gill was hurt all year so he couldn't play. But if he was playing, we'd have had a heck of a team. But Calipari came in and he changed it all. So he was asking who we blamed it on. I'll tell you. We blamed it on his butt.

Later that first year Cal and I were together, we were *still* losing.

I set up a meeting with Cal. I said, "Cal, I think me and you are not going to make it here in New Jersey. I think it's time for me to move on. I had my agent call up two teams I want to play on, and I think I should be traded."

And he said, "Jay, we know you've been practicing hard, and you've given us everything you have. So don't worry about getting traded." And he said, "The next time I'm thinking about taking you out of a game because we're getting blown out, I'll give you a few more minutes. I'll tell you, 'Go in there and do what you have to do, and after about six or seven minutes you're going to come out.'"

And then he brought up money, because at the time I was in the second-to-last year of my contract. He said, "Don't worry that I was only able to offer you a contract extension. I know you can only go up 20 percent on your contract. I know you wouldn't take that, because you're going to be demanding six or seven or eight million in a couple of years." (If he only had known.) "But I offered you an extension from the goodness of my heart to show you that we still want you to be a Net until the day you retire."

I left feeling good with Cal. And that lasted about a week.

I hurt my thumb, and I kept playing with it, even though my agent and my manager told me I should get surgery. They told me that playing while the team was losing wasn't going to help anyone. But Cal wanted me to keep playing, so I did. Finally, though, I couldn't. So I got the surgery, and Cal was pissed. And he wouldn't even look down the bench at me, where I was sitting in my street clothes. So I wouldn't look up the bench at him. And my first season with Cal ended on a sour note. It probably didn't help that I wrote a magazine article that year. I ended it by saying:

> *I just want to play basketball, and I don't want a man who's only eight years older than me yelling and hollering at me and telling me what I can do and say and what I can't do and say. He should just be worried about what I do those two hours on that basketball court. I've always done everything for the Nets . . . But I'm not going to let John Calipari decide what I can say and what I cannot say.*

*So me and Cal are gonna sit down soon. If Cal's gonna
leave me alone, then I'll be happy and play, and we'll have no
problems. But if he's gonna get mad at me, if he's gonna look
over and mess with me, then I'm not gonna be here. Because I
don't want to be putting my foot up Cal's ass in a contract year.*

I hated Cal the first year we were together. The second year, I
liked him. By the third year, when I had my long-term contract, I
knew we both wanted to win, and that Cal couldn't hurt me even
if he wanted to, so it was strictly a business relationship. Still, when
he got fired, I felt for the man.

It's Lonely in the Middle

Even though it's the coaches who wear the Armani suits and get the
big contracts and give the big motivational speeches, a lot of times
it's guys on their staffs who make a huge difference in what goes
on with the team. I'm talking about the assistant coaches. (Trainers
are a whole other book. Any player in the NBA will tell you, the
most low-down conniver in the world, the guy who will sell you
out in a second, is the trainer. Their job is being on the side of the
management and the coach. But a lot of times they try to act like
they're your friend. They try to play both sides. And a guy who
plays both sides is usually not a good guy.)

Assistant coaches are sometimes very, *very* important to a team.
You got your smart assistant coaches, like Tex Winter at Los
Angeles, who a lot of people say invented the triangle offense. You
got assistants who just rebound you the ball. And you got assistants
who serve as arbitrators between the head coach and the players.
And then on some teams you got the assistant who is smarter than
the head coach. But he only gets credit when it's bad credit. When
after something goes wrong, the head coach looks at him and says,
"Why in the *world* did you tell me to run that play?" Now, the last
forty times he ran that play, it worked perfectly, but once it doesn't,
he chews the poor assistant's butt out.

The best arbitrators in the league are Paul Silas and Don Casey, both of whom went from assistant to head coach in 1999. Those guys would help keep the peace between the head coach and the players. The difference in the two was Don Casey would talk to you in a way to get you to reconcile with the head coach. Paul Silas maybe wasn't quite as diplomatic as Don. Paul would talk to you in two ways. He'd talk to you like a man. And if you talked to him like a boy, he'd make your back dirty. I have seen Paul Silas fight Derrick Coleman and Benoit Benjamin. I've heard he went at Charles Oakley once. Sometimes you need a guy like that.

Paul Silas was probably one of the biggest influences on my professional life, along with Butch Beard, who was the head coach of the Nets for a while. Paul told me, "You're one of the best athletes I know. You're probably the strongest man in the league. If you can find one thing you can do real well in the NBA, then you'll always stick." And I found out my one thing was offensive rebounding. He and Butch helped me learn that I could be a star in this league if I really worked hard and put my social life on hold for a while.

The smartest assistant coach is an easy choice. That's Tex Winter. He might even be smarter than Phil Jackson. But Phil, with those suits, and those glasses, and the way he crosses his legs, he looks a whole lot better sitting on the bench.

Tex's triangle offense helped the Bulls win all those championships. And that is a tricky offense. I went to the Bulls some time ago and worked out with them for five days, when I was thinking about signing with them instead of New Jersey. They tried to teach me that offense for five days. I had sprained my ankle, and I was still limping around, working with Tex and about four other assistants and Phil Jackson. I could not get that triangle down. So the last day, I told Phil Jackson, "Phil, thanks for having me. You're a great guy, you've got a great team, you win a lot of championships, but with me you've got the wrong guy for that frigging triangle. Bye."

The Lowest Donut-Eater of Them All

The assistant coach I had the biggest problem with was a guy named Brendan Suhr, Chuck Daly's assistant when he was with the

Nets, and then his assistant when Chuck was with the Magic. A fat little guy, Brendan Suhr just got under my skin. He'd be smiling in your face one minute, next thing you knew he'd be telling others bad things about you, the fat little donut-eating, Barney Rubble–looking, fishwife-talking rat.

Brendan Suhr would always look you in the face when he wasn't playing straight. The man had more chins than a Chinese phone book. I used to like to look at him just to try figuring out how many chins this man's got. I saw him eat sixteen donuts once. Gobbled 'em all at one sitting. Not just regular donuts, either. Friggin' jelly donuts. When he talked, one side of his throat would blow up and the other side would go down, and I would just stare in amazement.

But he always used to talk like he was on my side. He reminded me of a three-card-monte dealer. I used to watch monte my whole life on Delancey Street, on New York's Lower East Side. "Yeah, yeah, yeah, I'm on your side, I'm going to help you out," the dealer would say, and "I'm going to help you get your money back." Then *boom,* he breaks you, and you're out of money.

I played for Brendan Suhr when he was Chuck Daly's assistant with the Nets in the early nineties, and I didn't like him then. But I didn't really have a problem with him till later, when he was with the Orlando Magic.

A teammate of mine—a guy we got from Orlando—told me that whenever the Magic were playing the Nets, Brendan would get up and go over the plays with the Magic players on the board in the locker room, and then he'd always say, "Williams is just not that good. He's a terrible rebounder. He just pushes and shoves. He don't want to win." Stuff like that. He'd be just killing me.

And I'd go out and get about 16 points and eighteen rebounds against the Magic, then this guy—the Magic player who ended up in New Jersey—would come in and find that donut-eater.

"Hey, Brendan," the player would say, "if Williams ain't a damn good rebounder, why don't you go out there with your fat ass and try to check him?"

The first year this player came to the Nets from Orlando, we were out to dinner, and he was telling me all the Brendan stories, and I was getting pissed off all over again. We were going to play Orlando the next day.

I go to sleep, and that next morning I stop at Dunkin' Donuts, and I buy sixteen donuts. Jelly donuts. And after our morning practice, the Magic come in for their shootaround. I wait until they're all stretching, and it's quiet in the gym. I walk over to that little Barney Rubble lying fishwife.

I say, "Brendan, I brought you another sixteen donuts, you fat little rat."

And I threw all the donuts at him.

Elephant Balls

Assistant coaches get abused, and head coaches might get fired all the time and have to put up with players like me, and you hear all the time how tough NBA players are, how we gotta be strong, and withstand pressure and all that. But I'll tell you who's the toughest guy on the court. That's the ref. You want to know the chief quality a ref needs to have in the NBA? That's a pair of elephant balls. The refs are the ones who have to withstand the pressure, the ones who have to break up the fights between seven-footers, the ones who have to hear all that abuse coming from the fans. Refs get booed eighty-two games a year, every game. In New Jersey, they get booed from the Continental Arena to Continental Airlines. At least each player has a home court where the fans love him, at least some of the time. The refs don't have anyplace.

I listen to some of the commentators complaining about how the refs let things go nowadays, how NBA players travel all the time, about how the guards palm the ball. But I got news for those guys, especially those older guys. Bob Cousy ain't playing no more. Players today are faster, stronger, and better. This is a different game, a different time. We got the best officials in any sport, any league, and the refs here, they'll let things go, as long as they let it go for everyone. There are a few exceptions, but only when a player has been doing something his entire career, and to start calling him on it now would be to hurt him.

People—usually Chicago fans—have been complaining for years that Patrick Ewing takes an extra step when he's going across the lane for that running jumper of his. Well, hell, if he's been doing it for years, what's going to happen when the refs start calling it now? I'll tell you what's going to happen. Patrick's going to lose about 6 or 8 points a game off his average. You think anyone wants that? So the refs don't call it. And it's smart of them not to.

If you're an NBA player, you learn to respect the refs. And you learn some other things, too. You learn that elephant balls ain't the only elephant things that refs got. I'm talking about their memory. If you show up a ref by yelling and gesturing to the crowd, especially if you're a rookie, then that ref is going to remember you, and you're not going to catch any breaks for a long time. So my advice to rookies is, when you get whistled for something, keep your mouth shut, because no matter how much you want to say something, it ain't going to be worth it.

Even the best refs miss calls sometimes. Illegal defenses, for example. And you *know* that teams use illegal defenses. Coaches say, "We're gonna make 'em call it on us." And sometimes they just don't.

Refs have it tough, and that's just one reason I didn't like the fact that some refs were thrown out of the league because of cheating on their taxes. They were allowed back in, eventually, but the NBA didn't handle it right. David Stern shouldn't have had anything to do with that. That's between them and the government, you know? How many times have athletes got caught with drugs, beating their wives, and that's not to mention cheating on their taxes, too? A bunch of baseball players got caught pretty recently, but they were allowed back in the league. Now David Stern comes and takes a guy who's been working for twenty-five years and takes his livelihood away from him. You should never take a person's livelihood away. These guys screwed up, so be it. They made a mistake and didn't report it to the government, and they're dealing with it. Everybody deserves a second chance. They should have been able to come back right away. Don't tell me that David Stern never "forgot" to put something down. We're all going to use the word "forgot." We all "forgot" to put something down on our taxes. I think it was wrong what the refs did. But I think it was a black eye for the league the way they handled it. We should have stuck by our referees. I told every referee that. I messed up my first two years in the league, and the league gave me a second chance. They should have given it to the referees immediately.

Chapter 13

What's Young & Skinny &

Can Do a 580-Degree-Double-

Pump-Backward Jam but

Doesn't Know How to Shoot

a Jump Shot or Set

a Back-Side Pick?

Meet the Future of the NBA

Can you name a great young jump shooter? Nah, I didn't think so.

The only ones who can sell sneakers today hitting jump shots are Glen Rice and Reggie Miller. Maybe Chris Mullin when he was in his prime. And that's it. And there's only one reason an NBA player can't hit a jump shot. Only reason you can't hit a jump shot is that you haven't shot enough of them. Young players don't believe they have to practice them *or* shoot them in games. They look at sneaker commercials, and they say, "You know what? My jumper'll be off today. I'll just go to the hole and keep dunkin', or I'll get fouled."

Honest to God, that's how they think. They want to dunk. When they turn on ESPN, when they hear "duh, duh, duh" or "duh, duh, duh, duh, duh, duh," they know they aren't going to be looking at no jumper from the corner. They're going to be looking at someone spinning around, doing a hook dunk backward on somebody.

You Don't Get Points for Degree of Difficulty

Whenever a player worries about dunking, he's in trouble. How often do you think the Chicago Bulls worried about dunks when they were winning all those championships? You think the Utah Jazz, as great as they are, lose a lot of sleep over how many dunks they're getting? Or the San Antonio Spurs? When you're losing, you're worried about the dunk, because only one person can dunk. When you're worried about the dunk, you're mostly worried about its aftereffects, because you want to be on *Sports Center,* and you're thinking, "How's this dunk gonna look?" In the meantime, your team is 25 and 50, and you're shooting 20 percent.

The Little Things Count

A lot of the kids coming into the league today don't do the little things. Things like backdoor cuts, hitting the open man, picking away from the ball. Part of it's the ESPN stuff, but players are worse now than they used to be. No one wants to get hurt; nobody wants to give their body up for their team. You wanna know one reason I'm making so much money now? Because nobody can do what I do in this league anymore. Charles Oakley is older, Charles Barkley is worn down, Dennis Rodman is over. I'm the best offensive rebounder in basketball history. I also set picks, I dive on loose balls, I can hit the little fifteen-foot jumper. I can get 14, 15 points a game, fifteen rebounds, and not many other players want to do that anymore. Even guys who make $100 million, they want to get 18 points and six rebounds, but not set one pick. They just want to do the things they think the crowd notices—the flashy dunk, the behind-the-back pass. I believe you have to play the total game. But not enough young players today believe that. Not enough young guys today play with heart and passion.

Antoine Who?

It's not like when I came in the league, ten years ago. Back then, you had to *be* a superstar to have a sneaker named after you. Now young kids come in, they're already entertainers, they don't have to earn their stripes. David Stern has made the NBA entertainment. Kids come into the league now, they're pushing product before they even *take* a jump shot. They are believing the promise of themselves.

Here's what I mean: We were playing a preseason game in Boston in '97, and our rookie, Keith Van Horn, was guarding Antoine Walker. And Antoine is saying, "This boy can't check me. He's a rookie." And "Gimme the ball. I'm going to show the rook something." Antoine won't shut up. He's giving me a headache. And during a time-out, I go over to the bench and I say, "How long has Antoine Walker been in the league?" I really didn't know. It turns out it's his second year. His second frigging year and he's yapping about his "I'm going to show the rookie" stuff. I couldn't believe it.

When Rookies Were Treated Like Rookies

Used to be, rookies were treated like rookies, and if you were a second-year player, you weren't treated a whole lot better. The refs wouldn't even remember your name. The refs will still make it a point not to know your name, or to pretend not to know your name, until you've been in three years. They do that to let the young players know that they're beginners.

Nowadays, among the players, when a rookie can come in and have a sudden impact—especially on a team that's been losing—no one wants to get him mad. A couple years ago, right when they came into the league, was anyone going to be abusing Allen Iverson or Tim Duncan? But back when I was a rookie, some of the veterans were downright mean. The good guys would take you under their wings. The bad guys wouldn't.

Bill Laimbeer and Rick Mahorn—I'm not saying they're bad guys, but they were hard when it came to rookies—they wouldn't even talk to you your first year. They just would not do it. And the veterans were always making the rookies do stuff like carry bags and fetch donuts. When I was a rookie, Rick Mahorn and Charles Barkley wanted a wake-up call from me at 6:30 in the morning one day, and they wanted donuts, but neither one could have whipped my butt, so I never worried about it. If they would have asked me nicely to bring them some donuts, I would have done it. I bring donuts to my teammates every day now, but it's because I *want* to bring donuts, not because anyone's *telling* me to bring donuts.

Today, you don't see many rookies carrying donuts for anyone. That's because today, anyone can read about great basketball players who are fifteen years old. Fifteen years old! And I hear about hockey players who are getting picked out, and groomed and taken care of, when they're ten years old. Treated like big shots at ten years old!

How do you expect a twenty-year-old kid to sign your kid's autograph when that twenty-year-old has been signing autographs since he was ten years old? He's been Mr. Big since he was just a squirt, and now he doesn't have time for anyone, especially you and your damn kid. We're creating our own monsters.

Me & Jimmy Hoffa

You know why teams are giving away first-round picks? 'Cause there's no such thing as a draft any longer. All the kids are coming out in the first year after college, or sometimes the second year. A lot of years, you don't have very good players in the draft. Until the league learns, until they put a cap on—say a guy has to play at least three years in college, get a certain amount of credits to come into this league—I think the NBA is being shortsighted. We don't need any more young stars, any more seventeen-year-olds. First of all, if a kid can come in here at seventeen and do what a man twenty-five can do, then that takes away from what the man can do. Plus, you're hurting the college game.

Too many kids coming into the league are wild. And that's because you got a lot of kids who leave college too early and get in trouble—knuckleheads. You know what college does? College doesn't make you any smarter than you were in high school. You're not going to learn much bookwise in college except for your major. But the important thing is you're learning how to deal with other people and responsibility. You're learning that you have a class at one o'clock and then you have another class at five. It's not like you've got classes all day and you have to be there. In college you've got time to go home, then you realize, "Oh, I got to get back to school." That's responsibility. And you learn how to deal with different people. Especially if you've come from an all-white high school or an all-black high school. In college you learn how to deal with a black guy, a Chinese, a Mexican. You learn social skills. College lets you know how to deal with people in different situations, different cultures, different races. It puts you with different persons in different situations.

Look at Tim Duncan and Keith Van Horn when they were rookies. They were kids who came in, they were articulate, they knew how to deal with people, they knew how to deal with pressure, because they'd been dealing with it for four years. When kids don't have that, they come in and they make mistakes. You give a kid with little or no college $3 million and he feels like he can do no wrong. As wild as I was after four years of college—a knucklehead with a degree—if I had come into the NBA when I was a teenager, me and Jimmy Hoffa would be lying right next to each other right now, telling war stories to each other.

The MTV Generation

Basketball is more like the World Wrestling Federation now than a real professional sport. We have done such a great job of marketing the younger players, the older players all seem to be forgotten. The new kids come in, and the sneaker companies want to give them a contract right away, but first they want to see you dunk on someone. It's only the older players who want to run the give-and-go, the pick-and-roll. The kids today are thinking, Who can make the best video, who can make the best commercial? They're thinking, Who can star in the most movies? Who can be on MTV the most?

It's not just the NBA. It's society. And the NBA changes with society. You look at MTV, and you'll see how the NBA is changing. A few years ago it was all the gangsta stuff, the hard-core rap. And you had players who seemed to embody that. You had a lot of knuckleheads coming into the league then. But then MTV changed to the grunge stuff, more pop, and you started getting more of the pop kind of guys, not quite as much attitude. Whatever you see MTV doing, that's most likely what the NBA will be doing.

Great Expectations

The last few years, two of the rookies everyone has talked about have been Allen Iverson and Kobe Bryant. And a lot of the talk was bad, and unfair. With Kobe, everyone kept saying he would be the next Michael Jordan, and then when he wasn't, he got criticized. Kobe Bryant is a good player. He's a very good player. But it's unfair to compare him to Michael Jordan. What people still don't understand is there will never be another Michael Jordan. A few years ago the two best players in the league were Michael Jordan and Scottie Pippen. If Michael Jordan was a 100 on the scale of basketball greatness, Scottie was about a 50. That's how great Michael Jordan was. Michael Jordan came into this league and he was scoring 30 points his first year. He also came out of a strong college program, with strong fundamentals. He was also one of the five strongest players in the league, and he had the most vicious killer instinct. Kobe wasn't any of those things. He wasn't as fundamentally sound, he wasn't near the top five strongest players in the league, and no one has the killer instinct that Michael did. So it was unfair to compare them.

Allen Iverson, though, he came into this league a major talent. Then he got busted with some friends for speeding, and there was a gun and some reefer in the car, and he got crucified. Everything that's wrong with the NBA, bad kid, out of control—that's what they said about Allen. Hey, I owned a gun once. One of my friends fired it in a parking lot and I took the blame. That's because I was raised to be Mickey the Dunce. You know, no matter what, you never rat on anybody (my experience in the YMCA notwithstanding). So I took the blame. When you're young, and Allen Iverson was young when he first came into the league, you're always going to have an entourage. You consider them your friends, and whether they really are or not, you learn that over the years. Well, I had my friends, Allen's got his. And I got in trouble, but I didn't get crucified like Allen did. I think the league might have considered my friends more acceptable than Allen's, because a lot of my friends were young Italian guys and Allen's friends were young African Americans.

I think part of Allen Iverson's problems might have been the unintentional result of college coach John Thompson. I respect John Thompson for a lot of things he did, but I do not agree with him in the way he kept such a tight rein on his players, how he wouldn't let them talk to the media. College should be about dealing with all kinds of different people and different pressures. How are kids going to learn how to do that if they can't ever talk to reporters?

I think it especially hurts the guys who don't end up in the NBA. Those guys, they finish at Georgetown and then they go out for a job interview, and the interviewer says, "Well, I know you played at Georgetown, but I never knew you had a personality. I don't know nothing about you, because you never said nothing in school." That's why I think Thompson should have given his guys the opportunity to articulate their thoughts to the media, even if it would have been a struggle sometimes.

What I say about Allen is, before you crucify him, look at yourself: What did you do when you were twenty-one? Everybody makes mistakes. I don't care if it's a twenty-one-year-old accountant, a twenty-one-year-old ballplayer, a twenty-one-year-old schoolteacher. And how do you think that accountant would be acting if he had a $40-million sneaker contract? I was no better than Allen when I was twenty-one. He'll learn, like I did.

In the meantime, don't crucify the kid. All that going out and running around will grow old with him. For now, let him go out and have his fun as long as he's not hurting anybody. He's entitled.

And a Child Shall Lead Them

As much as the old guys might be pissed off at some of the young knuckleheads coming into the league, it's in our best interest to be open-minded and to treat them nice. Because you never can tell when a future Hall of Famer is the goofy kid you're telling to fetch you donuts. When Keith Van Horn got drafted a few years ago, all that a lot of the players thought about him was he was white, skinny, looked about twelve years old. No one was exactly doing cartwheels. Then I practiced with him one day. The kid hit nineteen three-pointers in a row, and I mean from deep. And they were all with a guy sticking his hand in Keith's face. The twentieth one he misses, it bounces off the rim, and Keith runs in, gets the rebound in midair, double-cocks it, and dunks the ball. I mean, he *slams* it in. I immediately ran to Cal and apologized for every bad thing I'd ever said or did. I said, "I'm sorry I ever said I wanted to be traded. I want to play on the Nets forever now. I want to play with this boy." He wasn't just a great rookie, he was a great player. He could already shoot, drive, jump, everything. I knew he was our franchise.

But there were some guys on the team, even after they saw him, they didn't believe he was the franchise, and they didn't want to give the ball away. They thought, Hey, I'm a twenty-point scorer and I've been a star in this league before and hey, this is *my* team. But those guys weren't seeing reality, or they were just being selfish.

I told those guys, "This team belongs to Keith Van Horn for the next ten seasons. And when he's open, you *better* give him the ball." I told them that after Keith's rookie year, you know what he'll do to guys who still don't pass him the ball? I told them Keith would be able to yawn a command to the front office. I said he'll be able to just casually say, "Ah, ahem, get him outta here." And I told the guys that if Keith does that, that guy would be gone. I told them it would be best to stay on his good side, or they'd be in New Mexico or some other place they might have a CBA team. I think most of 'em listened, but if you check the little print in the sports pages and you see any former New Jersey Nets playing in New Mexico, you'll be able to figure out who wasn't paying attention.

 **Trash-Talking,**

Violence, Toughness &

Why Most Seven-Footers with

Big Muscles Wouldn't Know

What to Do If They Ever Got

in a Fight

 There are quite a few people in the league who think they're tough. They grew up somewhere in Virginia or some suburb. And they think all of a sudden they get in the NBA and they got a Nike commercial that they're a hard case. You see these guys, they talk junk during a game, like they want to fight. And who stops 'em? These guys are 6'11", 250, 260 pounds, and who breaks up the fight? A little referee who's about 5'8", 140 pounds. Get the hell out of here! Gimme a break. Those big pansies never wanted to fight in the first place.

Or you got guys like Dikembe Mutombo and Alonzo Mourning, they all got that Georgetown shtick to 'em. They try to intimidate you, they don't shake your hand on jump balls, stuff like that. What they don't understand is it's a basketball game, it ain't a knife fight. It ain't life or death. How the hell are you going to scare somebody in a basketball game? If you get scared of somebody else in a basketball game, then you shouldn't be in this league.

Tough Guys

Most of the big guys in this league have never been in a fight, and it's because they're so big and strong. They never *had* to be in a fight. And now they don't know how to fight, so they don't want to. The guys who are *really* tough in the NBA are the ones who grew up small, on the streets, the ones who had to fight in order to get by. Like me, because I haven't been big my whole life. Or the guys who are just flat-out tough, like Michael Jordan and Charles Oakley. Or the unpredictable guys, like Vernon Maxwell and Charles Shackleford. Or the guys who no one can figure out, and everyone gave up trying a long time ago, like Armen Gilliam.

One of the toughest guys I ever played against, or with, was a point guard. Scott Skiles. The man stood about about four foot five, couldn't jump, slow as a mule, but I'll tell you what: If you give him something physical—even by accident—he was going to give it back to you, hard.

He was playing with Orlando, and Shaq was a rookie then. And they had a play where Skiles would come across and set a pick on Shaq's man, who was me. So I'd step back five or six feet and and get a running start, and Skiles would be running to set a pick, and, bam, I'd knock him down. And I would do this three or four times, every time he called the play. You do that just once to most point guards, they'll quit calling the play. They're not stupid. But you know what? The scrubby little four-foot-five point guard kept calling the play. He kept calling it till I wanted him to quit. He was tough.

Another tough guy is Charles Oakley. Oak's got a great heart, he's a nice guy, loves kids, and does a lot of charity work. But when he steps on the court, or when he feels like someone's challenging him, he just puts on this persona. Mean. One time we were out at a club. Charles and I and about thirty-five guys. And one of these guys makes a wiseacre remark. And Charles goes over to this group of guys, says, "Which one of you mothers said something? Let's go. I'll whip all of you!"

Thirty-five people shut up, just quit talking. It would have been

Charles and me against these thirty-five guys, and I don't care how small they were or how big we were, with two on thirty-five, the two got some problems, unless the two are Jackie Chan and Bruce Lee. But that's the kind of guy Oak is.

They Don't Call Him Mad Max for Nothing

One guy I'd want in the foxhole with me is Vernon Maxwell. Absolutely one of the toughest guys in the league. Pure heart, and to go with it absolutely no idea that there are certain things you cannot do in this world. That's what makes him so dangerous. Vernon didn't take nothing from nobody. One time he got into it with Carl Herrera on the Rockets, when they were teammates, and they decided they were going to meet in the weight room and fight. So Carl gets there first and while he's waiting for Vernon he's doing some biceps curls. Vernon walks in a minute later, sees Carl doing the curls. Vernon grabs a ten-pound dumbbell, walks up behind Carl, and, *bong!*, throws it at Carl, hits him behind the head. End of fight.

Vernon would say stuff to your face, he'd throw a dumbbell at you. Hell, he even fought Hakeem a few times. Vernon was one guy other NBA players didn't want to mess with.

Naked

Armen Gilliam is a quiet tough guy, as I've mentioned. Very proper and articulate. He really didn't get so excited verbally, he'd just give you a look like he's going to kick your butt in the locker room. I've seen a lot of people try Armen Gilliam. Armen's father was a heavyweight contender. And Armen grew up boxing. Armen, he'd hit you four or five times before you put your hands up. Derrick Coleman's a good fighter but Derrick Coleman learned that from Armen Gilliam. Armen wasn't about talking. Charles Barkley and Derrick talked all kinds of smack to him. You know what he told them? He said, "Look, you can talk all night, but if you man enough, just put your hands up and we can get this over with. Just put your hands on me and we'll get it over with."

And they never put their hands on him.

I'll tell you something else about Armen. He's a guy who, once he's mad, talking isn't going to help anyone. One game Pearl Washington cheap-shotted him, and Armen took a swing, and they both got thrown out of the game. But Armen wasn't done. He didn't think he'd exacted what he wanted to exact. So he snuck in the locker room where Pearl was taking a shower. Armen wanted to fight some more.

Pearl ran out, soap all over him, Armen chasing him. Didn't quite make it to the concourse, which is a good thing. Would have scared a bunch of the little kids there.

Swings & Misses

Armen carries a big stick and makes no noise. A lot of other guys in the NBA, they make lots of noise but they don't carry no stick at all.

There are a lot of big talkers in the league. And if there's one thing I hate it's the guys who talk on the court, then don't back it up after the game's over. Those are the guys who when the game's over, they're the first ones showered and on the bus, and you can't find them. There are four guys who have agreed to meet me after the game to fight since I've been in this league, and every one of them, when we met in the parking lot, the first thing they said was, "Hey, man, I'm sorry, we don't have to fight."

The truth is the fights you see on the court are more like *Jerry Springer Show* fights than real fights. A lot of misses. With the money they charge for landing a punch in the NBA, a lot of people do a lot more ducking than punching.

I always believe if somebody really wants to fight, and they're really heated, then after the game, we'll just find us a little saloon that we both can afford to tear up, and we'll lock ourselves in there. And that goes for anybody. And then you take your business there, but you don't take care of business in front of the kids. I did that when I was a young knucklehead in the league, and I refuse to do it again. Because it's a bad example for the kids, and because I don't want to give the NBA any of my money for fines.

Have Some Gatorade

Speaking of being a young knucklehead, when I was with the Sixers, there was a guy who used to give me a real hard time. The few times I did get in a game, he'd always yell and scream and call me names and say I was a lazy bum.

I heard him. NBA players hear the fans, especially the ones close to the floor, screaming real loud, like this guy was. And as long as you're playing hard, you can't worry too much about what people are saying, because they paid sixty-five dollars or whatever to come there and yell and do what they want. As long as they don't put their hands on me, or throw anything at me, I'm usually okay.

But this guy was bugging me. And I could never figure out exactly who he was, because he would stand up and holler when I was shooting free throws, and I couldn't look in the stands then, and then he'd sit down real quick after the shot.

So I got some of my boys to sit in the section I thought he was yelling from. We got fifty tickets for each game, so I gave all fifty of them to my boys and I put them in the section I thought the guy was in and I asked them to look for this loudmouth. But I must have put them in the wrong section, because they couldn't find him.

So the next game I tried another plan. The first time I shot a free throw, I faked. I faked like I was going to shoot, and then I stopped and looked real fast at the stands. And sure enough, he had jumped up and was yelling.

After the game, before I even change, I ask him to come down and talk. He's still heckling and cursing me. I say, "Hey, I just wanna give you an autograph and talk with you a little."

He comes down and throws a beer at me, but misses. I take the whole big container of Gatorade, the one you're always seeing the football coaches get doused with, and I throw it on him. Rod Thorn from the NBA sees the incident and the league fines me $2,500. Best $2,500 I ever spent.

Strong-Man Competition

There are other ways than fighting to prove who's strong. I have challenged any player in the league to come to my gym and see who can clean, jerk, and snatch the most weight over their head. I'm the strongest guy in the league, and I've told all the other players I'll bet any of 'em $25,000 they can't beat me. Charles Oakley and I had a little competition one morning, about 3:30 A.M., and I beat him.

Last I heard, Kevin Willis said he was going to take the bet. He wanted to make it just the bench press. But he would have an advantage there because he's got alligator arms. Short, stubby things compared to the rest of his body. So I'm sticking with my original challenge.

The Protection Racket

If you're a tough guy in this league, one of your responsibilities is to protect your teammates who maybe aren't quite as tough. Especially the ones who have nice jump shots and fat scoring averages. Keith Van Horn is the best scorer on the Nets, but he ain't no Charles Bronson. I tell him, "Keith, you didn't grow up in no ghetto, no matter what you say about the Mexicans, and you're a lot of things, but one thing you ain't is a fighter."

Keith got a whole lot of hard fouls his first year. I'd tell him, "Just keep playing. You let me handle any retaliation. You let me get thrown out of the game." Keith never lost his cool.

Even one night in Miami, when a guard named Keith Askins almost killed him. Keith was driving for a layup, and Askins wrapped him in a headlock and threw him to the floor.

I was on the bench at the time, and I went crazy. Here's the future of our team, and this idiot from Miami's almost killing him. Just a dirty play, flat-out dirty. I was going to do something.

Alonzo Mourning saw how mad I was and he tried to calm me down. He walked over to me. "Jay," he said, "let it go. He was wrong. Just let it go."

I knew what would happen to a player getting off the bench and going after someone. So I tried to stay calm. And I told Alonzo, "We play you guys in New Jersey in a couple nights. And when you come up there, I'm taking his butt out. I am taking it out."

The refs must have heard what I was saying because not only did they throw Askins out of the game, they suspended him for the game in New Jersey. I was hoping and praying they'd let him play. Because I was going to go out and take vengeance.

After the game where Askins tackled Keith, I'm standing outside the locker room, and Keith's wife comes up. She's all upset. She's crying.

"Why didn't you protect Keith?" she yells at me. "You're supposed to protect him out there. What's wrong with you?"

And that ticked me off even more.

Why Life in the NBA's Not Fair

When you're just coming into the league, you'll get tested, you'll get challenged, you'll get fouled. But the truth is, if you get to that level where you're up there with the very best players in the league, a lot of times you won't get fouled. The first year I was an All-Star, when I'd be going up for a dunk, the other players didn't challenge me too much. They were like, "Oh, he's going to make that one, why hit him?" Whereas a rookie or a midlevel player going up for a dunk, he'll get hammered. Coaches and some fans might not like hearing that, but it's true. The other thing that players wouldn't do, especially the last five or six years he was playing, is they wouldn't do anything that might hurt Michael Jordan. Not that anyone was easy on him, but if he was going up for a dunk, and the only way to block it meant risking hurting Michael, most of the players would let him dunk. NBA players aren't dumb. We knew how much he meant to the league. And we knew how much he made all of us richer.

Big Daddy & the Gorilla

My father, Big Daddy, grew up down South, and he was tough from just about the minute he was born. When he was nineteen, he went to the county fair outside Ritter, and he lost all his money playing three-card monte. He knows he's going to get in trouble when he gets home with no money, so when the carnival folks—the carnies—tell him, "If you go in this here ring with this gorilla, we will give you ten dollars a minute," of course he goes. That was big money then.

So my dad gets in there, and here's this 500-pound gorilla. My dad grabs the gorilla from behind, right around the chest, and he thinks he's going to get rich now. He's counting those bills already. Then, all of a sudden, he says it felt like a balloon, that gorilla's chest, just getting bigger and bigger. My father's hands pop off and this gorilla turns around and my dad can see the gorilla's eyes.

"They were completely red."

That's the line my dad always uses when he tells that story. "Those eyes were completely red."

And the gorilla runs across the cage and bounces off a tire. Then he comes running back and knocks my dad down. Then he knocks him down again. And a few more times. And he's biting and scratching him. The state police had to come get my father out of there. But he was in there a whole minute. That tells you what kind of father I have.

Southern Discomfort

My mom and dad took me down to South Carolina when I was just finishing first grade, and we stayed there for three years. My dad was always a strict disciplinarian, but some of the worst trouble I ever got in, and some of the biggest lessons I ever learned, happened down South. If I'm tough, my years in South Carolina helped make me that way.

Once when I was at school, I was doodling on a piece of

homework paper. I swear I'm not exactly sure how it happened, but what came out was a picture of a billy goat with my teacher's face on it. My father used to check my homework every night at the dinner table, and this night he checks, and sees the billy goat drawing.

"What are you trying to do?" he asks. "Make fun of your teacher?"

"No, Dad," I say. "I don't know how it happened. I was just doodling."

But he calls up my teacher. In South Carolina, back then, parents knew all the teachers.

"Miss S———," he says, "is my son doing all right in school?"

"No, sir, Mr. Williams, he is not," she says. Miss S——— is an old white lady. And I'm listening, and I'm thinking, Uh-oh!

When my father gets off the phone he turns to me and he says, "Well, I'll be up there in the morning to the schoolhouse. And I have to pay a visit to your brother Stacy's classroom, too, because he's been acting up as well."

See, in South Carolina you used to get a beating in school. The teachers were allowed to beat you. And you know what? Sometimes the teachers used to make you beat each other. Like if you both got caught talking, the teacher might make you beat your friend's butt. And if you take it easy on him, the teacher'll beat *your* butt. So life for a fourth grader in Ritter, South Carolina, was no picnic. But now I was going to have to face something worse than the usual teacher whipping.

That next morning my father wakes up and says, "I'll be at the schoolhouse. You go ahead."

"Oh, Daddy," I say, "please, don't. Don't, Daddy."

He says one word. "Boy," he says. And that's enough. My father would never raise his voice. But he got his message across.

So I'm sitting at my desk, and I know he's coming at about nine o'clock. And sure enough, right at nine, there's a loud knock on the classroom door. Scariest sound I ever heard. It's the principal, and he comes in and he says, "Miss S———, Jayson Williams' father would like to talk to his son in front of the whole class."

My father gets up there and he says, "Now, boys and girls, I want you to know I love my son. But sometimes he thinks he's just a clown in front of you all. So I'm going to do something today to teach him he isn't a clown."

All my classmates are all goggle-eyed. And then my father says, "And for the rest of you who think you're clowns, some of your parents should do the same thing I'm doing today."

Then he tells me to come up there, and he says, "I'm going to teach you what humility is today." And he whips my butt. And I try to crawl through his legs to the door, and he catches my head between his legs and just tore my butt up. Sore for days.

And now he's going to the classroom next door, to get my brother Stacy. And Stacy sees him coming in the door and he jumps out the window and runs home. Stacy wasn't living with us; he was living with his mom, my dad's first wife. So he's safe that night. But Stacy ends up getting a lot worse.

Because that Sunday, while we're playing baseball—that was the only thing to do in Ritter on Sunday, and all six hundred people in the town would come watch—Stacy's at third base, waiting for a ground ball. And all of a sudden here comes my father's '73 Thunderbird, with his license plates that said ".45 Magnum." He comes tearing through the parking lot, spins around, he jumps out and catches Stacy at third base. Whips his butt in front of six hundred people.

Rack 'Em Up

My dad owned a pool hall down South, and that's another place I learned about discipline and toughness and standing up for yourself. I wasn't supposed to go in there, because I was so young, but of course, I would hang out there a lot and just try not to get caught.

One time I play a game against a guy named Grant. Grant's about nineteen, and I'm only ten, but I whip him. I tell him to give me the quarter he owes me. But he won't. I call him all kinds of names, and he hits me with his pool stick, but he still won't give up the quarter. "I'm gonna call Big Daddy," I say, and Grant just laughs. "Go 'head and call that potbellied old man," he says.

A few minutes later here comes that '73 Thunderbird with the ".45 Magnum" plates, swerving up. Grant's sitting on a stump outside the pool hall, holding his pool stick. And out from the car comes Big Daddy and he takes Grant's pool stick and breaks it right on Grant's stomach.

Grant takes one of those little bottles of beer and throws it and hits my father on the head with it. My dad goes back into his car and reaches in the glove compartment and pulls out his .45 Magnum. Grant starts running and my dad shoots him in the butt. Then Grant's lying in the road, and my dad walks over there and picks him up and puts him in the car and takes him to his mother's house and takes him inside and leaves him. And before he goes, he says, "Don't ever hit my son."

Then he takes me home, and he says, "Didn't I tell you not to be in that poolroom? Now you see what you made me do? I damn near had to kill a fellow over you." Then he rips my butt with a brand-new belt. And he lets me know exactly why he was doing it, like he always did. He would always ask afterward, "Now, why'd you just get that whipping?"

That question was supposed to be part of the instructional value of the whipping. Like the time I went to my friend Eric's house for dinner. There was twenty dollars on the table and Eric said, "Take it and we'll split it at school tomorrow." Well, I got caught, but Eric wouldn't tell his mom and dad that he put me up to it. So my dad whipped me. And when he said, "Now, why'd you just get that whipping?," I said, "Because I stole?" And then he said, "And what did you learn?" And because I was stubborn, and because I was so pissed off at Eric and his parents and my dad, I said, "Never to go to somebody's house for dinner again."

And I didn't. That's how stubborn I was. For about fifteen years I never would eat dinner at anyone's house but my own family.

By the Book

Getting whipped by my dad was bad. But getting whipped by his mom, my Grandma Elvira, was worse. Grandma Elvira had a sister,

Edith, my great-aunt, and the two of them made a team. Aunt Edith was a holy woman. She did something called "turning the Bible." In South Carolina there were a few people who could do it. What would happen is, if someone stole something, whoever it got stolen from would call Aunt Edith. And Aunt Edith would put a Bible in front of her, and you'd sit down and she'd start talking to the Bible. She'd say, "Well, did so-and-so steal it?" Nothing. Then she'd say, "Well, did Stacy steal it?" Nothing. Then, "Did Jayson steal it?" And the Bible would shake. And she'd ask where the hiding place was, and the Bible would fall and it would open to a page that described where the money was hidden.

I know it sounds crazy, but I saw it. I stole three dollars in quarters from my Aunt Edith and she turned the Bible, and she knew it was me, and that the quarters were under the shed, right where I'd hid them. There's no other way she could have known it.

I'll tell you what. After Aunt Edith turned the Bible and found out you'd done something bad, then you were *really* in trouble. Because Aunt Edith would tell her sister, Grandma Elvira, and Grandma Elvira would beat your butt with an extension cord. And if you were smart, you'd take your licks from that friggin' extension cord. Because if you complained about the extension cord, you'd get the switch. Grandma Elvira would make you go outside and get your own switch to get your butt beaten with. And if you came back with a little one, she would go out there and pull a whole tree down and whip your butt with it. So with Aunt Edith and Grandma Elvira, you learned to be honest—and to take the extension cord.

Ball Four

Family was extremely important to my father. Even though he had seven children by his first wife, he wanted everyone to get along. Once two of my brothers were playing baseball against each other. Stacy, the window jumper, he was pitching and Gregory was batting. Stacy was about fifteen then, and Gregory was thirteen. And Stacy's throwing high, hard fastballs, right at Gregory's head. Throws three in a row. Gregory says, "You better not throw another one up there." So sure enough, Stacy smokes one right at his head and hits him.

Gregory runs inside to the house where I live and he grabs the loaded .410 shotgun. He comes back out and shoots Stacy, twice. In the legs and back. At the time, my dad was working in New York, but he came back as soon as he heard. And as soon as Stacy gets out of the hospital, my dad locks him and Gregory in the same room. Just locks them in there, with one bed, and gives 'em food and keeps 'em locked in there till they start to get along. And after a few days, they got along. And they still get along.

Southern Gothic

It might sound like we had a wild, crazy family, but in fact, in Ritter, South Carolina, we were the peaceful, civilized ones.

There was a family that lived near us, and they had three boys, and let's say their names were Huey, Dewey, and Louie. Their real names were even weirder, but let's call 'em that. Well, they lived in an old farmhouse, and they didn't have electricity or any running water. We used to play together all the time.

I was eight at the time, and Huey, who was fourteen, was in the same grade with me. So that tells you something about the educational system in South Carolina. One day I'm on the school bus, and we're waiting on Huey. From the bus, us kids hear one of our neighbors, an old lady named Mabel Kinsley, yelling. She's yelling, "Huey, boy, get out of my pigpen. Gwan, get outta there, Huey."

And this big sow is squealing. *"Eeeeeee. Eeeee."* Huey was screwing this pig, I swear to God. Huey goes, "Right in a minute, Miss Mabel, I'm almost finished."

And he comes out of the pigpen, zips up his pants, and gets on the school bus with us like nothing special is happening.

Huey's brother Dewey was my grandmother's favorite. And one day he's sitting under her oak tree. Grandma Elvira and I are sitting on the porch and it starts to rain. And she yells out, "Dewey, come on up out from under that tree. I don't want you to get struck by no lightning."

"I'm all right, Grandma Elvira," Dewey says. Everyone called her Grandma Elvira, even the neighbor kids.

Grandma Elvira and I walk in the house then and *ka-bammm!,* there's a big thunderclap and we come back out and there's a bunch of smoke by the oak tree and Dewey's lying there, dead.

Louie, the other son, he goes and drinks a gallon of moonshine, and it makes him retarded. He's about sixteen and he's already married with a little girl. But now he's retarded. About a year after the moonshine, he falls asleep with a cigarette in his mouth, burns down the house, kills himself, his daughter, and his three nephews.

Huey's the only one still living. He got arrested for raping his aunt, then killing her.

Those were the kids I used to play with every day. Just one more reason I don't get too worked up when someone in the NBA starts acting crazy. Because I know what *real* crazy is.

Itchy

When we moved to South Carolina, I was finishing first grade. And then the school down there decided I should skip second. But then they held me back in fourth. And my parents saw kids like Huey, and I think they decided the school system there wasn't producing no Rhodes scholars, so we moved back to New York City.

And while Ritter, South Carolina, makes a kid tough, New York City doesn't produce any marshmallows, either. In fact, growing up in the city is one reason why my father used to have to whip my butt so much, and why I had to whip my children's butts when I was bringing them up in New York. Because this isn't the suburbs, where you tell your kid, "Don't go play over there," and he goes and plays anyway. And what happens? He comes back in with poison ivy. No big deal. You give the kid some calamine lotion and he's fine. But in New York you tell a youngster not to go play there in that section, he'd better *not* go play, because he might not come back. There might be junkies, derelicts, robbers, murderers, rapists.

In New York City—in *any* city—you can't just love your parents and respect your parents, like they do in the suburbs. In the city you have to love, respect, and also *fear* your parents. Because when you're a young lad, you're going to try and break the rules just for the thrill of breaking the rules. That's the way it is everywhere, with all young boys. So if you're in the city, you have to think, Now, if I break these rules, I'm going to get my butt whipped. And that might make your butt not do it.

When Gangs Were Good

Back in New York, when I was just a youngster, I got involved with gangs. Not the kind of gangs with guns, like you have nowadays. A good clean gang, if there is such a thing. That's what it seemed like to me. There was a lot of fighting and stealing between the gangs, but you stuck up for your guys. One time during a bus strike, some kids came over from Brooklyn stealing bikes. I think they were selling 'em to people who needed to get to work.

These kids tried to steal my bike right from under me, because I was a skinny little kid. But I wouldn't give it up. These Brooklyn kids—they must have been about sixteen and I was about twelve then—they went to work on me. I put my hands through the spokes and locked 'em together, and they just went to work on me.

By the time they got my bike, some of my boys from my gang could see what was happening. Frankie and Vinnie and a guy named Tommy saw me getting robbed, and they all started chasing the Brooklyn guys. They couldn't catch the kid on the bike, but they caught the kid who was running and they beat the hell out of him. The kid with the bike ended up getting arrested. I picked him out of a lineup and pressed charges. When I got my bike back, my little odometer said this kid had put four hundred miles on it. In a week! He must have known he was a fugitive or something.

Honor Among Thieves

Some of the really bad kids from the projects used to rob old people coming through the park. Three of the worst kids were named

Butter, Jim, and Edmund, all sixteen-year-olds, and one day I saw them rob an old Chinese man on his way back from grocery shopping. He was like ninety years old, little old wrinkled guy. He could have been Confucius himself.

Butter, Jim, and Edmund threw all his groceries down and took his watch, and they took six dollars from him. Usually they robbed people and ran. But they saw how frail this little Chinese guy was, so they just walked away. It made me feel awful. I helped the old man pick up his groceries and I walked with him into his building. Then I walked over to where I knew the robbers were, and I said, "You're all a bunch of punks! Next time I see you robbin' someone, I'm tellin'!"

The biggest of the three was Edmund. He was a big boy, about six foot five, and he punched me in my chest. I hadn't ever been hit like that in my life. He knocked me down and I couldn't do anything about it. And I couldn't come down out of my apartment for about three days, because I knew Edmund was waiting and he was going to beat me up.

One of my buddies, Boogie, who was with me for the whole thing, he kept saying, "Man, why do you bring this trouble on yourself? Why do you have to agitate those big boys?"

I said, "You can't be robbing old people like that. It's just not right!"

Edmund ended up in jail, for some other robbery he pulled, and he was there almost ten years. And when he came out, I was twenty-two, my second year in the NBA. I was hanging out at the park one day, and Edmund came up all friendly, like, "Hey, Jayson, what's happening?"

And I said, "Hey, you remember me? You remember punching me in my chest?"

"Nah," he said. "Nah, I didn't—"

"Now I'm gonna whip your butt, you punk."

My friends who were with me that day convinced me that Edmund wouldn't be worth it. But I was ready to kill him, all for something he had done ten years earlier. That's how I am sometimes. I have a hard time forgetting when people do me wrong.

Baloney!

Teenagers, as anyone who has ever been one knows, don't want to take anything from anybody. I was no different. I was fourteen years old, hanging outside my neighborhood pizza joint, and a cop named Fitzpatrick from the Seventh Precinct in Manhattan comes up and tells me to move.

"Move," he says. "Move off this block. Get outta here."

I wasn't doing anything but eating my pizza, and my friends were watching, so I decided to play it cool.

"Me?" I say.

"Yeah, you. Move outta here."

"Me?"

Fitzpatrick comes over to move me. He goes to put his hands on me. And I'm already a good fighter so, *pom-pa!,* I hit him a couple of times and he goes down. He's grabbing for his gun to shoot me now, and his partner comes over and grabs it.

"No! Don't shoot him," the partner says.

They arrest me and bring me down to the precinct and another cop there puts his hand on my shoulder, so I shake my shoulder. I know a lot of cops down there, so I figure the lieutenant watching will say, "He's just a young kid. Take it easy on him."

But the guy with his hand on my shoulder cracks me right across the head and the lieutenant doesn't say anything. They take me to the back of the building, and one cop punches me in the chest, another handcuffs me to a hot water pipe. And every time I lean back I hit the hot water pipe.

They put me in a cell with a transvestite, a guy who uses the toilet like a woman and who talks like a woman. And he calls me "hon."

When they bring dinner, he asks me in this real high voice, "Hon, you want that baloney sandwich?"

"Hell, no," I say, "my father will be here in a minute to get me. You can have it."

And at lunch the next day, same thing. "Hon, can I have that baloney sandwich?"

"Yeah, go ahead. My father will be here any minute."

When dinner comes that night, I'm ready.

Before he even says anything, I say, "You're going to have to take that baloney sandwich from me this time. You touch that sandwich, I'll whip your butt. I don't know when my father's coming, but this damn baloney sandwich is mine."

My dad is in South Carolina at the time, and he sends a lawyer to get me, but I got locked up on Friday, so I have to sit in jail all weekend. I never felt so good as when I got out.

It's not that I'm worried about nobody fussing with me in jail. Because I'm not. But I have claustrophobia. Horrible claustrophobia. So I worry about getting stuck in a little place, or being burnt all to hell if a fire breaks out when I'm in jail. That's one reason I built such a big house. Because I cannot stand being confined.

I tell people, when I die I want a big mortuary. I want to be put in a big country house. And leave the door open and don't put me in no box. I don't know what happens when you die. But if you come back, I don't want to have to dig through six feet of dirt. So just leave me in that big country house, leave the door open, and say good-bye.

God's Will

Not only am I a big-shot basketball player in high school, I'm a small-time jailbird and a tough guy. And the other kids know it. And the teachers know it. Even the priests know it. One day I'm in history class with Mr. Donahue, who is a great guy, would give everyone A's for just showing up. Me and my buddy George are sitting there in class pretending to listen to Mr. Donahue, and ten minutes later in walks the school bully, big guy named Jimmy, about six foot three, a drug addict, a guy so mean he was not only terrorizing the whole school, he was terrorizing the whole school down the block, too. Jimmy's always coming in late, disrupting the class, talking back to Mr. Donahue.

George says to me, "I'm tired of this bull. Jay, can't you do something about this? Jimmy's giving Mr. Donahue such a hard time he'll screw things up for everybody. We won't get no A's."

So I go up to the teacher, and I ask him to keep Jimmy after class. And the bell rings and Mr. Donahue leaves and it's the three of us, me and George and Jimmy. George is locking the door. And I say, "Jimmy, why you giving the teacher a hard time? He gives everybody A's."

He says, "Screw you. And screw you, too, George. Why are you closing the door? What—"

Bam! I hit him in the head. Knock him right out. And he hits his head on the desk. Jimmy's not moving. George is saying, "He's dead, he's dead!"

"Dead?" I say. "Oh, Lord!"

Now George is done grieving over Jimmy. Fastest grieving I ever saw. "We gotta get rid of him!" George says. "Let's shove him out the window!"

We're figuring we'll shove him out the fourth-story window, the body'll land in the alley, and then we'll get some help from the local underworld guys to hide it.

We're stuffing him out the window, but this big hoodlum has a big belly, and he's stuck. I'm getting set for the one big final shove when there's this loud knocking on the door. George opens it before I can finish the job, and Mr. Donahue and the school's ten priests walk in.

They pull Jimmy back into the room and Jimmy wakes up and starts yelling. He doesn't know where he is. He goes for one of the priests. So I hit him again and knock him out again.

The rumor going around the school the next day is Jayson and the ten priests knocked out Jimmy the bully. That was kind of cool.

Straight Shooter

Having a reputation as a tough guy can be a good thing. It can also be a weird thing.

Weekends in the summertime I'll have friends out to my house. We barbecue, relax, maybe shoot some baskets. One day we did some target shooting. Wayne Chrebet from the Jets was there, Jason Sehorn from the Giants, and some of my friends I grew up with.

"My boys," I call 'em. We were taking turns shooting the .50-caliber Desert Eagle, the most powerful handgun in the world.

It was my turn, and just as I shot, I heard something behind me and I looked backward. What I didn't realize was that Wayne was right in front of me, kneeling down to pick up one of the cartridges, because he couldn't believe how big it was. So when I fired the gun, it must have been just a few inches from Wayne's face, 'cause the noise knocked him out. Cold. I looked down, and there's Wayne lying there, with gunpowder all over his face. Jason looked at Wayne, and at me, and he tears into the house. I send my boys in to see what's wrong, to make sure he's okay.

I'm sitting there with Wayne, shaking him, and after about thirty seconds, he comes to. He's a tough little guy. And by that time, Jason is peeking his head out one of the windows. But he won't come outside. So I go in, and there's Jason sitting with my boys. Jason says, "Jay, can I speak to you a moment, in private?" We go in to another room. We both sit down.

"If Wayne was dead," he says, "your boys would have killed me, wouldn't they? That's what you sent them in here for, wasn't it?"

I look at this guy, and I can't believe it. I'm doing my best to keep from laughing. And I say, with a straight face, "Yeah, man, they sure would have. They would have had to silence you. 'Cause I don't think you could have held that secret."

Soft & Cuddly

Even big, strong guys who get in fights have a soft side. And mine gets activated with kids and with animals.

Back when I was starting in the league I was trying to see how fast my 750 BMW would run. Rick Mahorn had told me it would go 170, so I was on an empty stretch of country road, pushing the pedal.

I'm up to about 165 when I hit something. I slow down, go back, and there in the middle of the road is this little raccoon. I feel real bad, so I go in the trunk of my car and get a first baseman's mitt and I pick up this raccoon and take him home, try to nurse him back to health. I'm giving this wounded raccoon cat food, water, everything I can think of to try to make up for almost killing it with my 750 BMW. Twenty-four hours I'm trying to help this raccoon. But he's not getting any better.

I call the Wildlife Association. Say, "I'm Jayson Williams. I'll pay whatever it costs, I don't care how much. Just come take care of this sick raccoon."

They say okay and I go upstairs and fall asleep. That night my parents come over. I hear my dad yelling, "Holy smokes, Barbara, there's a coon in the house. A raccoon. Get the gun, Barbara, I'm gonna kill it."

I go running downstairs.

"Dad, don't do it! Don't do it! That's my raccoon. I hit it and I'm trying to help it."

He says, "You hit a raccoon, you brought him home, put the thing in the middle of the living room. You going to nurse this raccoon back to health in the middle of your living room?"

Luckily the wildlife people came the next day.

Cost-Benefit Analysis

Getting in all the scrapes I have got me a reputation. And it's not a reputation that really helped me. So the past few years I've really tried to behave better, to give people room, to stay away from violence and guns and stuff. And it's worked. The summer of 1998, I signed a big contract with Bob's, a chain of stores in New Jersey. I go in, sign some stuff, and they give me a lot of money. One day my dad came with me to Bob's.

During a break, I said, "Dang! If I would have known I could have made all this money by being a good man, I would have stopped all the fighting and drinking and stuff eight years ago."

My dad looked at me. He said, "If *I'd* have known all the money you could make being a good man, I'd have been whipping your butt even harder *ten* years ago."

Matters of Life and Death

Both my sisters, who were also my best friends, died when I was just a youngster. One of 'em got cut up bad by a man trying to rob her. She was the most beautiful woman I ever knew. Still the most beautiful woman I've ever known. She had to get blood transfusions she got cut up so bad, and from the transfusions she got the virus. Then when she got out, she was all messed up, and she died of AIDS, along with my other sister. For a long time I wanted Jesus to take me, too, so I could join them. I was filled with hate. And all of it was for that man who cut up my beautiful sister.

He got six years for that crime and you know what? I waited. I waited and my friends waited. And the day he got out, we were there. We caught up with him in the neighborhood and we all took him to a neighborhood park. I hit him. And I hit him and hit him and hit him until he was bloody. And then one of my friends gave me a gun and my friends all said, "Finish him, Jay. Square things now, for you and your sisters."

Then they walked away, gave us some privacy. And I was holding that gun and looking into the eyes of the man who killed my sister—my sisters—and I couldn't do it. I consider myself strong, and I consider myself tough, but Jesus would not let me take that man's life.

I saw him looking at me, and I told him, "You better run as fast as you can, because if my boys see you still alive, they won't be like me. They'll definitely shoot you." And then I smacked him one more time on the head with the butt of that pistol, and he ran, and I never saw him again. But I still think about him sometimes. My sisters I think about every day. Every single day, when I wake up and when I go to bed.

I told that story to Michael Jordan at dinner one night. It was his second-to-last year in the league.

And he said, "Jay, you and me are alike. We play hard, real hard. We're hard guys. But I don't know if I could have done what you did. If I ever came face-to-face with the guys who killed my father,

I don't know if I could have gone your route. I don't know if I could have let them go."

I said, "Mike, it's just been a few years for you since your father died. I had a longer time to grieve for my sisters."

I told Mike that time would heal. I told him that time would heal almost everything.

Chapter 15

The Swamp Called the Meadowlands— My Up & Down, Loving & Hating, Bench-Riding & All-Star Career with the New Jersey Nets

When I first decided to write about my life in the NBA, I had just been named an All-Star, and the New Jersey Nets were headed into the play-offs for the first time in four years. John Calipari had been named coach of the team the previous year, and even though we had had our differences (not helped by the magazine article where I talked about putting my foot up his butt), I was looking forward to not just *making* the play-offs but doing some damage in them. I figured the Nets were just a couple steps from what all NBA players want—a championship ring. I signed my big contract. I predicted a championship in the next few years. I expressed my love for Calipari.

We started the 1998–99 season 3-17. Cal got fired. I broke my leg. The Nets were out of the play-offs early in the season. How could such a promising team, with great players, great owners, and what seemed like a great coach, turn so bad so fast?

Are we really ready to be one of the premier teams of the NBA now? Did we just run into a patch of injuries and bad chemistry that are being fixed right now? Or are the New Jersey Nets, no matter the new owners, the new players, and the new coach, still the same jinxed bunch of short-bus guys I joined ten years ago?

Losers

I don't think a player was ever happier to be traded from the 76ers than I was. I'd be close to home, close to family. And I thought this would be a place where I could finally start getting some playing time, proving that I belonged in this league.

Then I met the short-bus crew. Derrick Coleman and Kenny Anderson, as I mentioned, and Chris Morris, who used to write "Trade Me" on his sneakers. Then Armen came to the Nets, and that added to the nuttiness.

There were some great athletes on that team, but they were great athletes with issues. I think some of the players on that team, as great as they were, preferred losing to winning. And I think there are more than a few players in the NBA like that. They're players with the really flashy stats, who have never been on a winner. Why players like that prefer losing to winning is, if you win, everybody's going to be watching you, and then you're going to have to get better. As long as you lose and you get your stats, you get your paycheck and there's no pressure. If you play well every day and you help your team play well, people are going to pay attention. And then you've got pressure, and some players just can't stand that. That's why you've got great players on some bad teams, and when you move them to a good team, they're failures.

The Hardest Worker I Ever Knew

My first year with the Nets was the 1992–93 season, and I thought we might have something special. Chuck Daly was the coach, and Drazen Petrovic was our shooting guard. We'd have practice at noon sometimes, and when I'd get there, Drazen would have been shooting for two hours. Then we'd practice, and he'd shoot another two hours. Sometimes he'd go home and shower and then come back and shoot some more.

When that season was over, Drazen told us he was going back to Europe, to play in a tournament with the guys he grew up with from Croatia. I asked him why he was doing that, there being a war going on and all.

He looked at me. "Why do you go to your neighborhood where you grew up all the time?"

I told him because it's my neighborhood; it's where I'm from.

"And it's like there's war all the time down there," he said, "with shooting and things, but still you go. Same thing with me."

The day he left to go back home, Drazen knocked on the door where I was living. I had been bitching for about three months how the cable TV company hadn't sent me my remote control yet. They kept saying they'd get me one, but they never did. So here comes Drazen, his bags all packed, headed to Croatia, where there was a war going on, knocking on my door at 5:00 A.M. He wanted to give me his remote control. And about a week later he was dead. Killed in a car crash.

The year after Drazen died, Chuck left. The next season, 1994–95, we had the lowest field goal percentage in the league, the lowest number of steals, and the lowest number of forced turnovers. We finished 30-52. The year after that, Derrick Coleman and Kenny Anderson were traded in the middle of the season. And we kept losing.

Security Check

Even when good players came to the team, it was tough, because a lot of times they were so unhappy playing for us. That's how it is when you're losing.

When Kendall Gill first came here from Seattle in the 1995–96 season, I walked up to him to welcome him, tell him how happy I was to be playing on the same team with a player like him. But I had heard how pissed off he was at George Karl, that maybe he was a little bit crazy, that he was mad about being traded to New Jersey. Stuff like that.

We were at the airport, and we were about to get on a plane. I noticed that Kendall had a briefcase, and it looked like it was hand-cuffed to his wrist.

I say, "What you got in that briefcase, brother?"

"None of your business," he says.

"C'mon, man, open it up and show me."

"Nah, it's none of your business."

We go on and on like that for a few minutes, until security makes him open it. There was a computer in there. And I shook that damn computer up and down. I thought with all that talk about him being crazy and all, he might be coming on with a bomb to kill every-body. But it was just a computer, and what I thought were hand-cuffs was just a bracelet Kendall wore.

Three days later I come into the back of the locker room before a game and I see Kendall taking a needle. I think, Oh, Lord, have mercy. The boy's a junkie. But I don't say anything.

A couple weeks later we're getting to be pretty good friends, and I'm shooting a free throw during a game, and Kendall comes over to me.

"Hey," he says. "You know that shot you saw me take two weeks ago? That was for my migraines. I get migraines, so I have to take my medicine."

"Goddamn," I say. "You're gonna tell me about your migraines now, when I'm shooting 60 percent for the season?"

After that, Kendall and I became great friends.

Chalk Talk

Every NBA team, the coach writes a bunch of stuff on the black-board before games, going over the plays and stuff, what to do if the other team does certain things. After hearing this stuff all sea-son, you got it memorized, and you don't want to hear it anymore. So most players would tune out then. Charles Barkley would take a crap.

In my early days with the Nets, the only thing that livened up the Nets' chalk talk was every day our assistant coach Clifford Ray used to walk to the training room to work on his knees, and coming back, he'd walk in front of the blackboard, buck naked. Clifford has a body like an alien, real fat up top at seven foot and little skinny legs. Like Fred Flintstone, or even Barney Rubble if he'd been taller.

Every day Clifford walks by in his birthday suit and a bunch of us kind of look at each other and roll our eyes, but we keep our laughter in, because we know our coach, Butch Beard, will get pissed off if we're cracking up before a game. Especially because we hardly ever won. Butch was really cranky then, telling us we played like bitches, which really pissed everyone off. Chris Childs tells P. J. Brown and me one day, "If Butch calls us bitches again, there's gonna be trouble. I'm not gonna stand for that no more."

After the tenth game Clifford walks by naked, Chris Childs can't help it anymore. He busts out laughing. He won't even look at me, because he knows if he does, I'll start laughing and then he'll laugh even harder. By the thirtieth home game, Chris is laughing hysterically. And by now the rest of us are giggling, too. Me and P. J. Brown, my fellow decoy duck, especially. Everyone's laughing but Armen Gilliam, the son of a preacher man who can't stand anything improper.

Butch hears all the laughing and he stops his chalk talk and stares at us.

He says, "You guys remind me of a bunch of bitches. You guys play like a bunch of bitches, and now you're acting like a bunch of bitches."

We'd heard Butch's "play like bitches" speech before, but never the "act like bitches" stuff.

Butch is screaming now. "You guys are all a bunch of bitches." And P. J. Brown and I, because we're the team clowns, and we like stirring up trouble, we're rolling our eyes at Chris Childs, because he'd been the one talking all about how he's not going to stand for any more "you guys are bitches" talk. Chris is a tough guy, had just come over from the CBA. We're nudging him, whispering to him.

"What you gonna do now, man? He's calling us bitches again."

Butch is still talking. He puts down his chalk. Then he says, "Are you all going to go out and play hard or are you all going to be bitches?"

"Butch," Chris Childs says, "can I ask you a question?"

"What?"

"Why do we got to be a bunch of bitches?"

"Because that's how you all play. Like bitches."

"Butch," Chris says, "I'm a man. I want to be referred to as a man."

"You might look like a man," Butch says, "but you play like a bitch. You act like a bitch. You a bitch."

Now they're in each other's faces, talking bitch this and bitch that, and motherf——— this and motherf——— that. Spit's flying, veins bulging. Armen Gilliam, the Hammer, he's sitting behind Butch. And he gets up because all the cursing bothers him.

"Excuse me, gentlemen," he says, because he's so proper. But they're ignoring him.

"Gentlemen, gentlemen! We don't need none of that profanity. Can't we all just . . ."

And Butch, without even looking back, just sticks his arm behind him and points his finger in Armen's face.

"Shut the f——— up, Hammer!" Butch says.

That was the end of the "bitch" fight, because Chris was laughing so hard. To this day, if you want to crack Chris up, on or off the court, all you gotta do is say, "Shut the f——— up, Hammer!"

On the Beach

After a while everyone got used to the losing. The players. The fans. Even the opposing teams. Other teams used to love playing us. Well, that's not actually accurate. The truth is it was no big deal to them. I'd look over at the layup lines of the other team when they played us and guys would be over there kissing their wives, talking to their friends, making their dinner plans for after the game. The only ones on the other team running the layup drill would be the tenth, eleventh, and twelfth guys on the team. And even they looked kind of bored.

Teams came in figuring we'd be an easy "W," and they would

stay out in New York City all night, the night before they played us, then they'd come in hungover and tired.

The Nets' arena in those days was like one of those sound studios. You could hear everything it was so empty. Once some joker got ahold of the loudspeaker somehow, and he said, "Will the lady who lost five children please claim them. They're beating the Nets 70–65."

No matter what we did, we kept losing. It felt like there was a black cloud over us. It was like a bad marriage, or what I hear bad marriages are like. Some days are okay, some days are better than others, but most days are really bad, and you want to get out of the marriage. You keep telling yourself it might work, but really, you have a strong feeling it never will. That's how I felt when we were losing all the time. I think a lot of players felt that way.

The only good thing about playing on the Nets then was the end of the season. All the players would pull up in their convertibles, for those last few home games, when play-offs were coming, and it was like we were camels and we smelled water in the desert, and we were running for it. And what we were running for wasn't the play-offs, because we knew we weren't going to make those. We were running for our summer vacations. Even players who came from winning teams got to like that part of the season with the Nets. Those guys might have made plane reservations the past few years for vacation, then had to cancel them because their team made the play-offs. But with the Nets, they never had to worry about canceling any reservations. They could count on their season being over on April 20.

Problem was, though, even a long summer vacation got sour in a hurry. I was lying on the beach in the Bahamas once just a few days after the season ended and we didn't make the play-offs. I was lying there, drinking a piña colada, saying to myself, "Ain't this great." Then this guy comes up to me, and he says, "Hey, you know the score of the Bulls' game?"

I felt like a loser. And I was one.

Cal's Promise

And then the Nets hired John Calipari, and he came in with his talk about demanding excellence, and his loyal staff and his Pete Sampras routine. Like I said, Cal could sell fried ice cream, and Cal wanted to win as much as anyone I've ever met.

Cal told us he would get a couple of All-Star talent players, and he'd sign back our best free agents, and he'd get us playing together and then we'd start winning, and winning a lot.

I didn't believe him at first. I figured that no All-Star was going to come in here in order to turn the franchise around. I saw it as a catch-22 situation. We were winning twenty-five games a year, so what kind of All-Star is going to sign with us to turn us around? Would a young man like Grant Hill, who was then twenty-seven or twenty-eight, want to come to New Jersey and try to turn a franchise around that had won just twenty-five games? Why would a young superstar like that want to go someplace and put all that pressure on himself? I figured you would only have one kind of All-Star that would come into a situation like that. That would be an All-Star who would be here for one reason—the money. And there's a number of All-Star players who would do just that. But is that the kind of player who's really going to help an organization like the Nets? Or would you rather get someone who really wants to come here because he likes the coach, he likes the organization, he likes the players he's going to play with? A guy who comes just for the money is going to treat it as just a job. He'll want to do his job and get out. He's not going to give his heart and soul.

So I had doubts about Cal's plan.

Growing Pains

Cal wanted excellence, and we wanted excellence, but sometimes we differed on how to be excellent. For example, Cal wanted me to be more of a hard case with the other players. He and some of the rest of management thought I was too nice with the fellas. They wanted me to be a tougher guy, especially since I was a tri-captain then, along with Robert Pack and Kendall Gill.

But I thought I could help by being more rewarding and giving compliments and saying things like, "C'mon, man, let's go," instead of "Aw, man, what the hell are you doing?"

If I was to do that to somebody, say, "What the hell are you doing?" then I'm disrespecting them. And then they might come back and disrespect me and tell me to go screw myself. And then that guy would be losing some teeth. And then I think morale would be very low. That player would have some speech problems, because I don't tolerate disrespect. And that's why I don't disrespect anybody. Because if I do, and then they disrespect me, I'd have to knock them out.

But Cal and I eventually learned to get along. We told each other it's not like we're going to have to get married. We both realized if Cal doesn't win, he's going to be in trouble, and if I don't play well and win, then I'm going to be in trouble. We both agreed that for us both to be successful, I would have to play wise, and he would have to coach wise.

How Times Change

By the middle of Keith's first year, teams knew we weren't the same old Nets. No one was ordering dinner in the layup line or kissing their wives. Even Michael Jordan was coming in, clapping, yelling at his teammates, saying stuff like, "C'mon, there ain't no easy win here tonight." And that felt good.

And we made it to the play-offs. That felt *really* good, even if we lost in the first round, in a tough series to the Bulls. And it felt real good to think about the next year. We figured we'd go far in '98–'99.

When Bad Things Happen to Good Teams

When we started that season, I'm thinking that we're going to win the Eastern Conference finals. And then Rony Seikaly goes down in practice. And after that, Sam Cassell goes down, and then Chris Gatling.

In my view, one of Cal's problems was he always let Sam do what he wanted. And when Sam didn't play when he was injured, that hurt. A lot of things cost Cal his job, but what it boils down to is we wouldn't have been 3-17 with Sam playing. And that's eventually what we were: 3-17.

Bigger Isn't Always Better

Team owners will try a lot of things when their franchise is going bad. Trades, yelling at the coach, all that kind of stuff. Our owners went further. They hired Tony Robbins.

Tony's the Personal Power guy you used to see in infomercials all the time. The guy with the teeth. A couple days before they got rid of Cal, the owners had Tony come in to meet with the players. Of course a lot of the guys thought he was full of it.

First thing Tony does is he asks me to stand up. I had torn ligaments in my thumb at the time, and I'm pretty sure the Nets had told him that even though I was in pain, they also thought I didn't have the enthusiasm that I did before, back when I was jumping around on the court, chest-bumping, slapping high fives, and stuff.

So Tony Robbins has me stand next to him and he says, "You're a warrior, you play hurt, you play hard. Now, let me see your warrior look."

And I'm not really into this Tony Robbins business, so I'm standing there with my shoulders slumped, my head down. Tony says, "Show me how you feel when you're winning."

My head comes up a little, my shoulders go back. "Now walk like a winner," he says. So I'm strutting around a little. Tony's going now, he's into his thing. He's talking about winning, and being a warrior, and being excited. And I don't know how he does it, but he puts me in a trance.

I'm walking around the locker room, all big and barrel-chested. I'm growling. Tony says, "Jayson, what word describes you now? What's the one word?"

"Big," I growl, really loud. I'm breathing hard.

"I'm big," I say. "I'm *big!*" My eyes are closed, and I'm sweating, stomping around that locker room, and now Tony's yelling, too.

"Get big! Get big!"

"I'm big!" I scream, and I punch the blackboard and it flies about twenty-five feet and smashes into the wall and breaks into a bunch of pieces.

And then I snap out of it, but I'm still all sweaty and breathing hard. And Tony's all happy, smiling. He asks for two more volunteers, and no one raises their hands, so he asks who are my two best friends on the team and I tell him Kendall Gill and Keith Van Horn, so he gets them to come up next to me.

Now Tony wants to do the same thing again, but with all of us. So he's talking about getting big, and I'm breathing hard and sweating again, just starting to get into it, and I can hear him yelling at Keith and Kendall to get big, too.

"Get big, Keith," Tony's yelling. "Get big, Kendall. Get big, get big, *get big!*"

My eyes are closed, and I'm just about completely in my trance, but I still sneak a look at my buddies, to see how they're doing. What I see is Keith and Kendall crouching down with their hands up over their heads, because they're scared I'm going to knock something else across the room, and they don't want it to be them.

That was the last of Tony Robbins.

Team Meeting

It's one thing to be yelling at your players when the team's winning. But when we started losing, some of the guys started tuning Cal out and bad-mouthing him. And I tried to warn Cal.

After one of our losses—we were about 3-8 at the time—I remember going to the front of the plane. I sat down next to Cal.

"Man," I said, "you know, you've got guys on the team who are not happy right now the way things are going. You've got to be careful. With all the yelling and stuff."

Cal looked at me. He didn't say anything. I said, "Not me, but people can lead a revolt. And it can hurt you."

The next day Cal tells us before practice someone's here to talk to the team. And Lewis Katz, one of the Nets' owners, comes into the locker room. And he says, "Cal will be our coach for many, many years to come. The Nets are deeply committed to Coach Calipari."

And as soon as he left, a bunch of us look at each other. And we're all thinking the same thing, whether we're happy or sad about it. That thing is, "He's gone."

That's the way it works. As soon as the owner says something like that, you know the guy's gone. Same thing with players. As soon as you hear, "Oh, we believe in you; you're part of the franchise; you're going to be here for five years," that's trouble.

Green

The last thing the Nets did before they fired Calipari was trade for Stephon Marbury, the point guard who grew up on Coney Island. We gave up Sam Cassell and Chris Gatling, and there were three teams involved, but to the Nets, the big thing was getting Stephon.

A lot of the press reported that getting Stephon might save Cal's job, but in fact, it was probably the thing that meant Cal was definitely gone. Because first, the players knew Stephon was coming before Cal and the coaching staff did. That's partly the nature of the NBA today, when so many superstar players have the same agent, and the agent talks to the players and the players talk to other players. Second thing was everybody knew Stephon wasn't the kind of guy who was going to come in and sign a long-term deal at a place he was going to get yelled at every day. Stephon got told before he signed with the Nets, by his agent, "Don't worry, no one's going to be yelling at you for long."

Translation: "Cal ain't going to be here too long."

So when Stephon came in, most of us knew Cal was leaving soon. And though a lot of people were talking about how great it was going to be to have a point guard like Stephon, I was a little more philosophical. People always say the grass is greener on the other side. Well, I've turned over a lot of grass. I've laid over 200,000 square feet of sod around my house in the past three years. Grass is never greener on the other side. It's dirt.

What's That Noise?

Cal or one of the owners must have talked to Stephon, because after one of his first games, which we lost to Philadelphia, Stephon gives a speech in the locker room. He's yelling at the team about how we have to stick together, we have to have heart. He's screaming about how we don't have to like each other but we have to respect each other and play together. He's going on and on about turning the season around and sharing goals. It's the same stuff Cal has been yelling about the whole season, so most of us figure Cal asked Stephon to make the same speech. And Stephon is into it. He goes up to each player and yells in his face.

Then, while we're all in the shower, Stephon is still yelling in the locker room. One of the guys says, "That kid is a world-class yeller." What we learned was, he's an even better basketball player. He talks the talk all right, but he really walks the walk.

The Music of Good-bye

The day after Cal got fired, he flew up to Toronto, where we were playing, to say good-bye to everybody. I give him credit for that. He got together with the team, right before we were leaving for practice. And he said, "I failed." Which was just like him, the man who said, "Bet on me." Now he's taking all the responsibility, saying, "*I* failed."

He went around the room, shook everybody's hand, looked everybody in the eye. He told Keith Van Horn, "I hope you have a great career." He said a few words to me, to Kendall Gill, to Kerry Kittles. And Jimmy McIlvaine is yelling from the corner of the room, "Cal! Cal! Cal! Come on over here. I got this CD for you." Jimmy pulls this CD out of his gym bag. It's a CD Jimmy had mentioned to Cal at the beginning of the season, because the band has a guy in it named Calipari. And *now's* the time he's decided to give it to Cal.

Cal looks at Jimmy like he wants to take that CD and break it over his seven-foot head. Cal's like, "Are you serious?"

Why Rush Things?

When Rony Seikaly got hurt, some people doubted that his injury was very serious. That happens to players sometimes in the league. Unless you have a broken bone or some obvious swelling, there are always people who are going to say you should be playing. But I knew he was hurting.

Still, we needed a low post scorer. I knew Rony could help the team. So after Cal got fired, Keith Van Horn and I took Rony out for sushi and we talked to him for two hours. Told him he could really help the team, and help himself, if he'd just get out there and play just a little bit. Told him it would mean a lot to the guys, that it would show what kind of teammate he really is. Told him the owners would like him better, too.

"Okay," he says, "I'll play."

Next night he's on the bench in his uniform, Don Casey calls him to get up, and he goes in and plays for four minutes. When he comes out, I pat him on the back.

"That's the man," I say. "Way to go, Seik. Thank you for those four minutes. It means a lot." And I meant it sincerely. And I say, "Now, tomorrow, you know, maybe you could give me twelve minutes."

"Tomorrow?" he says in that accent he talks in. "Tomorrow? What do you mean, tomorrow? Are you trying to ruin my career? I can't play tomorrow. I can't play back-to-backs."

I couldn't believe this guy. I say, "Back-to-backs? You played four friggin' minutes. You got to play a *back* first, before you can play a back-to-back."

Rony played one more time, about three minutes in Cleveland, and that was it for the season.

Wearing Colors

I always wanted to be in the spotlight. When the play-offs come, I know all eyes are on me. I love that. I love coming out and seeing all the media. I love seeing Bruce Willis and Danny Aiello in the stands. I love our owners.

I stayed in New Jersey because I love it here, and because New Jersey fans are the best fans in the world. Back in the bad old days, kids used to be scared to wear a Nets jacket. Hell, *I* was scared to wear a Nets jacket.

A couple years ago, when we were starting to win again, I bought twenty-five leather Nets jackets, at $800 a pop. Keith Van Horn said to me, "Jay, boy, you sure like to wear Nets gear."

I told him, "Boy, I used to wear Nets gear when I first got here. And that took some balls then. You'd go into a bad neighborhood, they'd beat your butt because the Nets was so bad and you were wearing their jacket.

"Now," I told him, "we got respect and I can wear stuff like that and be proud. And I want everybody around me to wear it and be proud."

Then we had that nightmare in the '98–'99 season. That's why I'm working harder than ever before now. I want to wear that Nets jacket with pride.

Chapter 16

**What the NBA**

Has Taught Me

About Life

When I came into this league, I didn't
want to play basketball. My sisters
had just died, and I was pissed off at
the world. Sometimes I was even
pissed off at Jesus. I thought because
Jesus took my sisters, he gave me the NBA. I thought he gave me
fame and fortune and now he thought we were even.

But I didn't want to play. I didn't want the pressure. I was wild,
I was crazy, I was drinking too much, and I didn't take anything
from anybody. Somebody said something to me, I would just go
crazy on them. And I was scared of losing the rest of my family. I
know that now. When I entered the league, I planned to take my
$2.5-million contract and invest it, and buy a home, and then, after
three years, I'd have enough money to join my father in the construction business.

There's nothing wrong with a plan like that, but the way I went
about it was fighting and drinking and being irresponsible. And that
was my downfall.

I don't talk about it a lot, because I think religion is a private thing, but a short while after my mom and dad sat me down and talked to me about cutting back on the drinking, and growing up, I quit thinking that Jesus had decided to torture me by taking my sisters and giving me fame and fortune. I started seeing what gifts I had received. And about six years ago, I started thinking, How can I cut a deal with Jesus? How can I give back to him things in order to make up all the gifts I've received?

And the answer I figured out is that I can give him back things by giving things to people. That's something I'm grateful I learned, because many NBA players never do. The NBA has the best marketing in all professional sports, and that, combined with the fact that there are only twelve players on a team, creates a situation where young guys come into this league and they're stars from the beginning. It's not like baseball, where it takes time to be a star, or football, where there's so many other players. The guys who come into the NBA have been stars all their lives, in high school, in college, and now in the NBA. So, many of them come in with a mind-set of "me, me, me."

You know, it's good for everybody to be able to have a white house with a white picket fence and dog and two kids. That's the American way. But it's not the American way to forget your community where you come from. And I'm not talking about just going back and fixing up the friggin' basketball court in the park. Spending $10,000. Any idiot can do that. You put your time in. You go visit some hospitals, bring a smile to a kid's face. You do it more than once a summer.

You got to give back. That's what God put us on this earth for. That's something I learned, and I'm grateful for it.

Is Anyone Listening?

I've always prayed. I pray before I leave the locker room. I pray after the national anthem, after I hold my hand over my chest—I love America—and I pray before I go into the game.

And then in 1998, after I signed my big contract, I started praying even more. I started praying because there was so much pressure on me to win, and to perform, because I was making so much money.

I started going, "God, please, let me play well. God, please, let us get a win."

And God said, "This kid calling my name again?"

He said, "Okay, I'll give you something to think about. I got problems in Kosovo. I got problems with these cops in New York City shooting somebody forty-one times. I got riots. I got rapes. I just gave you a hundred million dollars, a big house, your health. And you don't even understand what you have received. And you're asking me for a win, for a good game?"

God says to me, "I'll give you something to think about. It's something to think about for a little while."

And then God went *snap,* and he broke my leg.

And then God said, "Now, I'll tell you another thing. You pray for me to help you win? You think I care? I don't even watch the Nets, because I only have so much time, but I'm damn sure going to watch the NBA during the play-offs and y'all ain't going to be in them."

God talked to me when I was sitting in my wheelchair, watching my father work, looking over 135 acres, turning my head and looking down a hallway in my house that goes down four hundred feet. That's when I realized what got me in trouble. Vanity. Vanity set in and got me thinking how important I was, and wanting more and more, and asking God for wins and good games.

The Importance of the Off-Season

Every summer, as much as I like lazing around, what I do is work out and do charity work. You hear some NBA players say they work out and do charity work in the off-season, but when they say they're doing charity work and working out, you have to understand, it's like me saying I'm brushing up on Shakespearean tragedy, when what I'm really doing is watching *Scarface,* which by the way is one of my favorite movies of all time.

Some NBA players, they say they're working out, what they

mean is they're going out, playing eighteen holes, drinking a few beers, and taking a nap. Some of them that are really working out will jog two miles in between the golf and the beers. I lift weights every day, I play basketball, I come into the season strong, and running and jumping. When I see one of these golf-bag-toting, Budweiser-drinking guys fresh from his summer vacation, you can bet my eyes get big as Tony Manera's, the *Scarface* guy, right before he got down to his business.

Decisions, Decisions

Everyone faces tough choices in life. Should I take that drink or not? Should I go into this business or that? Best to ignore someone's hot words, or stand up and fight? And when I'm faced with tough situations, I always try to imagine what my dad would do. Not what Jesus would do. We know what Jesus would do. He would always do the morally right thing. And sometimes we can't always do the morally right thing, which is a shame.

So I think, What would Dad do? For instance, a few years ago an NBA player named Oliver Miller opted out of a $9-million contract because he thought he could make more. He ended up taking a bath, not getting anything. And whenever a business decision came up, I thought of Oliver Miller. And my dad. Because I know what my dad would have done if I had been Oliver Miller. My dad would have had two heart attacks right after he shot me in the butt three times if I had opted out of a $9-million contract.

We Are Family

Fame and fortune are great, and even if I didn't think so, no one would believe me. And all the riches and the popularity have allowed me to do things I never would have been able to otherwise—to not have to worry about working after I retire, to build a nice house, to touch people's lives. But when my career is over, all

I want to do is to get married, have two or three children, ride off into the sunset, and that's that. I'll still do the charity work, especially with kids, but that's it. No more work. Well, maybe try being a general manager, or if Mike Jarvis has moved up to the NBA, coach St. John's. But if not, I'll just sit at home with my family. Because all I want to do when I retire is love my family, my wife and my kids and my parents.

By that time, my first kids—my sisters' children—will be all grown up, and my grandson will be a young man himself. And I'll probably spank him from time to time, just like I spanked my sisters' kids when I took over raising them. When I did the child-abuse commercial for the NBA, I told them, "Look, I spank my children. I don't whip them, I discipline them. Probably spanked each kid about five or six times in their life." Like my father did me, only I got it about thirty or thirty-five times. But he never hit me where I had scars. He'd hit me with a belt, and my butt might be stinging for about three or four hours, and that was it. And that's the way I brought my children up. It's tough raising kids, and I know I've got a temper, and it was especially hard controlling that temper when I was a younger man. But I did control myself, because I had a good upbringing. I had the best lesson of all. I know what it felt like to be on the other side of that belt.

My parents stay with me now about three days a week. There's a house on the property that's theirs. They squabble sometimes, usually about who's done what when it comes to being a parent. When they come to Nets games and my dad's all proud, my mom says to him, "Oh, *now* he's your son? He wasn't your son the first few years." She lets him have it, probably because she's pissed off he wasn't around much when I was a baby, he was working so much.

They're both in their sixties now, but they're still young at heart. My dad gets out and works every day. And my mom, she still drives about a hundred miles wherever she's going, and she got a tattoo when she turned sixty, a little angel right on her ankle. She was diagnosed with Parkinson's a few years ago, and that's slowed her up, but she's still got her sense of humor.

When she first got diagnosed, I took her to the doctor. She was just starting to shake a lot. The doctor asks me, "Is she drinking a lot of coffee?"

"Hell, no," I say. "She spills most of it." She got a kick out of that.

Learning from Losses

If you read the newspapers or watch television, it's easy to start believing that the most important thing in the world is whether your team won last night, or how many points your favorite player had. Players get involved in that, too, and to a point, we need to focus on what we're doing. It's our job.

But every once in a while something happens that makes me realize what really counts.

In the summer of 1998 I visited my uncle in the hospital. My father's brother, who I had spent a lot of time with growing up, had leukemia. He went for a checkup one day, and the next week he's in the hospital.

His head was all swollen up, he'd lost fifty pounds. I saw him right before he was rolled in for surgery. And driving home, I had an anxiety attack. I had to pull off the highway for about twenty minutes because I couldn't breathe. I just sat there, trying to breathe, thinking about things.

I finally got back home and I made my father come with me everywhere I went that day. I wouldn't leave him. He didn't want to sit in the gym and watch me work out for three hours. He didn't want to watch me run on the track. But he understood. He did it.

Sometimes we all lose sight of what's most important in life. NBA players, with our million-dollar contracts and our pictures in the paper, might lose sight more often than others. It's easy to lose sight of what we love the most.

A week after that first visit, my uncle died. I spent time with him every day that week. But that first day in the hospital, as bad as I felt for my uncle, and as much as I prayed for him, I was grateful that visiting him helped me remember what mattered most.

When Plans Change

Every morning at 7:45, when I'm not on the road, my dad and I meet. We get in my car, we drive to the deli, I get a coffee, he gets coffee and a bagel, and we drive back and we talk about what we're going to do that day. I'm going to practice; he's going to work on a house, or a hotel, whatever. We get our day straight. And then when I get back in the afternoon from practice, I call him again, about three o'clock. If I miss him, I call him that night. If I don't get him at night, I panic. Same thing with my mom. If she doesn't pick up the phone when I call her, I panic.

People who see me on TV think I'm the most happy, funny guy in the world. But people who know me best tell me I shouldn't be so uptight—I need to stop worrying so much. But you've got to understand, I lost my two best friends when I was a boy, my two sisters.

And for years after, I wanted to join them. I used to walk into places where pistols were flying. I took the one guy's gun at my bar and slapped him with it. I got in stupid fights. I drove 170 miles an hour. Why? Because I wanted Jesus to take me, to let me be with my sisters.

Jesus wouldn't do it. Jesus said, "You ain't getting out of here that easy." Jesus had other plans for me.

Portrait of the Rebounder as a Middle-Aged Man

I want to be remembered as a good son and a good father. I want people to remember me as a good friend. And when I retire from basketball, I want people to say that I worked as hard as anybody who ever played. I want to be an All-Star six more times, and I want to win at least two NBA championships. I want to grab more offensive rebounds than any other player in history, and I want to help make the Nets franchise great.

When I'm retired and have some gray hair and a potbelly, and when I'm sitting in some high school gymnasium, watching my son's and my daughter's basketball games, and on one side of me is my mom and on the other side is my dad, who'll both be in their golden years by then, I want people to look at me and say, "That's a good man." Even the ones who say, "Isn't that the guy who used to be so wild, who used to be drinking and fighting so much, who was always getting in trouble?" Especially them. I want those people to look at me, sitting with my parents, watching my children, and I want them to say, "He sure straightened out. He sure learned what's really important."

INDEX